THE ORDER OF THE WOUNDED HANDS

SCHOOLED IN THE EAST

Intention in the cover design:
Jerusalem's citadel, or 'Tower of David', on the north-western slope is reproduced here from the well-known 19th-century print by David Roberts. It has long been the symbol of the unison between religion and power, between faith and force. David was the founder and exemplar of 'Davidism', having unified the north and south of Israel/Judea by the capture of the ancient Jebusite stronghold. Thus he bequeathed to Solomon the raising of the Temple and the supreme flourishing of Hebrew rule.

It was here in due time that 'Umar, second Caliph of Islam, and centuries later a Salah al-Din achieved for Islam the same amalgam of *regio* and *religio*. It may well date in part from still earlier reaches of remoter history.

It was here in turn that the Crusaders made their last stand some nine decades after its triumphant capture at their hands. For they, too, pursued the same policy of forceful acquisition on the principle that unless we enthrone we cannot pray, unless we rule we may not inhabit. That same philosophy has been renewed by a 20th-century Zionism necessarily understanding itself, after bitter experience of powerlessness, as an inherently intrusive entity requiring to be power-bent.

From a sketch (by David Archer) two hands belong where the Tower rears but in determined contrast to regimes where their vocation has its different ministry, drawn from and for the authority of 'God in Christ'. They detach their Gospel from any unison with the pride of force and power. Beyond an ever corrupting and corruptible power nexus, they see and learn a more patient task of conscience and concern amid the necessary ordering of government and politics.

In our contemporary global scene, the cover's dual imagery signals how there are larger liabilities to love and truth than power, for all its legitimate necessity, ever avails to satisfy.

THE ORDER OF THE WOUNDED HANDS

SCHOOLED IN THE EAST

Kenneth Cragg

MELISENDE

© Kenneth Cragg, 2006

The right of Kenneth Cragg to be identified as the author of this work has been asserted by him in accordance with the Copyright, Designs and Patents Act 1988.

All rights reserved. No part of this work, its text any or part of the illustrations and drawings, may be reproduced, stored in a retrieval system, or transmitted in any form or by any means, electronic, mechanical, photocopying, recording or otherwise, without the prior permission of the copyright owner.

The Order of the Wounded Hands
First published 2006 by Melisende
London
England

ISBN 1 901764 48 6 (10 digits)
ISBN 978 1 901764 48 2 (13 digits)

Melisende Publishing Ltd, London
and
Rimal Publications, Nicosia
For information on our publications, visit our website
www.melisende.com
and for
Rimal Publications, Cyprus, www.rimalbooks.com

Editor: Leonard Harrow
Printed and bound in England at the Cromwell Press

CONTENTS

FOREWORD BY THE ARCHBISHOP OF CANTERBURY	vii
AUTHOR'S FOREWORD	ix
INTRODUCTION	1
1 WITH THE PSALMIST TO THE CHRIST SANCTUARY	12
2 THAT SANCTUARY IN FACT AND FAITH	25
3 THEREFORE	37
4 WHERE MOST INDEBTED MOST FULFILLED: JUDAICA	53
5 WHERE MOST EXCLUDED MOST ENGAGED: ISLAMICA	80
6 WHERE MOST DISCOUNTED MOST INVOLVED: THE SECULAR AGNOSTIC	109
[EASTER EUCHARIST: A COLLEGE SERMON]	133
7 ALL YOUR CARES AND STUDIES	137
8 THE OBEDIENCE OF TIME	160
BIBLICAL REFERENCES	167
QURANIC REFERENCES	169
INDEX OF NAMES, TERMS AND PHRASES	170
INDEX OF THEMES	177

With such love as 'twas then—

MELITA

—the love that abides

FOREWORD
by the Archbishop of Canterbury

We shall understand what is distinctive about Christian ministry when we understand what is distinctive about Christian faith itself. This is the assumption from which Bishop Kenneth Cragg begins in this demanding and extraordinarily renewing book, a book which is almost a systematic theology in unsystematic form. What is uncompromisingly new in the Gospel is the definitive overturning of the *lex talionis*; there is no place now, in God's new creation, for the arithmetic of settling scores. There is only the stubborn power of a God who has declared himself vulnerable, and who therefore does not resort—in a significant sense, *cannot* resort—to any strategy in which the other is denied or coerced.

Only wounded hands can reshape the world; it is into this that Christ's public ministers are ordained, and Bishop Kenneth powerfully evokes the cost of lifelong commitment to this summons. In a way that is uniquely informed by his own long lifetime of engagement with the 'other' of Judaism and Islam, he insists on the central paradox: it is when we are clearest about our Christian distinctiveness that we are best able to relate in integrity and humility to the other, and, in that relating, to find ourselves questioned by Christ, as well as questioning in his name. We may put the question to Judaism about the inevitable vulnerability of any God who commits to human history. We may put the question to Islam of how the greatness of God, celebrated in every call to prayer, draws us to a recognition of its incomparability with any human greatness and so to the saving weakness of God in Christ. And the secularist is engaged boldly and directly, challenged as to the real meaning or value of any statement that we are 'simply' the way we are: there is no 'simply' about the complex dignity of human beings.

En route, Bishop Kenneth sheds new light on the 'messianic secret' of Mark's Gospel; he confronts the 'two covenants' theology that

The Order of the Wounded Hands

has influenced many pursuing Jewish-Christian dialogue and shows that it does no favour to either Jew or Christian; he comments with uncomfortable perception on the stalemate of current Anglican debates. Above all, he makes the reader *discover* the Gospel and hear it anew.

At no level is this easy reading; but it is vital reading for any re-energised Christian theology of ministry or of mission. This is reflection of the highest spiritual and intellectual quality and it bears the closest study. It is a fitting crown to decades of exceptional theological work and equally exceptional pastoral service to the Church worldwide.

+ Rowan Cantuar:
Lambeth Palace
St Michael and All Angels 2006

AUTHOR'S FOREWORD

Faith, whether religious or secular, is the grist of autobiography. One lives one's way into awareness. Conceptions of meaning ride with reception of experience. Thus life can come to propose to itself a form of its definition which it will deliberately volunteer to adopt as the context and capacity of its own pursuit.[1] For others a certain drift of indecision may contrive the opposite of a personal destiny, except insofar as economic factors do not impose some necessary pattern.

Of the first description is the invitation into Christian ministry, as it is set forth in the age-long 'Ordinal' for the making, ordaining or consecrating of deacons, priests, and bishops in a historic threefold sequence since the formative centuries of Christianity. Autobiography is thus a deep dimension of that story within the individual respondent, open in registering a given summons and thereby active in making the response. The narrative is thus intensely private, yet expressly public, a personal availability gathered into a warrant. The issue is 'ministry of Word and Sacrament'. These will abidingly belong with the further course of autobiography. Something of the same duality of 'me' and 'thus', present in the first origins, will abide in the long issue of time and circumstance.

It is the purpose of these pages to study the incidence of this mutual reality of 'ministry' via the 'laying on of hands'—the ritual which from the outset has been the pattern of the Ordinal, in capturing the central tradition by which the present entrusted from the past into the future 'the inestimable riches of Christ'. It is a study which can only transcend the personal in being inherently so. 'As it happened'—as we

---

[1] Using 'capacity' in its sense both of 'ability' and 'warrant' in respect of action proposed: having what an 'office' or 'duty' 'takes' and deploying it effectively.

say—the story, as studied here, led through the same geography which long marked the pilgrim way to Jerusalem (often from the north and the Lebanese foothills of Hermon) which generations of Christian priests adapted from the psalmist when each sang (as their Vulgate has it): *Introibo ad altare Dei.* (Psalm 43. 4)[2] 'I will go unto the altar of God, the God of my joy and gladness.'

They meant, of course, the Christian sanctuary and the celebration of the Christian Eucharist. The perceptive genius who wrote the New Testament 'Letter to the Hebrews' had educated them how to transpose what the Hebrew psalmist intended by his distant access to Jerusalem into what a Christian priesthood meant, loaded and precarious as the transposing was.[3] To the former, Jerusalem meant the Temple and its daily holocaust of animal sacrifice; to the latter it meant the city of the Gethsemane and the Calvary of the redeeming Christ of God.

That 'office', with the 'ministry of the Word' which they had received by 'the laying on of hands'—it is here argued—could have been none other than from the wounded hands of that same Christ. The mandate, not to say the energy, of ministry could come from no other source. Whether deacon, priest or bishop, the Ordinal would have each know that their commission had no other origin than from One saying:

> 'Mine the ordering wounded hands
> And the thorns that crowned Me.
> Evermore My passion stands
> Energising round thee.'

That logic belongs further to Chapter 3 following and the clarion word: 'Therefore' throughout the New Testament.

Is there perhaps a remote shape of analogy in the usage of civil or political life from which we have 'the Order of the Garter', '… of

---

[2] Psalm 43 is generally seen as linked to Psalm 42, where the context would seem to indicate a singer, yearning for far-off Temple from the slopes of Mount Hermon where mountain torrents pouring down the hillside were the 'waves and billows' of his unwanted exile. Visualising his former part in the ceremonies, he yearned for their renewal.

[3] Inasmuch as there can only be painful discontinuity between arbitrary, ritual, animal, endlessly repeated 'sacrifice' and the historic, volitional, redemptive suffering of Jesus as the Christ. See further in Chapter 4. The writer is at great pains to discern such continuity as he can, in token of his 'good faith' with the old order.

Author's Foreword

the Bath', '... of the Thistle' and anachronistically ' ... of the Empire'? It is apposite indeed to understand Christian ministry as 'the Order of the Wounded Hands', seeing that the Ordinal can claim no surer sanction of validity, whether from history or theology. Any impulse, however, to ponder as some Timothy: 'Let no man despise thee,' keeps ever in mind how 'He was despised'. The heavy 'discounts' of Christian ministry must come in Chapter 6 and surviving them in Chapter 7.

Meanwhile here, Chapter 1 traces in psalmody the Hebrew advent to Jerusalem as its memoriter of its own past and the faith-accents of its constant present. Jerusalem and its Temple, in their single relevance, enshrined the whole story and the entire logic of a 'people of God'. In coming into their sanctuary they were possessing themselves, celebrating identity, transacting their heritage. We have to trace the elements of this heritage in people-focus, land tenure and historic story, via Moses and Exodus, Joshua and conquest, David and Solomon in kingship and how these issued into that deep 'psyche about sin and its seriousness' that characterised the whole Levitical system and the structure of sacrifice. For these were the matrix of the Christianity which, in the New Testament, entirely transformed them into an open peoplehood and a world-wide *parochia*.[4] That fulfilment belongs in Chapter 2.

The Introduction following will explain how—reverting to what in all else can only be autobiographical—a personal journey into Jerusalem came via the same Lebanon and thereby initiated me into a perspective from which to comprehend it. In a strangely significant way, the route the psalmist took southward from his Hermon loneliness had been repeated as a private discovery, in that the origins of the journey had educated its conclusion.

In both cases of course, his and mine, there were antecedents prior to that formative Lebanese sojourn and its route to Jerusalem. My 'Orders' were from the Diocese of Chester and had set me in a lively parish in Tranmere, a district of Birkenhead with a view across the River Mersey to the Cathedral of Liverpool still in the making.

---

[4] Not the severely local English 'parish' into which the Greek term was corrupted, but a community—as the Letter to Diognetus has it—of 'people who are nowhere "alien" and can be everywhere at home.' *Parioikia* 'to dwell as a stranger', or 'here the more in not belonging'. See 1 Peter 2.11.

xi

The Order of the Wounded Hands

But my three years there were issuing into transit to the Middle East and the Anglican Diocese in Jerusalem, then led by Bishop George Francis Graham-Brown.[5] I was to be non-salaried Chaplain of All Saints' Church, Beirut, with duties in teaching in a local mission. These, unknown to me at the outset, were soon to develop into a strenuous inter-fusing of the ecclesiastical and the educational in terms that brought me into strangely formative contact with Dr Charles Malik and with his Christian vision of the vocation of Lebanon in the spiritual topography of the Middle East. The immediate story falls to the Introduction.

It was a truly salutary process of 'learning' from which to encounter the ethos of Jerusalem, ancient and Zionist in the forties of the last century. Here in Chapters 4, 5 and 6, Jerusalem stands to be read, within any Christian reckoning that knows 'the wounded hands of Christ', in three dimensions, namely as the sacred city of three faiths and as representative, in contemporary terms, of a deep secularity. Since the Christian character of the city and its significance is explicit in any ministry the Church brings, this leaves us with the three 'measures', the Judaic, the Islamic and the secular.

Currently, the State of Israel covets and proclaims the city as the inalienable, exclusive capital of the Jewish nation. Its internationalisation, prescribed in the UNO vote of late 1947 which gave Israel juridical right to exist, has long ago been forgotten.[6] The status of Jerusalem is therefore seen in Jewish eyes as the symbol and the sanction of the entire validity of Zionism in the total repossession of ancestral territory and the token exclusion from it of a Palestinian partnership.

---

[5] Born 1890, he became the sixth Bishop in Jerusalem in 1932. He died in a tragic accident at a railroad unguarded crossing as he drove down the Beirut to Haifa coastal road which criss-crossed the train track at frequent points. He was en route to Jerusalem from the inauguration of St Justin's House, Beirut, and other episcopal duties. He brought a strange amalgam of steely leadership and humble diffidence towards the role of 'chief pastor'. He had officiated at our wedding a bare two years earlier in Beirut and had baptised in Gaza our first son, John. My debt to him on every count was great and grateful. N.B. the usage 'Bishop in Jerusalem' was in steady recognition that any Anglican 'presence' deferred to the long ecclesial status of the Orthodox Patriarch. The origins of the Bishopric in 1841 had caused disquiet in some English minds lest it should be otherwise as some 'trespasser'.

[6] It needs to be remembered that the Balfour Declaration of November 1917 had no legal status. It was a gesture of goodwill on Britain's part, 'favouring' 'the establishment of a national home'

Author's Foreword

Nevertheless, the sharpest irony, Jerusalem remains an inalienably Islamic city, unless and until—unleashing all demons—the twin Islamic shrines in Temple Mount are no longer in place. Islam still has this rooted stake in the identity of a 'holy city'. 'The rock of Abraham' persists as 'the rock of Muhammad'. Jerusalem was the first *qiblah* of a nascent Islam and remains cynosure of all Muslim eyes. There are also the long centuries, before and after the Crusaders, when Jerusalem was ruled within Islamic caliphates or by Muslim tenants. The steady, deliberate attrition of its Islamic ethos has not diminished its Islamic identity while diminishing its Arab population. What might have been 'international' is steadily the more 'one-national'—which leads to the third category of the strongly 'secular'. Religions may well mutually exclude each other. There is nothing that does so more than certain moods of the secular mind. Israeli Jerusalem is, therefore, a symbol of a deeply secular abeyance of the religious reckonings of statehood. What is tragically evident is the quiescent role of Orthodox Judaism in the politics of Israel, except in terms of applying any leverage power to the material interests of the synagogue communities. Where is protest about the direction, the violence of state policy in recent days? The essential thrust of Zionist action ever since Theodor Herzl, despite the deep land-emotion, has been secular. If we find it 'Messianic', it is so in its politics and cult of power. Ben Gurion, in his day, could placidly rely on the docility of a spiritual Judaism in the vigorous pursuit of his essential policy of a thrusting pragmatism. The willingness in the summer of 2006 of Israeli arms, planes, warships and aerial gunships to devastate the city of Beirut, the highways and infrastructure of Lebanon and to decimate its economy, livelihood and dignity, is tragic witness to

for Jews in Palestine. Its studied ambiguity made no mention of 'a national state of ...' though later, under the Mandate, the Jewish Agency insisted that it did. Thus the Mandatory Power was trapped by its own subterfuge into a costly and tormented task of holding the ring for incompatible purposes, Jewish and Palestinian, the one assertive, the other defensive. In the changed world of post-1945 the Mandatory could only own itself defeated by the chicanery of gross ambivalence in its origins. It is virtually the same impasse which has accompanied the story since 1947 around the intention and the haplessness of United Nations' Resolutions. Israel's story is that of a steady, cumulative 'self-implantation' into a not vacant territory and a series of steady *faits accomplis*, manual, pragmatic, martial and physical and of a sequential encounter with another people, already present, much excluded, and pre-possessed by just the same ingredients of identity (tribe, territory and time) as the Zionist 'self-implanter'.

The Order of the Wounded Hands

a secularity utterly reversing the dictum of the prophet: 'Not by might nor by power but by my spirit' 'says the Lord of Hosts.'[7]

It falls to Chapters 4, 5 and 6 to trace the task of Christian ministry in theological terms in respect of these three measures of what the scene must evoke of patience and passion. From these will stem all that must follow in Chapter 7 for 'all those cares and studies' the Ordinal enjoins.

When the first generation Christian Church alerted itself for 'service for Jerusalem', it was in terms of 'collection for the poor' of the Mother City—a strange commentary on the old Hebraic idea of 'nations coming to pay tribute to a sovereign Zion.' This was a Church that had reversed the old centripetal direction of tributary worlds into a centrifugal one that took in the world. Any northern Englishman, resuming some 'Jerusalem direction' in a 20th century, and doing so in 'the order of the wounded hands', would be heir to all that dispersion had brought to his erstwhile remoteness. He would be repaying a debt. He might hope to do so the more wisely thanks to his route through Beirut.[8]

---

[7] It must seem incongruous here, in a world of armed force and power politics, to cite Zechariah 4.6. For he belonged with post-exilic frailty in a world where 'Israel'—in the last analysis—had only spiritual resources of patient trust in Yahweh's fidelity and what might be the good offices of pagan powers. But the incongruity is only a measure of how different are 'then and now'. It also poses the deep question of how Judaism relates to Zionism and Zionism to Judaism, on which there are endless answers. But what of the 'conscience' which surely must belong with either? Or does it mean, as the old psalmist had it—'There is no fear of God before their eyes'? A deep theme of the present time must be how the great Biblical prophets—Amos and his fellows—would now be addressing the State of Israel.

[8] Only in respect of what Beirut came to mean in any novitiate, thanks to the challenge legible in the American University of Beirut, its long self-giving American dedication to a land a sequence of their generations adopted as 'natively' theirs, and to the interpretation of his Lebanon which I had from Charles Malik. See further the Introduction following.

*Absent thee
from felicity awhile
and in this harsh world
draw thy breath in pain
to tell My story*

INTRODUCTION

It was in the dire quandary of near despair that a psalmist cried: 'While I was thus musing the fire kindled.' (Psalm 39. 3) 'His heart was hot within him' over the problem of evil and all its tragic exhibits in the human scene. He could have been writing in the grim summer of 2006 as the crime of the devastation of Lebanon unfolded to arouse 'the dreadful astonishment of God'.[1] It is part of the kindling of this book.

But what follows—as Forewords have indicated—belongs with a retrospect of 'Holy Orders', i.e. of seventy years from a diaconate in England and half that length of episcopate in the jurisdiction based in Jerusalem. (The 'ordaining of priests' normally follows the year of diaconate.) The coincidence of times, dark and glad, dates these pages. It happens that a crucial fusing of the disaster of Lebanon with the anniversary year of ordination set my private retrospect with deep emotion in the defining context of its early tuition in the same territory.

I was on the point of leaving the English domesticity of my first and only curacy for the new fields beyond those frontiers. It is always to be assumed that Christian ministry has to be ready for the world in transcultural as well as geographical terms. Nothing is to be counted alien so long as the venture is not intrusive. That must turn on the temper of the venture, its capacity to learn. There were two dimensions waiting in my education in the emigration from Tranmere/Chester to Beirut/Jerusalem.

It would be useful to come to them by staying briefly on that psalmist's talk of 'muse' and 'fire'. At his inaugural vision 'a live coal' was

---

[1] A striking phrase once used by William Temple in marking how far humans will go in defiance of the divine mind. The note he strikes is akin to the question from Allah to assembled humankind in Surah 7.172: 'Am I not your Lord?' See William Temple, *The Church Looks Forward*, London, 1944, p. 71.

the token of the prophet's call, 'taken from off the altar' where—it was enjoined—'the fire should never go out.' This imagery has long passed into Christian employ as, for example, in Charles Wesley's plea:

> 'Kindle a flame of sacred love
> On the mean altar of my heart.'

where he even managed to weave 'inextinguishable' into his metre. Such 'live coal' imparts and imports, in community, what Paul called 'the glow of that which gloweth.' Sundered from such mutual society 'coals' disintegrate and die.

The metaphor is apt indeed for venerable entities which need, like fires, the ministry of bellows to rid them of the accumulated ash of their past combustion, thus to renew their living contact with the oxygen of the present hour. Ecclesial fires are not the least likely potentially to extinguish themselves by their past histories, unless they accept this vital condition of their continuity.

In a curious way seasons of Christian ordination are known as 'ember days'.[2] The implicit parable is only incidental. The language of 'embers', however, is deep in the New Testament not least in the Pastoral Epistles where Church growth had had time both to develop and know frailty. 'Stir into a flame the gift of God which is in you,' Timothy is warned (2.1.6) where the reference to birth and rearing might translate 'the gift of God which is you.' For personality was ever the fuel of God. The Ordinal prays:

> Come, Holy Ghost, our souls, inspire
> And lighten with celestial fire.
> Thou the anointing Spirit art
> Who dost, Thy sevenfold gifts impart ...'

Veni Creator Spiritus is ever the heart prayer of ministry. There is also the 'stirring of the wills' in the last post-Trinity Collect in the Book of Common Prayer.

---

[2] 'Ember' seems to have had quite another origin as the name given the three fast days (Wednesday, Friday and Saturday) in the four weeks of early Lent, Trinity, Holy Cross day (September 14) and Lady Day in December. These came to be times when ordinations with accompanying 'retreats' came to be held. Hence 'Embertide' and 'Ember Days.'

Introduction

The Methodism of John and Charles Wesley, one such example of the 'art of the bellows', knew itself in what they called something 'strangely warming' in the soul. Theirs was in echo of the psalmist's *in meditatione mea exardescet ignis* as the Vulgate of Psalm 39. 3 has it. 'The fire kindled ...' Only so had come their response to the query of the Ordinal: 'Do you think that you are truly called to this ministry ...?'

That the pattern of the divine mind is always 'truth through personality' is evident enough throughout the Christian faith and its tradition. 'Laying on of hands' is fitting expression of this meaning. For 'hand' or 'hands', whether 'laid on' or 'being laid', signify an entire self. 'Hands to the plough'—that other telling image of vocation—speaks an entire self for a self-engrossing task. 'The hand' is the part for the whole—as in 'hands on deck' of ship-board—and, effectively the whole in the part. 'Give me a hand' means 'Come to my aid.'

Thus, in 'laying on of hands', the Ordinal brings together the ongoing future of a continuous past in a living present. The continuity is supremely personal. It takes 'office' to bequeath 'office'. A mutual present signals the transition and what 'comes to pass' is one with what has been. The sequence witnesses to the staying power of the faith in the Church, of the Church with the faith. The authority under which either acted and either received could only ever be that of the hands of the wounded Lord Christ, from whom all authority derives—and derives in that, by his teaching, he had abrogated that deadly law of retaliation and had died in its repudiation in and beyond the Garden of Gethsemane. Since we most truly 'measure' God in those 'wounds of Jesus' it can only be there that ministry will trace its origin and know its authority. The *lex talionis* being the dire curse of history, the Cross and its 'benefits' would be its benediction.[3]

Such being the 'muse' and the 'fire' by which ministry had being, it was these that ushered me from a first Chester to a new Beirut, from curacy and the tried, to chaplaincy and the untried. This brings a story round to the two dimensions to be understood via the Beirut route towards Jerusalem. One might be described as an

---

[3] The theme recurs here throughout, being vital to the Christian theme of redemption. The limitation (one for one) allegedly benign, is no solution. It witnesses to how any revenge is liable to pursue itself further. In any event a further injury is done or a life lost, so that—in contrast to forgiveness—there is no return to the *status quo ante* and no end to mutual 'damage'. Jesus and the apostles repudiated *lex talionis* completely. Was there not, in Gethsemane, a clear suggestion in those 'swords and staves' for Jesus to resist in like kind? Remember poor Malchus?

'educational patience' both ways, in the fulfilment of ministry. The other was akin, namely a mediating capacity such as the example of the Lebanese Charles Malik taught me as the ambitious significance of his native land. It was a lesson desperately urgent in and for the angry passions to which all Jerusalems are liable. To dwell with his double tuition was my Beirut journey into them.

What can be meant by an 'educational patience'? There are and will always be 'diversities of gifts'—those, for example, of the 'televangelist' with a declaratory—even a declamatory—Gospel who must by all means 'save some'. But such does not 'stand at the door to knock.' He is more like a town-crier speaking God's lines. For Matthew 11. 28f. there was no doubt of the urgent invitation but it said: 'Learn of me that I am ...' as 'meek and lowly of heart'. Its call was to what we would 'find' rather than where we should sign.

During a six-month interim sojourn in what is now 'the Gaza strip' I had known the puzzlement of trying to 'commend the faith' to peasant groups in villages like Khan Yunis or Bait Hanun, squatting beside the endless red-fleshed green rind local melons piled in welcoming heaps around us. There was no doubt of the warm human nexus .We were visiting ex-patients of the Gaza Hospital after first calling on the *mukhtar*, or 'mayor', the persona of the place. But how to make fruitful and incisive the familiar issues between rival convictions, with much illiteracy, not to say poverty, daunting the whole idea? Ought the Hospital to be content with a ministry of healing and forego one of propagation except insofar as the clues were in the former? A steady perplexity was ever waiting on that question.

To be sure, the world is much more than 'Sophomores' being initiated into philosophy. But serving thus in the American University of Beirut alerted me to how matters of faith could be handled from inside a measure of neutral detachment from the dogmatic, only the better to clarify its meanings, so often impeded as these were by the prejudice they kindled in their way. Maybe, 'by indirection we could find direction out,'[4] as a Shakespearean situation phrased it.

---

[4] William Shakespeare, *Hamlet*, Act 2, Scene 1, line 66. There can be a 'take it or leave it' attitude in competing dogmas which will not stay to elucidate, what may be opaque to the other party, or unaware of the pitfalls in a single word. Familiarity—we might say—breeds impatience unless it is ready to think 'tangentially'.

Introduction

The University, meanwhile, would sustain the open field of intellectual honesty and in that context more explicit 'witness' to 'the mind of Christ' could usefully proceed by aid of the mutual respect that the questing ventures of philosophy had served to generate, whether in the labyrinth of 'knowing', or the experience of 'being', or the ultimate bafflement of death. At least, by way of appeal to 'diversities of ministry', there could be a case for an 'educational patience' in and with the trust of truth and its task towards 'the knowledge and the love of God'.

What was also impressive was the wide field of comparative literature, the sympathies between Arabic and English contemporary writing in themes that impinged on the cares of doctrine and yet quite bye-passed them in old controversial terms. The despair in the Palestinian tragedy took poets like Tawfiq Sayigh, Salah 'Abd al-Sabur and Mahmud Darwish into keen admiration for the mood and the broken metre of T S Eliot. Even his poetic drama about an Archbishop of Canterbury (1170) could be recruited to illumine a Sufi Muslim martyrdom in Baghdad (922).[5]

Essayists and novelists like Yusuf Idris, or Najib Mahfuz,[6] responded to the 'contagions' (if we so regard them) of Europeans like André Gide, Albert Camus and J P Sartre with their grim inquests into the human condition. There could be no doubt about the exposure of the Muslim reading public to the sense of 'lostness' in the western search to find and be found. All of this meant a salutary exposure of the assurance of religious structures, whether benign or malign, to the probing light of scrutiny quite other than the old and self-indulgent controversies. Pioneered by the likes of Taha Husain there was also a steady stream of translation for a widening Arabic literacy.[7]

---

[5] See my *Troubled by Truth*, Edinburgh, 1992, pp. 166-86, for discussion of Salah 'Abd al-Sabur's use of T S Eliot, in his verse drama on Al-Hallaj, the martyr of Baghdad. Several poets were also deeply influenced by his themes and style.

[6] On several writers, see, e.g., Ismat Mahdi, *Modern Arabic Literature, 1900-1967*, Hyderabad, 1983. On Yusuf Idris, see P M Kurpershoek, *The Short Stories of Yusuf Idris*, Leiden, 1981. There are numerous studies of Najib Mahfuz, as e.g. Sasson Somekh, *The Changing Rhythm, A Study of Najib Mahfuz' Novels*, Leiden, 1973, or Rashed el-Enany, *Naguib Mahfouz: The Pursuit of Meaning*, London, 1993.

[7] From his own experience in France (at the Sorbonne) he sought to have Egyptian culture acknowledge fully its Mediterranean dimension, for which he pleaded in *Mustaqbal al-Thaqafah fi Misr* ('The Future of Culture in Egypt'), Cairo 1938.

Increasingly, there was also the rise of a strongly articulate Islamic feminism raising, in truly existential terms, the vexing issues of the Qur'an's authority and the cultural conditioning of human sexuality. In the grim flux of things perhaps the soul of salvation had to take priority over salvation of the soul.[8] Mere polemic had no place in such a world. Truth and ministry had to ally themselves with gentleness as the 'yoke' that bonded them and was the way of their 'learning'.

So much I began to understand in a prolonged transit through Beirut with intent towards Jerusalem. Meaning, in a word, was for mediation.

Such was also the second significance of Lebanon via a concept as Charles Malik envisioned it. It might seem an odd idea now to dwell with a theme of sixty years ago when Lebanon first became independent at the end of the French Mandate. Moreover, it has been desperately tarnished and compromised in the turbulent years since Malik dreamed of it. It could well be realist to hold it whimsical and forlorn, were it not the Lebanon which Israel again in the summer of 2006, trampled underfoot, as earlier it did in 1982. For it is a vision of mediation which Israeli Zionism itself needs for its soul-health and sanity.

For the Malik vision and version of Lebanon perceived a geography of 'in-between-ness', nurtured doubtless in philosophy but striving to fulfil itself in politics. It had to do with the 'original' Christianity of Lebanon with Maronite and 'catholic' identity, but its experience of the impact of Greece, of Plato and the entire western tradition of the Mediterranean, where its shore-line lay. All this had been corroborated and enhanced by the ideals of the American educational enterprise Malik's own nurture had absorbed.[9] It equipped his native soil he believed, to interpret this heritage, as thus a genuine Middle Eastern thing, to the hinterland of Arabism and Islam to

---

[8] A trite way of making the partial differentiation there can be between what seeks the individual in every faith-equation, and what cares about ministering to the whole ethos of another faith structure.

[9] Charles Malik, see *The Challenge of Human Rights, Charles Malik and the Universal Declaration*, ed. H C Malik, Oxford, 2000. He left his Chair in 1945 to be the first Lebanese Ambassador and thence President of the General Assembly of the United Nations, where he became the main architect of the Declaration of Human Rights. He died in Beirut in 1987, aged eighty-one. He lived for the ideal of his native Lebanon as mediating between the Islam of the Syrian hinterland and beyond and the western values with which Lebanon was linked via France and the Mediterranean, and more recently in part thanks to the AUB of the United States.

Introduction

which no less territorially it belonged. It could thus aspire by dint of geography itself—if not also by temperament—to serve as a bridge of cultures. It could hope to be, as it were, by native genius, an essay in compatibility. Doubtless its potential asset this way was its supreme experience of risk. It is not seldom that agencies of conciliation in history are subject to conspiracies that will ever threaten them. Cynics will say that the viability of a Lebanon in Malik's terms perished long ago in the dire civil war that erupted in 1974 and lasted bitter years. Was the very geography to which it appealed also its undoing? For the Mandatory Power in 1920 had enlarged the fragment of Mount Lebanon (which Charles Malik had most in mind) by the addition of Shi'ah Muslim areas around Sidon and Tyre and also Sunni Muslim areas to the north beyond Tripoli. His ideology was thus jeopardised by the size on which it had to rely in its appeal. That dilemma has sharpened in the intervening years. It may well have become insuperable

Nevertheless the vision of 'something mediatorial' in the Middle East is ever more urgent of realisation. It is a light too precious to be extinguished The reasons are profoundly Israeli, did Israel 'know the things that belong to her peace.' For Zionism has always been, inherently, a quest for compatibility pursued in terms that disavow the pre-requisites of compatibility.[10] Its active, inner ideology precludes its actual outward success, so that—in the words of its foremost anthologist—'Zionism has neither failed not succeeded.'[11]

He had been himself a student at the University and thence had gone to Harvard where he read philosophy in the days of Alfred North Whitehead and William Ernest Hocking, whose 'measures of thought' he brought back into his own teaching. The long sustained idealism of the University down to the late forties was a splendid sample of genuine internationalism, of inter-human community which Malik sought to translate into his local Lebanese world and, via Lebanon, into the whole Near East.

[10] There is a 'pathos' in the word's root that needs to be noticed. It carries the archaic sense of 'suffer' as 'let' or 'allow' (cf. Jesus saying 'Suffer the children to come …'). We cannot relate positively without a measure of readiness for cost at our expense. Hence the futility of perpetual *lex talionis*.

[11] The verdict in paradox of its anthologist, Arthur Hertzberg, *The Zionist Idea: A Historical Analysis and Reader*, Forge Valley, 1959, p. 17. 'To date', he wrote, 'even after the creation of the State of Israel, Zionism has neither succeeded nor failed.' By 2006 both are more desperately clear. It has a threescore history as a vigorous *fait accompli*, a phenomenal achievement of vision, energy and resolve, but the where and how of its realisation condemn the ideal of a peaceable place among the nations to seemingly irreducible frustration. By its very ideology it never meant to integrate; its leaders in rule have been its leaders in war. Does its will

The Order of the Wounded Hands

As Abba Eban, with others, would eloquently insist, Israel had no mind to be 'Levantine'. It had no intention to belong in and with the region. It intended a homogeneous Jewishness in national, political terms for which the region between Jordan and the Middle Sea was the truly destined locale, despite the undoubted—and at the outset—the overwhelming presence of an other people. From these, they, in Jewry and for Jewry's meanings, would be 'dwelling apart'.

These, the inherent terms of its ideological presence, desperately needed to be somehow reconciled with the reality of their location. For all its inward preciousness of 'promise', divine pledge and proper destiny, its actual strategy was intrusive Its necessary pragmatisms were endlessly ambiguous in the very business of being effectual. From Herzl onwards, through the Balfour Declaration and the chronic years of the British Mandate and in the long aftermath of the UNO Partition Vote, all remarkably progressed by a sort of creative stealth, avoiding to define its ultimate dimension. Thus, through harsh ineptitude and much bungling and mischance, the 'other party' has been bitterly frustrated in its own countering struggle for kindredly 'Zionist' objectives, namely land and statehood by which alone to 'be ourselves'. There is no human denying the corresponding human claim to the same 'attaining to be'. Yet the Zion that is Israel, the Israel that is Zion has steadily excluded from genuine reckoning the terms on which that claim might come to pass with Israel's honest, full and forthright concurrence.[12]

The steady *fait accompli*, first of settlements and then roads to link them into nuclei, serve an 'apartness' which elsewhere is relentless encroachment and, for the land-loving, tragic displacement and, for the angry and the violent, relentless provocation. What then is 'the self' whose 'right to exist' and 'right to defend itself' is constantly trumpeted?—how large? when final? whenever mutual? These, the questions that alone 'make for peace', have remained unanswered.

If, simply, we ask: What confronts what? the answer can only be an abiding, political Israel and a demographic Palestinianism,

---

to be exclusive, ideologically and territorially, darkly militarise its survival and thus deny authentic Zion to Zionism?

[12] At many points in Jewish self-understanding there are issues about what Zionism is implying about Judaism and about how or whether Judaism is at peace with Zionism. If the one is essentially a religion, how is the other an armed regime? What of diaspora Jews who truly find their 'promised land' where they are? And what of the paradox Israel is sustained and viable by dint of those who do not choose to dwell in it? See also previous note.

neither reducible by or to the other. Whatever be the other burning themes—repatriation, refugees, the status of Jerusalem (which 'Oslo' tried fruitlessly to take *seriatim*)[13]—these are the twin reality. They speak only one logic—compatibility.

Now it would seem that, at long last, by means of the notorious 'Wall', Israel is preparing to define itself but in age-long terms of calculated apartheid, and to impose it as if it resolved all obligation towards that demographic Palestinianism. There is no peace this way. There is only, on the one part, a still more irreconciled hostility and on the other a destiny to remain embattled, a state never at ease either with its location or its conscience and doomed to be ever at odds with its own Zionist soul.

Of all the Arab neighbours of Israel, Lebanon is unique in its tradition of aspiring—or maybe of having once aspired—to the art of co-existence within itself.[14] Such a neighbour could be a priceless asset to Israel. For Jewry also has the same Mediterranean littoral in more southerly terms, long European perspectives and a deep Arab hinterland.

It is not remotely suggested that Lebanon, under present humiliation—or ever—can be of any relevance to Israel, except perhaps with the lesson that for every identity there is a necessity to inter-belong. No particularity is exempt. For Lebanon this necessity is within its own nationhood: for Israel it belongs with its own location. In the last analysis 'a people dwelling apart' is a contradiction in terms. Israel must find it within her to co-exist and do so in her own required terms of 'landed liberty via acknowledged statehood'. There was no wisdom in context in degrading and decimating a neighbour potentially learning or exemplifying this lesson.

It is perhaps relevant in context to note how, via the resolute leadership of Charles Malik, this Lebanese humanism gave being to the

---

[13] 'Oslo' was the nearest point of some ordered co-existence but its Israeli mentor-pioneer was assassinated by Israeli hand amid very inadequate protection after he had been cruelly vilified. Soon after an election took Oslo 'out of the way' that the old order of provocative stalemate might ensue. The difficult policy of encouraging a 'negotiable' moderation was always baulked, so that increasingly Palestinian hopelessness, 'prospectless-ness', deepened its obduracy, in face of a mutually crippling impasse.

[14] Its sundry elements leave it no other option. Its only hope is to learn to 'inter-belong' with a precarious 'national' concept. The Druse and Armenian elements apart and a Christian diversity, it has the common duality in all Arabism, between a Sunni and a Shi'ah Islam.

United Nations' 'Declaration of Human Rights'. He had, to be sure, the determined backing of that brand of American sanity represented by the formidable personality of its 'First Lady', Eleanor Roosevelt. It is fair to see the Declaration as the fruit of a Lebanese mind in creative reckoning with the world at large.[15]

It was in this double; education that Beirut and the Lebanon initiated me into any further journey of my ministry to Jerusalem with all its exactingness in the comings and goings of four decades until the mid-eighties of the century. Inevitably the pain of the events of the summer of 2006 forced its way into this Introduction as prelude to ensuing chapters. It is necessary now to stand back and seek patiently the measure of the task any Christian relation has to 'the Jerusalem that now is.'[16]

In geopolitical, global terms, it is certainly to resist and disown the notion of an inevitable 'clash' of an East and a West, with the one Muslim and violent, the other secular and liberal. This way there is, and can only be, folly, futility and tragedy. Thus—'it is not and it cannot come to good.' It is grievous danger to have it seem that Israel is somehow a 'proxy' warring, with US weapons and political clout, on behalf of world sponsors, while Hizballah/Hamas are seen as 'the source of the problem' in representing an inherently violent Islam. There are no monopolies of 'terrorism', direct or indirect. There are resources of sanity, wisdom and humanity in Islamic faith and civilization, there to be retrieved—if need be—from its darkest image. There are also regimes which—for all the dubiety (in western eyes) of their 'democratic' credentials—are already alert to being global and co-existent by Islamic/secular norms. Deep issues still remain in this situation. A presumption of global confrontation does nothing to resolve them. The West is culpable enough to add further or longer, by its fears and phobias (or its readings in these terms) to assertive confrontation. 'We are fighting terrorism' is a wilfully naïve and cynical stance unless what shapes its practitioners is patiently undertaken, both in its human sources and its doctrinal sanctions. It is from within Islam that Islam defines and fulfils itself. The rest are not spectators. Nor are

---

[15] The story is documented in Habib C Malik, *The Challenge of Human Rights, Charles Malik and the Universal Declaration*, Oxford, 2000. Cf. note 9.

[16] Borrowing a phrase Paul used in another context in Galatians 4. 25.

they masters of hostilities. They could be neighbours to an issue of hope, sanity and peace.[17]

Here, to be sure, belong the essentially doctrinal ministries of a Christian theology. Evident enough are the three realms of the Judaic, the Islamic and the secular as integral to the contemporary Near Eastern scene.

It is well to begin with how the psalmist made his own way from a Lebanese sojourn towards the Temple for which he yearned and how that access into 'ultimate sanctuary' had Christian realisation in the inauguration of the Church as the faith that found, in the fact of Christ, 'the place of the Name' where God made redeeming rendezvous with us humans in His world of our divine intent. For only so did the ministry ensue which had that truth of us in its worldwide care.

---

[17] What might well fortify that conclusion is the irony we have noted in how the Israeli Zionist and the Palestinian nationalist have in common the very same demands and criteria of identity, namely 'Ourselves, our land, our State'. It is madness to call the one 'legitimate' and the other 'terrorist'. Neither avails honestly without the other.

Chapter 1
WITH THE PSALMIST TO THE CHRIST SANCTUARY

I

'Lord, I have loved the habitation of Thy house and the place where Thine honour dwells'. (Psalm 26. 8)

The 'tabernacle of honour' brings together two defining words in the Hebrew tradition, alike of history and of worship The dual concept in their juncture abounds in the language of the Christian New Testament in the sense of an indebtedness to be explored here in Chapter 4. There are sundry Hebrew terms for 'honour' as belonging to Yahweh with synonyms like 'majesty', 'glory', 'excellence', which can be compounded together in the reiteration of the 'praise' that comprehends them all.

'The place where Thine honour dwells' ... but how can these mysteries of God have territorial locale? Can geography tell theology or the art of mapping yield doctrine? If the Biblical theme were not so familiar it would surely seem utterly incongruous. The founding idea of a place of rendezvous with the divine, so pivotal in Hebrew faith, translates into the Christian esteeming of the personal drama of Jesus as the Christ.[1] Even with Jewry's Jerusalem, mere locale (if we may so speak) was gathered into history, out of the long antecedents of Exodus and conquest in pursuance of covenant under Joshua and ultimate capture at the hand of David, with Solomon's Temple

---

[1] 'Esteeming' is appropriate here inasmuch as, while faith ensued upon event, it was event which engendered the faith that hailed and told it. This inter-action is crucial in all religion between 'things held' in belief and the believing that possesses them. Hence the need for faith to have a critical scholarship within itself which takes this situation in hand. See Chapter 7. The theme of 'rendezvous' also draws on the fusion between drama and dramatist, or music and the musician on which Dorothy Sayers drew so usefully in *The Mind of the Maker*, London, 1941, and re-issues.

With the Psalmist to the Christ Sanctuary

then ensuing to finalise a Hebrew tenure of 'the holy Mount' of an ancestral Abraham.

Thus transpired 'the place of Yahweh's honour'. Situation geographical was known for meaning historical. Time and territory contained in their strange unison the drama of a people and their destiny.

All four—story, scene, society and soul—came together as a saga of faith but only, also, as being a city of sacrifice. The Temple ritual, so meticulously set down in the Book of Leviticus[2] and assiduously pursued in daily and seasonal offerings of blood and animal slaughter, was—as it were—the measure of that 'honour' of God duly accorded Him, but in terms which would come to seem incredible and unseemly.

The theme and the faith of these pages now is that 'the place where God's honour dwells,' remotely yet effectively from these antecedents, came to be discerned in Jesus and the Cross that ensued from his Gethsemane. There were things perpetuated, namely place, event, occasion, suffering and sacrifice but all these were transformed in that—as magnificently the Letter to the Hebrews told it—'the blood of his sacrifice was his own' (9. 12). What was contrived, artificial, a device of ritual and ceremony, the practice of animal immolation on an 'altar of burnt sacrifice', was displaced by a living drama of intensely moral history. What Temple-wise was no more than a vicariousness arbitrarily inflicted on unknowing, unconsenting beasts became a conscious shouldering of a world-size wrongness in a crisis of legible history.[3] A 'priesthood' that had been external and unscathed within a ritual consisted now in a Saviour's own redeeming wounds. The recognising faith all kindled in the sequel—to be told in the chapter following—carried the language of Psalm 26 into the confession of 'the Lamb in the midst of the throne', and the 'majesty on high' read from 'the crown of thorns'. The Church found itself saying of the whole Christ-drama:

---

[2] With its strange breadth of legislation both liturgical and moral, ceremonial and social. Ezekiel later demonstrates how instinctive this devout 'legalism' was to the Hebrew mind. We might speak of 'a cultic correctness' as purists do elsewhere.
[3] 'Legible' in being as Paul had it—'placarded' for all to read, like the *titulus* over the Cross: 'world-sized' in having to do with 'the sin of the world'. See below.

'Lord, we have loved the habitation of Thy house the Place where Thine honour dwelleth.'

and found itself in knowing it so.

That Christian perception of the 'place' of supreme rendezvous with God where being redemptive takes on the weight of human guilt and the cost of forgiveness in a 'suffering' that bears it, needs careful exposition elsewhere. For much confusion and distortion have flowed from imperceptive connection between 'altars' and the Cross. Here we need to linger with the psalmists. How resoundingly they celebrate their Temple-geography saluting their people-history. Doing so, they enlist the whole range of musical sound, from harp, cornet, trumpet and the ten-stringed 'psaltery' (33. 2, 68. 23, 87. 7, 92. 3, 150. 4). For

'Honour and majesty are before Him: strength and beauty are in His sanctuary.' (96. 6)

Is 'the sanctuary' at once the natural order of external nature, the splendour of the landscape *and* 'the building made with hands,' as if the whole scenario of the 'hills that stand around Jerusalem' usher their mystery into the single shrine.[4] The sparrows of Psalm 84 found those 'altars' of the Lord congenial for their nesting place, as sharing the blessedness of the human 'dwellers'.

In chastened mood also and out of deep despair, the divine sanctuary is where re-assurance avails. 'Out of His holy hill' 'the Lord heard my voice,' cried the sad-at-heart in Psalm 3. 4 assailed by scorners who saw 'no help for him in his God'. Perhaps the classic text in this vein is Psalm 73 puzzled by the pain of lonely perplexity—things altogether 'too hard'

'... until I went into the sanctuary of God, then understood I ...'

'Flesh and heart' alike—that duo of psalmists (40. 12, 73. 26, 84. 2 and 139. 23)—are mutually righted by 'help from the sanctuary'.

These deeply personal emotions around the Temple shrine were only the more poignant from the corporate significance—'whither

---

[4] The founding/founded 'city of faith' as the centre of the earth.

the tribes go up.' The place of people-thronging seized powerfully on the private heart when absence in distance precluded being present. Thus Psalm 42 with its echo in 43 would seem to belong with such a haunt of privation—if we read aright the note about 'waves' drowning him—was far off in the foothills of Hermon where mountain torrents were cascading down the slopes to feed the native streams of the Jordan. Memory played its plaintive part—

> 'I went with the multitude to the house of God, with the voice of joy and praise ...' (42. 4, 6 and 7)

—memory heightened by 'festival', the other great virtue of 'the hill of the Lord'. 'The multitude' for which the psalmist yearned 'kept holiday'. Time and season lent their aura to the themes of music. Ritual with calendar weaved text and the texture of thanksgiving.

In this rich amalgam in the saga of psalmody of the pilgrim, the choir-master, devotee, the celebrant of festival, it is noteworthy how relatively rare—as compared with the Pentateuch—are references to the sacrificial system. Questions of dating are, of course, involved since psalmody is contemporary with long evolutions of Hebraic story and identity. The long Christian tradition of aligning Psalm 43's: 'I will go unto the altar of God' with the table sacrament of Christian redemption would be tenuous indeed without larger reason than 26. 6: 'So will I compass Thine altar, O Lord,' where the singer is protesting his avoidance of sinners. 'Then will they offer young bullocks on Thine altar' (51. 19), albeit deeply penitential, is remoter still. We need to let the deep piety of psalmody lead us beyond the 'altar' theme in priestly ritual terms to its larger implications, if the word is ever to comprehend justly the Christian mystery of 'God in Christ'. How the Letter to the Hebrews struggles to do so concerns us in Chapter 4.

II

Another dimension presents itself in the concept of 'kingship', essentially that of Yahweh and derivatively that of the David tradition. The umbrella title: 'The Psalms of David' however spacious across centuries until the Exile, captures the royal role within the music.

The Order of the Wounded Hands

So many psalms, far more numerous than those which accompany a ritual, salute an accession or a coronation or celebrate a royal birth. There are more than seventy echoes of this theme across the Psalter, with Hebrew kingship strangely fused with the sovereignty of Yahweh. 'Yet have I set My king upon My holy hill of Zion.' (2. 6) Zion is 'the hill of God's holiness' entrusted to the governance of His appointed custodian—'My king'. Psalm 2 can be sharply confrontational vis-à-vis the nations, because it is as if Yahweh has—as it were—taken on 'a son' via this earthly rulership that presides in the seat of God's holiness. Thus Jerusalem monarchy symbolises and transacts the majesty of Yahweh. The psalm's theology is thoroughly 'anthropomorphic' in its conviction about a divine-Hebraic unison in city-throne. The opening of Psalm 50 might be read as linking that unison with creation itself:

> 'The mighty God the Lord, has spoken and called the earth from
> the rising of the sun to the going down of the same'. (50. 1)

to be promptly followed by

> 'Out of Zion, the perfection of beauty, God has shined.'

Are the words here anticipating, as it were, the Johannine, Christian fusion of the light that commanded at creation and the light of the Incarnate Word (John 1. 1-18)? Or is the reference to utterance from Sinai—hardly 'from orient to occident'—given the privacy of 'all *our* fathers under the cloud'? Either way, this near-identity between Yahweh and Zion draws the psalmist into an entire and forceful rejection of the whole sacrificial system of ritual altars (v. 8-15). Here is a 'theological royalty' which dispenses with forms in claim for the integrity they too often exclude.

Elsewhere confidence in the divine investment in Hebrew sovereignty is blithe enough to salute even royal weddings (45. 8-16) and heir-ensurings with eloquent poetry in song, celebrating—in the same strophes—'Thy throne, O God, is for ever and ever.' 'Love of righteousness' is the common property both of Yahweh and 'His king'. The singer (v. 1) is touchingly confident about the warrant in his inspiration and the gifts of 'tongue and pen' he brings to it. 'Grace is poured from thy (his?) lips.' In Psalm 24 'Who is the King of glory' can have only one answer yet 'the gates' He is to 'enter' belong to 'all the earth' and to the 'holy hill of Zion' whose king will match the criteria of righteous sovereignty. Royal longevity is the care of 61. 6, integrity of 99. 4, victory over rivals of 135. 10-11 and 136. 17-20. King-psalms are thus more frequent, more poetic than priest-ones; the theme of righteous power more central for psalmody than that of ritual priesthood.

We will need to note elsewhere the strong role of prophethood in the antecedents of Christian ministry as the Anglican Order presents it. Here is it clear enough that any sequence from psalmists to deacons, priests and bishops, entrusted as these are with the ordering of worship in which those psalms have long played so large a part, will have to focus on their salient concern with the features we have studied which anticipate 'Messiah'. For all that is 'kingly' in their salute to sovereignty intends that Messianic issue. But it is one that will only be fully understood, via Hosea, Isaiah, Jeremiah and their kindred, as—to use Rabbi Heschel's words—'the Messiah of divine pathos'. There will be every Hebraic reason for knowing Christian Ordination as 'the Order of wounded hands'.

III

This realisation conveys us to another task in sequence from psalmist to the Christ-sanctuary. *Introibo ad altare Dei* will be a strange cry in the heart for any approach to Holy Communion in 'bread and wine', unless we register the fortunes—or misfortunes—of vocabulary. Words go up and down and 'altar' has always been a curious one, oscillating between 'high hill', 'place of slaughter', 'place of troth' and 'site of ceremony'. It has yielded many compounds like 'cloth', 'fire', 'frontal'. From its *altus* origin we might think of it as 'a place of heights', whether of aspiration, of solemnity or of 'steps that lead there.' What can contrive much of meaning incurs much of ambivalence. We might strike analogy from 'prestige' which has moved all the way from its Latin 'delusion/illusion', to 'a conjuror's trick', to 'high deserved reputation'. Or that of the Greek 'character', moving all the way from a 'mark on clay' to an 'actor in a play', to a 'man of great parts' like an Abraham Lincoln, bearing in his face all the features of his leadership.

Only in some such progression can we inter-associate what happened in the Temple's daily holocaust and what happened in the

Cross of Jesus.[5] The Letter to the Hebrews anon will serve to study how, with its admirable anxiety to connect long Hebrew usage and mind-set with the Eucharist in Christ. Deferring that theme of the things of the Temple and the things of Holy Communion, there is another motif within both which belonged with many a psalm but only because it stood for a deep perception of history. This tells itself as 'the place of the Name' and takes us back to the exciting narrative of the call of Moses and its splendid issue in the Exodus. 'This place of which Thou hast said "My Name shall be there"' echoes through Solomon's Prayer at the dedication of the Temple (1 Kings 8. 29) when he takes thought for all the vicissitudes through which the nation might pass when they would look towards it in hope and yearning. Place and time could thus come together in the economy of Yahweh and so also in the circumstances of the people.

'The place of the Name' has its origin with Moses in his wilderness sojourn, brooding doubtless on the fate of his people and the meaning of his own fugitive state in exile from them and—thanks to these—his arresting vision of 'the bush that burned' from which there came the summons whereby he was to be the great emancipator. Addressed in these incredible terms, he answered Yahweh (at this first 'knowing of the Name') with misgivings at the condition of his people so long enslaved and broken. 'When I say to them: "Yahweh sends me to lead you out of Egypt" they will say to me: "What is His Name?"' The meaning surely is as Martin Buber has it.[6] They, the people with their question are looking for re-assurance, even for guarantee. Is this 'Name' trustworthy, dependable, real? For Egypt, the creation of a river and fringed with daunting desert, is not a country rashly to leave, least of all for an oppressed and craven band of slaves. 'What', Moses enquires, 'shall I say to them?' Then comes the divine answer as to 'any place and any Name'—not an illegible riddle 'I am that I that I am?' How would that motivate or inspire? Rather the sense is that of a promise, not of an enigma. 'I will be there as whom there I will be.' In

---

[5] It is sometimes forgotten that the origin of the dread word 'holocaust' was precisely the ritual 'burnings' of the Levitical system (*holos kaustos*—'a whole burnt offering').

[6] See Martin Buber, *Moses*, Oxford, 1940. However, later—brooding on 'Messianism'—he drew a contrast between Moses as a figure of 'history-making power and authority' and the powerlessness of the great prophets who had to witness against 'power in evil'. Thus the 'Mosaic' (with Samuel) belonged to an early phase of Israeli story. See ed. N N Glatzer, *Martin Buber on Judaism*, New York. 1967.

the experience of exodus the God of Exodus will be known. Future, but pledged, it has to be. Only in the going will be the proving. The rubric is not 'guarantee' unless as 'trust'.

So, at length, in the event it proved to be. They learned Yahweh's identity in emigration under His wing. What happened to them 'happened' a conviction in them. It then became a ready theme of memory and a memory in festival. 'All our fathers passed through the sea.' When that history culminated by entry to the land it became the geography of fulfilment. The story became the architecture of the Temple as symbolising the meaning of the whole land as the dwelling place, alike of Yahweh and His people. It, *qua* locale, was 'the place of the Name' in the precedent history having first been so *qua* narrative-experience. 'I will be there' (Exodus) became 'I dwell here' (Jerusalem.) So for Isaiah 18. 7 their capital city is 'the place of the Name', and likewise for 60. 13 and 66. 1 'the place of His sanctuary'.

There are similar allusions in Hosea 1. 10, and in the language of restoration in passages like Jeremiah 28. 3, 29. 14, where 'the place whence I called you to be made captive,' becomes again by sublime irony, 'the place of My Name' anew. A 'there' in history becomes a 'there' in geography: a 'here' in experience translates into a 'here' in conviction.

It is evident enough that this imagery of a time into a place, or—better—of a time as a place, passed fully into the Christian mind concerning the entire ministry of Jesus where and in whom God had—as it were—'place-timed' Himself and had done so supremely in the event of Good Friday. Why, else, called 'good'? Event had again been where 'the Name' was housed, read, made legible, pleadable and sure. It lingers in that strange detail in Matthew 27. 36 about the watch of the Roman soldiers beside the Cross. 'Sitting down they watched him there,' 'Him there' such a person in such a place, a paradox at the heart of history where Christian theology has anchorage, the 'locality' where the Greek in Paul's defining words is 'locative'—'God in Christ'—this way, by this language, this place of identity.

Must not this be the point of that strange language in the Gospel about 'the temple of his body', before 'body' can become the incorporate nature of his people? It is characteristic of the Fourth Gospel written out of the Synoptic situation but from the perspective of the incarnational theology developed, as it only could be, from the experience of Jesus 'risen', the development that has to be traced in the succeeding chapter. We have in the Johannine scene the Jesus of the parables and of the Sermon on the Mount but now comprehended as having the language of 'the Word made flesh'.[7] Thus the term 'the temple of his body', so enigmatic to the Jewish leadership, could be credible by dint of analogy concerning 'where God dwelt.' (2. 21).

The physical Temple was

> '... microcosm of the macrocosm. The building gave visual expression to the belief in Yahweh's dominion over the world and all natural places.'[8]

Being thus a place of historic 'theophany', it was well suited to attest the meaning of the 'Christ for all nations'. Its 'cleansing' by his hand would tell 'the zeal of God's house' in double sense. As, and even when that literal Temple was 'destroyed', all places in Christ would find themselves equidistant from divine rendezvous, as Christian expansion in mission would assume. David's vision and Solomon's builders had fulfilled their task.

IV

What then, it remains here to ask, can the Christian celebrant or 'president', the individual communicant, mean by the *Introibo ad altare Dei* of his/her approach to 'exceeding joy', as once did the psalmist compassing his Jewish precincts? Let us leave to Chapter 4 the rationale of the Letter to the Hebrews with its partiality for the logic that controls it. We are arguing throughout that the aegis under which 'presiding' happens or communicants 'approach', is from 'the wounded hands of Christ', seeing there is no other mandate into 'Holy Orders' and their ministries than Christ's from whom all human ones derive.

It is necessary first to concede how incongruous the analogy is between Christian Eucharist ('God my exceeding joy') and the Levitical

---

[7] It is vital to know this quality of John's Gospel as, indeed the factual situation but told in the speech of its *post-facto* experience of 'the Son of Man' being 'the Word made flesh'. Only as the latter could so many of the sayings, like 'I and my Father are one,' be comprehensible *in situ*. John's Christ speaks as 'the incarnate Word'.

[8] R E Clements, *God and Temple*, 1965, p. 67.

With the Psalmist to the Christ Sanctuary

system of repeated sacrifice. All is implicit in the range of that word 'sacrifice' now used so carelessly and at all times so variously. We must disown with Jesus crucified all 'passive victimisation'.[9] The psalmist en route to divine rendezvous at 'the hill of God', whether under Levitical or Deuteronomist ritual regimes, brings a realist sense of the seriousness of sin but a sadly minimal, almost mechanical concept of the transactions of forgiveness and the cost of pardon.

He is sharply aware of the wrongs done, the onus of evil in life and society and in the private bosom. Not for him the notion of time that can 'draw a line' under the past and get on with life, resumed as if memory had no part in the liability of personhood.[10] But this commendable sense of the entail of wrong done, of the issues of sin, is answered for him in a mere ritual of animal immolation. The writ of the *lex talionis* is still in place. Indeed, it preserves a vital role in the legislation even to the point of barbarous cruelty in penalties of guilt requital, and punitive revenge.[11] There is no occasion for the costly suspension of these, so that crime done and wrong inflicted merely have their sequel in the perpetuation of them which occurs in what only avenges and so fails to redeem.

Perhaps we may see this realist view of wrong and sin in the Temple ritual as the corollary of the very 'holiness' of Yahweh. For that quality is everywhere in emphasis. It requires the meticulous care for all the details of due 'sanctity' of garments, vessels, furnishings, persons and offerings of the sanctuary. It has almost a physically antiseptic aegis over all details of its drama in liturgy.

Is it here that we should look for the clue to the inadequacies of the strategies (if we may so speak) of the pardon it allows? For what is genuinely 'vicarious' in the theme—or the objects—in burnt

---

[9] It is strange to find 'passivity' attributed to Jesus in Gethsemane and its sequel when the whole event is an active, costly negation of the *lex talionis* (that curse of all history) and a *will* to redeem. See further, the odd thesis of a 'passive victim' is in eds., N Solomon, R Harries and T Winter, *Abraham's Children: Jews, Christians and Muslims in Conversation*, London, 2006, p. 119.

[10] These frequent contemporary phrases of guilt dismissal are expressive of a sad trivialising of moral wrongs in social relations. 'Done nothing wrong' is easy exoneration for what is thus merely 'episodic'.

[11] A striking example comes in Deuteronomy 21.18-23 concerning the: 'rebellious' ('prodigal'?) son hailed before 'the elders of the city'. Did this passage kindle its 'overthrow' in Jesus' famous parable in Luke 15 about the kiss and the robe, the shoes and the feast? How ready with 'the stones of stoning' was that Pentateuchal world.

offerings? In their animal status there can be no conscious acceptance of any pained relationship implicit in the deeds of inter-human wrong, no engagement with the honest price of foregoing revenge and willing into being the *'status quo ante'* as active forgiveness will and must.

How could the Hebrew mind configure the theme of the 'scapegoat' driven into the wilderness laden, only ceremonially with the guilt of the wrong-doer imposed by the hand of ritual?[12] Its grim exit into vacancy may have impressed the soul with some notion of a 'vacancy' now ensuing as a 'farewell' to guilt, but what avails of genuine reconciliation with the injured party? All is a very self-centred transaction, pre-occupied as it is with an inward sense of 'righteousness' which ignores the true breadth of relatedness to God and neighbour. Have not Leviticus and Deuteronomy reduced divine forgiveness to a priestly mechanism in which the 'priestliness' has not 'entered into God'? The divine dimension is, as it were, appeased, requited, satisfied but not otherwise involved. We put the matter in another form if we enquire about 'things vicarious' as only formal and as genuine and integral. What 'lamb(s) of God' can there truly be? We have to pass from the animal plural to the eternal singular.

The cry, according to John the Evangelist, of John the Baptist concerning Jesus (1. 29) may have derived in part from the Pentateuchal liturgy but it only had its truest matrix from the biography of Jeremiah prefiguring things Messianic.[13] The Evangelist or his namesake, would later 'behold that Lamb' there 'in the midst of the throne of God', in token of how 'the love that suffers is the power that reigns.' We are only on Christian ground reading 'the Lamb of God' this way, far other than impossible precedents from the rituals of the original Temple rendezvous with Yahweh.

We reach the same necessary conclusion in Chapter 4 by another route, in other bearings of Jewish-Christian themes. Meanwhile,

---

[12] The deep irony is that, via Anti-semitism, Jewry has been made to suffer the role of its own imagining in the scapegoat.

[13] The 'lamb-likeness' of Jeremiah is his own tragic imagery for the burden, pain and anguish his vocation exacted from him through the long saga of its costliness in lonely privation and public scorn and final death in exile. See 11. 19 and cf. 8. 18 and 21, and 15. 18 with the bitter protest of 20. 7-9 with its own violent address to Yahweh: 'You raped me' in 'enticing' me into this utterly fated ministry which I never sought. See below and John Skinner's classic study, *Prophecy and Religion: Studies in the Life of Jeremiah*, Cambridge, 1922. There is no doubt that his suffering prophethood was a paradigm of a suffering vocation for any Messiah, studied further here in Chapters 2 and 4.

it remains to note how salutary for the Christian faith has been the witness of that Temple rendezvous to the seriousness of sin and wrong, yet how dire its legacy when readings of Christian redemption have drawn uncritically on its notions of external sacrifice as ever being congenial to the reality of 'God in Christ reconciling the world'.

To the deep prejudice of our 'learning of Christ', preachers have insisted on a rigorous, literal immolation of Jesus in almost Levitical terms as 'the sacrifice for sin', in a way that excludes God altogether from the meaning of Gethsemane and its sequel in 'Christ crucified'. So doing they have betrayed the classic New Testament theme of 'God in Christ', where the particle 'in' is indeed 'transitive'. 'I have been there as who there I have been' is the truth of the divine nature and the heart of theology.[14] Just as human wrong is integral to the reckonings of divine righteousness, as the Pentateuchal scene knew well, so is the cost of human forgiveness integral, as the heirs of Leviticus and its cultic pardon could only learn via the reality of Jesus as the Christ.

'Burnt offering', animal-style 'atonement' could never worthily presage the redemptiveness that is both divine and Christly in terms the Temple could never be. The far distance in that contrast was memorably stated by O C Quick.

> 'What the Christian calls redemption is the process by which the relation of instrumentality to goodness is universalised ... Wherever, and in so far as, any evil has been overcome and made, in result, instrumental to good, the evil has been redeemed and atonement made. And, when it is asserted that the Atonement wrought by the Cross of Christ is universal and all-sufficient, we desire to understand that the Crucified Saviour, is in space and time the one perfect sacrament of the power by which, in the end and in the whole, all evil is redeemed'.[15]

---

[14] Letting the echo of Exodus 3.14 ruminate through the Passion narrative and its inherently divine meaning. This is the wholly distinctive theme of the Christian tradition which must on no account be allowed 'to perish from the earth' in the sundry ventures of 'dialogue' probed here in Chapter 3.

[15] Oliver C Quick, *The Christian Sacraments*, London, 1927, p. 84. The capital letters are his own. Note: 'We desire to understand ...' 'In the end and in the whole' are vital provisos. Other ways of 'mitigating' evil leave remainders of unfinished-ness. Only 'the love that bears' bears away. It is entirely clear how this sense of things, in both senses of the word 'crucial' to Christianity, utterly contradicts and reverses that *lex talionis* which plays—as we see here throughout—so large a part in Judaic and Islamic ethos. It is evident so tragically in current history in the perennial pattern of retaliation which fills the Israeli/Palestinian scene.

The Order of the Wounded Hands

The psalmist's and the Christian's 'sanctuary'—in Temple and the Christ—are measure of the contrast inside Biblical religion. We must learn it further from the different angle afforded by the Letter to the Hebrews in Chapter 4. Meanwhile, how *ex eventu Christi* the faith that underwrites the Christian Ordinal was historically reached, is the theme of the chapter following.

Chapter 2
THAT SANCTUARY IN FACT AND FAITH

I

Historians have to know themselves as the 'high-priests of memory'. For they are in trust not only with the meaning, but with the honour of the past. There is, therefore, always a mutual element between fact and faith, between event and record, between truth in either and truth in the other. If there is fact within faith there must be faith about fact.

It was eminently so in the arrival of Christianity, as being the possessing in mind and soul of the drama of Jesus being the Christ we have traced in the preceding chapter. It was a possessing which awaited and needed its possessors in the good faith of their discipleship. Theirs was the discerning of what, in Christ, was the discernible. Faith came to be because fact had been. For it was not self-generating but responsive to what kindled it. Yet that kindling was essential to, and dependent on, what the fact contained as what fact could mean.

There is nothing Christianly unique here. For such is the quality of all history as a recognition of the recognisable. Truth is forever twinned as having an incidence and carrying an import. Even sciences like medicine and chemistry so physically concrete carry significance for the soul. Diagnosis of the onset of cancer is one thing in the laboratory, another for the heart. Microscopes become tragic in what they may disclose. What, we might ask, is the 'history' of Napoleon retreating from his Moscow, a city in flames, his soldiers decimated in the snows? Or of Abraham Lincoln brooding on the field of Gettysburg about 'the last full measure of devotion' no oratory can think the better to 'dedicate' with other telling than its own? These histories become sordid or splendid, tragic or majestic only in the verdict encompassing the fact. There will always need to be the imagery our reading brings to them. Yet the imagery on which interpretation relies may well be what event itself will yield. But the inter-fusing of what happened and what what happened meant is unmistakable in all narrative making faith, all faith from narrative.

The present task is to trace this mutuality in the Christian faith-event. It requires a careful distinction in the term 'the New Testament'. It has to mean both a concept about 'covenant' and a document of Scripture, the latter being the text about the other, the 'textile (we might almost say) in which the other is woven where it may be had in hand and open to the eye.

Significantly, this documentary 'New Testament' is composed of Letters and Gospels, with a linking narrative between. By and large the Letters are chronologically prior with Gospels their antecedents in *kairos*.[1] The reason for this sequence is rooted in the fact/faith situation we have noted. The document is one of expanding witness in the bosom of growing community. How, otherwise, Letters relating back to Galilee but penned in Corinth to Rome or from the road with meanings for Ephesus?[2] The scattering of missives this way belongs with a scattering of folk who are inherently one—as the phrase now is—'in Christ' but distant from each other and from their faith-origins. Being new to faith they need nurture and education in its moral ordering of their lives, under the watchful often hostile eye of Roman imperial power and newly recruited from its pagan culture. Such 'tuition' needs to come from the apostolate which has the authority of their oneness and the trust of their dispersion.

Hence the epistolary nature of New Testament texting of its 'covenantal' character, keeping faith with itself within itself, as both many and one. But this situation space-wise is also happening in lapsing time. The Church is becoming a matter of generations. Custodians of personal memories are thinning with the years. We note a reference to Mnason, 'an old disciple' with whom Paul was to lodge en-route to Jerusalem from Caesarea(Acts 21. 16). Such were clearly a diminishing folk.

---

[1] Noting the distinction between time as a 'when *(chronos)* and time as a 'what' *(kairos)*—timing by simple date and timing for content as in 'season', 'festival', or 'crisis'. Letters thus 'preceded' textualising of the Gospel record but the *kairos*, significant time, within them happened first.

[2] See below for discussion of how much 'Galilee' is mirrored in the Epistles. We have to disqualify the curious notion, often current, that Paul and the author of 1 Peter were disinterested in Jesus and Nazareth.

Here surely is the genesis of the textual Gospels to ensure the documenting of precious memory before human frailty might forfeit its cherished origins in Jesus, at Galilee and from Nazareth to Jerusalem. For his words had ever only been vocal on the air. He had himself left no scripted text. At the culmination of his ministry and Passion there was nothing to abide save a bunch of fragile folk and they, emerging from the deep trauma of his dying into the 'alive for evermore' of their confidence concerning him. All this precariously awaited its textuality—a documentation that came to be achieved, with endless risks involved, in four—to be canonical—Gospels. These together with those ardent Letters would be the documentary shape of his enduring through the Christian centuries as 'whom we have believed.'

The clue here to the very identity and genius of Christianity is the entire dependence of its textual on its historical, so that the precious fabric of Jesus' ministry only passed into history in the wake of the world-entry of his community. The unison of the two attests the whole order of fact and faith we have argued as reciprocal to one another. We only have the story of Jesus as the Christ in and by the taking of that Christhood into the Mediterranean scene as symbolising the human scene at large beyond its middle sea, 'the uttermost parts of the earth' being its stated vision.

This dispersion, unlike the sundry scatterings of Jewry whether under post-Assyrian/Chaldean tyrants or after Titus and Hadrian of Rome, was never for refuge or necessity, but for mission and 'presence' purposive and urgent. It might be fair to say that had there been no 'going' Church there would have been no 'knowing' Scripture. They could only co-exist. The fact and faith were mutual both in genesis and expression. What gave being to the church gave being to its Scriptures fulfilling either in the reality of both. It was essentially in seeking the world that the faith understood itself. This is a situation we need to anticipate in the setting of 'dialogue' across cultural and religious frontiers, due to be pondered in the following chapters. It often proves that interpreting into what prejudice misreads or incomprehension distorts gives the interpreter also a livelier understanding. Faith-awareness is in fee to faith-witness with a faith's integrity turning on their unison.

II

The impulse for the world, crucial in the documenting of the faith, was no less definitive for the structure of the faith-community. The travelling folk who needed 'letters', and prompted Gospels also occasioned 'holy Orders'. Leadership was an obvious requisite of such a society and leadership needed to be both central and local. The tradition of hospitality required credible commendation of 'guests in Christ' in a world of spies and persecutions. The bona fides of people passing through meant the bona fides of their faith. Who should vouch for these or who vet them if not known figures in all locales, people like Philemon of known stature, and 'in whose house' where—often enough—the Church gathered for prayer and sacrament? There is a clear reference in 3 John 6 to this practice of 'speeding onward worthily of God', whereby fellow members could both anticipate and receive the ministries of hosts to guests, the debts of guests to hosts. Name-lists like that in Romans 16 are evidence enough of 'faithful on the road' becoming familiar to each other by this means.

Thus the emergence of a Christian ministry was as spontaneous—we might almost say pragmatic—as the attaining of Christian Scriptures. With the lapse of time we arrive at the Pastoral Epistles where 'appointing elders in every Church' gives official shape to a first shaping 'Ordinal'.

That linking story, the Book of Acts, narrates the urge for 'deacons' in the administration of alms and the ensuring of probity and equity in the economic realm. The stresses of the Roman situation, not to say the vagaries of human nature, necessitated the development of structures of authority. The bond between these local and these central was vital for the due loyalty of faith and the identity of worship. Jesus had bequeathed the pattern of the 'twelve apostles' and it is clear how deeply this tradition was honoured, but—otherwise—just as he had left no writing, so he had left no organised system. When the apostles, as Luke graphically has it at the close of his Gospel, 'returned to Jerusalem' from the commission of the Ascension in all its mystery, they were all there was.

This emergence of Christian ministry, so impressive in its initial haphazardness,[3] matched the parallel emergence of Christian

---

[3] That seems the right word for the situation in respect both of textualising and structure. The

Scripture in being effectual and actual only in the will of the faith for the world of, and beyond, Jewry. It was faith alone, its content and its reach, which gave being alike to 'holy writ and holy orders', Scripture and Ordinal, Word and sacrament, text and charge. It generated its verbal and ministerial fabric out of its own character concerning 'God in Christ'. The faith and fact sequence we are arguing is like the blood in the veins, the river and its banks credentialing each other.

III

There was, according to the Luke of Acts, a signal occasion of this reality in quite definitive terms in the Council in Jerusalem concerning the taking of the faith to non-Jews. This—characteristically—seems to have been an initiative by 'lay' unknowns, 'men of Cyprus and Cyrene', pioneers indeed but nameless in the annals of faith. Peter in the encounter with Cornelius had needed much circumspect diffidence in a similar 'temptation' (as it first seemed to him).

When 'Gentiles' had responded in Caesarea and Antioch and elsewhere and their faith in Christ seemed genuine, central authority in Jerusalem—thus far free of these dubious moves with their utterly revolutionary implications—sent Paul and Barnabas to investigate. With the satisfying evidence of their report, this 'first Synod' of Christian history decided to approve, enjoining—not circumcision any more—but certain provisions re idolatry and morals.[4] It was a watershed and a waymark from which there could be no reversing. The decree the Council issued gave otherwise unqualified approval to the new departure, entirely congenial as it was to the genius of the Gospel and to the fact-faith sequence we are studying.

---

risks, which have properly given rise to endless scholarly discussion are the very charm of the scenario. That scholarship has to be noted in Chapter 7 and 'cares and studies'. Everything might have eventuated so differently—a fact which the 'canon', for example, sought to take care of. But there is no doubting the essential faith that emerged about Jesus, from the apostles.

[4] The demand for circumcision as requisite for interested 'proselytes' had long been a major deterrent for enquirers about Judaism. 'The mark in the flesh' was a prime token of a 'chosen people', hardly to be reconciled with those 'not born of that flesh'. The idea of admission of 'Gentiles' also fell foul of the rigorous ritual and ethical laws of Jewry. It was a major concern of apostolic nurture that the churches should be well taught in conduct worthy of Christ and thus to silence the sceptics about their inclusion.

The missive used a phrase that might give us pause. 'It seemed good', they said of their decision 'to the Holy Spirit and us.' 'The Holy Spirit and us!' What a strange use of 'and'! Surely what 'is good to the Holy Spirit' is good: what has 'and us' to add? But they had captured the whole meaning of fact into faith and faith out of fact. This kind of 'and' is always present where God and grace are at work. The human agency is taken up into the divine end.

Of course, they were rightly concerned for their authority as 'the mother Church' in Jerusalem. The 'us' was significant.[5] Authority was claimed and meant and was to be acknowledged such. Is not the formula 'the Holy Spirit and us' plainly realised in those twin metaphors of Pentecost, 'wind and fire'. What avail is wind without sails to harness it, or sails windless 'as idle as a painted ship upon a painted ocean'? Where is fire if not in coals or wood and fuel? But what are these when ashen, black and cold where no heat dwells? There is something thus integral between the theme of faith and the substance of the faithful.

There was something of this order—but in its own divinely sacramental quality—in the Incarnation itself.[6] Of her annunciation might meaning say to Mary:

> 'It is his love's prerogative
> To come by need of you ...
> In every enterprise of God
> Some human part is due.'

so that response can only be: 'Behold the handmaid of the Lord.' The faith incorporates the faithful just as the faithful embody the faith.

IV

But, moved to realise within ourselves this 'fact and faith' at the 'Sanctuary' of 'God in Christ', and borrowing the psalmist's 'altar' language 'of his joy and gladness', we are still in pursuit of how and

---

[5] 'It seemed good to the Holy Spirit and me' would be a risky formula for fanatic or enthusiast to claim. Consensus is from *fidelium*.

[6] It is right to think of 'the Word made flesh' as 'incarnational' in that here the physical 'embodies' the spiritual, as in the analogy of 'the face of Christ'. Facially all is sinew, nerve, tissue, muscle but, in all these the smile, the joy, the frown, the anxiety and wonder are made visible.

That Sanctuary in Fact and Faith

what the decision was by which 'fact' concerning Jesus became the 'faith' as to 'God in Christ', how a cumulative event became an inclusive theme of preached conviction, with the Master the ground of the one, his disciples the possessors of the other. We are handling the substance of a verdict issuing into the genesis of a community.

All happens in the context of Messianic anticipation, the long antecedents of which in the Hebraic setting are the concern of Christian relation in Chapter 4. Aspects have been with us also in the previous chapter in moving from the psalmist to the Christ. All is in the single realm of 'sanctuary' understood as a place of divine/human encounter, and on that count, of cost and sacrifice and pain. The deep issue is whether these belong with the divine mind or only in their occasions in their 'sanctuary', whether 'sanctuary' be the acts in ritual or a deed in life.

Unmistakably— for the Christian faith it fathered[7]—it was that 'deed in life' which belonged with the person, ministry, the life and death of Jesus of Nazareth received by sequential faith as the Messianic actuality, fulfilled in time and place as being eternally in the mind of God.[8]

Narrative requires that we see how central to the Gospel meaning was the expectation of Messiah. The Baptist's question: 'Art thou he that should come?' enshrines it. 'He that should come' was certainly also a question in the minds of at least some of the disciples, seeing that at least two of them were former (or actual) Zealots. Some scholars have argued against the importance of the Messianic factor, even implying that it was an 'invention' of the disciples afterwards. These argue from some alleged 'Messianic silence' in that the point was so rarely broached. The clue to that, however, is clear enough in that 'publicity' about Messiah would have been a highly explosive matter, subject to endless and contentious ambiguity. The 'who?' question could only be known when the 'how?' question had been answered. Jesus well knew that identity would be in action, never in hearsay and speculation. Sundry messianic 'actions'—violent, ascetic, ecstatic or magical—were widely debated.

---

[7] Both in the sense of bringing it into being *and* causing it to know expressly what 'Fatherhood' in God truly was as manifest in the 'Sonship' of Jesus.

[8] The course of thought here has brought us round to the 'we desire to understand' of the O C Quick citation in the previous chapter, p. 23.

There are conspicuously three indices to this underlying theme of 'the Son of Man' and promised righter of all wrongs inside the narrative of Jesus. The first is the insight the Gospels give of the 'testings' of Jesus in the desert, following his baptism by John. None of those suggestions could 'mean', in the absence of this dimension from prospective ministry. For each of them had to do with patterns a 'Messiah' might envisage. 'Stones into bread', economic plenty, the *materiel* of the golden age. Or, sheer miracle—the heavenly figure descending unscathed into the crowded Temple court, men's credulity taken captive but their souls unredeemed. Or some supposedly viable compromise with the inevitable evils of a world power-regime— 'seeking first and last the political kingdom'.

That all three were rejected, on the ground of the Scriptures Satan himself employed, made certain the final decision in Gethsemane. They had been the only options. 'Satan left him for a season,' keeping them all in the frame as if to obviate 'the cup his Father gave.'

The second index is that significant episode when Jesus briefly withdrew with his disciples from the scenes of ministry to the foothills of Hermon well north of Galilee, as if to reconnoitre ministry's tally in mid-course. 'Whom do men say that I am?', 'who do you say, my disciples?' The questions are not asking for mere information, still less for a response of sycophants. What matters is how the evidences of the ministry are pointing, what the experience of hostility indicates and whether there is a pattern emerging as a clue to what the cost (as index to the task) of how Messiah should be? From Peter's ardent but artless reply, it is clear how central the theme was, while Jesus' rebuke told how critical both the matter and its comprehension were to the mind of Jesus. It was from that point that the 'We are going up to Jerusalem' explicitly supervenes, the city that 'kills the prophets.'

The third index stems from an enigma in the translation of a clause in the Lord's Prayer—that 'daily' in the familiar version about the bread which is its plea. There is no problem with 'this day' but what and why is 'daily', seeing that the rarest of Greek words, *epiousios*, is plainly about 'futurity' in some sense—'the bread of the coming'. Can it well be 'of 'tomorrow', inspiring innumerable sermons about 'trust'? There is nothing about *epiousios* that requires 'day'. Why not 'the bread of the coming one'? Then the meaning would be 'Let us have Messiah's bread (i.e. task) this day'. Had not Jesus said, according to John: 'My bread is to do the will of Him that sent me.' (4. 34) Were not the disciples aware of the idea of 'Messiah's banquet', and coveting the places of honour there? 'Let us be day by day partaking in Messiah's task' would be a fitting prayer for them to learn. They would certainly become apostles later in learning to do no other work. This reading of *epiousios*, though disputed by those who neglect the translation problem, tallies with sundry other clear 'Messianisms' in the Prayer.[9]

These three evidences of the 'Messiah' theme within the Gospel frame apart, there is the clear role it played in the trial of Jesus before Pilate. It was precisely the issue between a political 'pretender' and a relatively harmless maverick rabbi that so puzzled and tormented the Roman procurator. It was the former Jewish priestly authority alleged (as the only way of getting a capital sentence). It was the latter Pilate thought he detected in that highly charged interview outside the Judgement Hall into which Jesus' accusers 'would not enter'.[10] Had 'Messiah' not been the crux at issue, Jesus might never have been charged, sentenced and crucified. All lay in the tragic costliness of being a redemptive and in no way a politically violent 'Messiah'.

It is important to realise how this 'place for a decision' thus so brutally at stake in the climax, was vividly present throughout the entire ministry, the 'trials' with which—as he said—the disciples had been 'with him'. (Luke 22. 28) There were elements of confrontation

---

[9] They are evident enough in the first three petitions the 'hallowing', 'coming' and 'doing' of 'the Name', 'the will' and 'the Kingdom'. They are also present in the necessary translation: 'the time of trial' (not 'temptation' in the popular sense of inveighing into wrong). If Messiah's task was to be achieved with persisting 'remainders' beyond it, he would be disproved. Therefore, it was assumed—and feared—that 'the days prior' would be a time of dire distress one might not wish to see. Hence the theme of 'Messianic woes' first. In paraphrase that clause might read: 'Do not let maximal evil overwhelm us but ...' (quickly following) 'deliver us from the evil.' See further Chapter 4, pp. 65-67.

[10] The exchanges in John 18. 33-38 are a striking example of how crucial can be the bearing of a word. Pilate, brusquely, confronts Jesus—it is all in all a tiresome case—with the words: 'King of the Jews, they tell me?' Jesus cannot answer either: 'No, I am not' without denying the sense in which he could be. Nor can he affirm 'Yes, I am' without giving to Pilate, a Roman, a false meaning that does not belong. He can only try to clarify what the word might signify. 'Pilate, are you using this word as you would as a Roman or are you quoting from another source?' Pilate is impatient about seeming equivocation and demands: 'What have you done that you have been brought here before me?' Still with the crucial word, Jesus speaks of the nature of his 'kingdom', to which Pilate retorts: 'So you are a king then?' Jesus replies: 'King is your word ... my subjects ... bear witness to the truth.' Pilate, sceptical of any 'truth' concludes that Jesus is 'innocent' of the only 'kingship' that matters to a Roman. Jesus is sentenced, we might say, over the confusion about 'Messiah' that had attended all his way.

The Order of the Wounded Hands

with the way of the world as Jewish authority and Roman imperialism incessantly shaped it. The Roman measure was to be 'borne', tolerated with e.g. 'going the second mile' as forced labour was imposed, 'borne' in welcome to perceptive 'centurions' and 'suffered' as in a common humanity.[11] There was no *lex talionis* in the armoury of Jesus but, instead, a 'meekness' that left the crimes of Rome—when such they were—to 'the judgement of God' that had 'room' enough for them in its unfailing justice.

As for the regime of Jewish order, sundry encounters arose which engendered—on the one side the will to oppose, on the other a will to undergo with patience what the situation demanded, while identifying by word and example the disavowal it deserved. There was the Sabbath, misappropriated into Sabbatarianism of a crippling kind when compassion was denied. There were the dietary laws in their apartheid from 'Gentiles', and minutiae about 'unwashed hands' and the ever present danger of self-righteousness, coupled with an enmity to 'tax-gatherers' and other miscreants.

What clearly emerges is that the whole ministry, foregoing—as it did—the *lex talionis* of retorting in the same kind and turning issues into envious, rather than moral, contests, was a narrative of 'bearing', of 'taking upon oneself' what society exacted—in its being at odds with his preaching—of blame, calumny, enmity and hate. This was the exacting price of the message itself in our sort of world. His behaviour this way was the only right corollary of who he was and the Messiah he must be. 'Bearing' this way was *per se* the art of 'being' what Messianic calling alone consistently fulfilled. The climax in Gethsemane only sealed finally what had been explicit throughout. The 'swords and staves' of violent arrest would neither argue nor provoke retaliation in kind. For his truth's sake, he would undergo what they exacted.[12]

---

[11] Some Muslim writers, arguing from the different order of things in Muhammad's Mecca where Hijrah into regime was possible, have surmised that Jesus was only content to be powerless because Rome was invincible and all rebellion forlorn. The difference is then seen as a mark of Muhammad's higher rank of prophethood as being competent politically to actualise some regime of Allah and so complete mere preaching. This does no justice to the counter evidence of the Gospels or to the radical presence of the issue of suffering throughout.

[12] This is the dramatic rejection of the *lex talionis*, so prominent in Judaic and Islamic culture and a curse over all human history. Paul had learned from Jesus that sublime word: 'Avenge not: leave room for the judgement of God.' The 'swords and staves' were a clear signal for a reaction in kind—the strategy that may well have been the devising of Judas to precipitate *in extremis* the 'Messiah' he wanted Jesus to be as one of the Zealot order.

It was thus in the very texture of events that the Messianic decision was defined and taken. It was this inclusive act of Jesus in its cumulative significance that moved the disciples, beyond their own dark crisis, to discern, possess and announce it as the making of the Church. Recognition of the recognisable transpired as the legacy of the Resurrection which can well be understood as the drama of the understanding of the Cross.

v

'Definition' of Messiah this way on the part of Jesus in the very fabric of his public story came via convictions of a 'sonship to the Father' into which faith cannot penetrate except via what thus tangibly it meant. What was concrete in his ministry and person was the insignia of his whole identity for a reverent theology. All the ambiguities about Messiah could be resolved in a narrative. There were precedents from the Hebrew prophets. It was they with whom the hope of this 'all-righting' figure was born out of the bitterness of exile and that exile read in the light of the 'faithful Creator' of original creation and His positive engagement in human story. These architects of Jewish hope had suffered too and had learned to read their suffering as the ready price of their fidelity to truth. The bonding of these two, fidelity to truth and truth-serving suffering, was plain to see in the likes of Hosea and Isaiah and even more tragically in the life of Jeremiah. They, we may be sure, were often in the mind of Jesus in the encounters of his ministry.

Yet what also is incontestable, is that the relevance of such prophetic precedent to the very figure of Messiah, faith owes entirely and singlehandedly to the mind and policy of Jesus and—thence—to the mind and preaching of the apostolic Church. Christian faith is bold to take that sequence back beyond Church, the Cross, Gethsemane, Nazareth and Bethlehem, into the 'very gate of Heaven' and the caring sovereignty of God most high. *Introibo ad altare Dei* can mean no less in faithful coming to Christ's 'bread and wine'.

We need to understand that this truth of Christ's Cross as, in these terms, 'the power and wisdom of God', is no cult, as some have alleged, of pseudo-martyrdom, nor a morbidity about 'blood and tears'.

The Order of the Wounded Hands

Nor is it a culpable negligence of the tasks of legitimate power. All is active, positive, vigorous—a taking on of evil, not a shrinking away. The cost it incurs is free, being its own discerning 'power-policy' in entire assessment of what redemption means and takes.

As for governments theirs is the due orbit of justice, law and right order and peace. 'Things Caesar's and things God's' are not two separate realms but territories where both reciprocally have writs—those divine conditionally entrusted to the human, those human obligated to the divine. But these in their legitimacy will never 'redeem', seeing how there are always reaches of evil beyond their aegis and sometimes beyond their awareness. And they always leave 'things undone' if we are handling guilt, forgiveness, mercy and compassion. Power and law are tempted to be vindictive in the act of being regulatory and punitive, arrogant and self-preening in the business of control. They always need the monitor of truth to whom they are accountable, a monitor above their practice and their intimidation. The very fallibilities of power are reason for the higher sovereignty of what alone redeems.

Thus 'the suffering Messiah' is the only authentic Messiah there can be. It would seem to follow that the God of such Messiah's 'sending' is authentically God as God must be. If such is how Christian faith concludes in being the Christianity it is, it must be seen to cherish a truth of vision, a vision of truth, that have reason and warrant to be ever present in the world with voice and heart and song and liturgy, with their 'bread and wine'.

But if it is truly their 'presence', it will be neither raucous, nor arrogant, nor assertive. What it believes about this God in this Christ dictates a mission only loyal to its own quality. This must mean it is ready to come in that temper to the contemporary, popular pursuit of inter-cultural dialogue. Doing so, it has a special duty towards the Judaic to which in the Messianic theme it is so far indebted, the Islamic where its central witness to the Messianic dimensions of divine compassion is so far disallowed, and the current aggressive 'non-religion' where what it cherishes is so far banished.

These are the tasks of three succeeding chapters. But first there is the 'therefore' which bids 'Holy Orders' be.

Chapter 3
THEREFORE

I

The logic of the fact and faith we have reviewed in their mutual evidences is the Christian ministry of Word and sacrament. Since 'the words and acts of Jesus ... possess a significance adequate to generate and sustain the faith of the primitive Church',[1] that faith-church unison fulfilled itself in 'the service of its servant-King'. It was ruled by a 'therefore' which became one of its most favourite words.

Whether a sort of annunciation to the heart or as the sequel to a case-made in argument, it recurs throughout the Biblical scene, alike from Hebrew and from Greek. Jesus used it frequently, Paul also in urgings on his Roman readers. To trace New Testament 'therefores' in their *argumenta* would be a sound tactic for any serious study of the nature of obedience as the clue to faith.

Consider Jesus' directive drawn from the very practice and character of God, as 'sending His rain on the just and the unjust'. 'Be ye therefore inclusive *(teleios)* as your heavenly Father is.' (Matthew 5. 48) Or his impulse to preach with an urgency due to the Kingdom of God.

> 'Let us go into the next towns that I may preach there also: for therefore came I forth.' (Mark 1. 38)

The writer to the Hebrews has learned the same thrusting call when he writes in comment on the costliness of things:

> 'Let us go forth, therefore, unto Him ... bearing His reproach.' (Hebrews 13. 13)

---

[1] Edwyn C Hoskyns in *Mysterium Christi*, London, 1936, p 70.

The Order of the Wounded Hands

There is hardly a theme in ethics, or theology, that does not clinch its meaning as to grace, or fellowship, or ministry, with this word. 'Ye are bought with a price, therefore glorify God in your body ... (1 Corinthians 6. 20.) 'Therefores' lead out of Nazareth, into and beyond Gethsemane and on to Ascension. They dominate the assurance of the first Apostles. 'Let all the house of Israel know that God has made this same Jesus both Lord and Christ' opens with Peter's resounding 'Therefore' (Acts 2. 36) Whether as 'because of', or 'in deed and truth', or 'so then', or 'wherefore', it persists throughout the reach and the motive of faith.

It is no surprise that the Christian Ordinal, in turn, holds ample feel for it, with its initial 'Take heed ...', its introit with the Litany and its careful catechism as to due intent, awareness, resolve and discipline, its 'consider' before its 'authority' and its plea: 'Thy blessed unction from above' to 'visit our minds, our strength renew.'

Thus, in the mandate to be deacon, priest or bishop as inter-standing offices in the Church of God, there runs the inward logic of a watchful, personal consecration of the very self. A 'thereunto are we called' via a 'thereby' of 'take thou authority'—an 'authority' that is wholly 'taking us'. But where? Into the parish. But just as the parish has to be the immediate world, still 'the world has to be the parish.' Sundry factors may at length explain why a particular geography supervenes to fix the question 'where?' But not geography more than incidentally ... on behalf of something richly and arrestingly theological.

Open allowing and private affirming are gathered into the symbolic act of 'the laying on of hands'. The tradition was inherited by the apostolic Church from long Levitical usage, where it had to do with Aaronic priesthood or could even, incongruously, load the scapegoat with the guilt that would goad him into the wilderness. Its use in the Book of Exodus for the consecration of offerings was eloquent for borrowing in the call and commissioning of Christian ministry.

'Hand' or 'hands' have long been synonyms for the self where the part does duty for, and as, the whole. 'Hands' 'laid' or recruited, transact identity. 'What is between your hands' is—in Semitic usage—a definition of 'the you you are' whether as orator comprising his emphases in a gesture or as lovers embracing the theme of mutual love. 'Give me your hand' invites to faith and partnership: a 'laying on of hands' does so 'from a beyond-that-is-akin', from a realm of abiding authority seeking a continuity that is akin, as from age to youth, in a sequence of unfailing warrant.

Thus it was according to Acts 6. 6, in the first 'making of the seven deacons' and (Acts 13. 3 and 15) the sending of Paul and Deacon Barnabas on their first historic journey beyond the initial borders of the faith. There are sundry references in the Pastoral Letters to the same pattern—Timothy himself thus commissioning and commissioned (1 Timothy 4. 14 and 5. 22) and Titus (1. 5) 'appointing elders in every city' of Crete. The long 'ordinal' tradition of the Church of England and of the Anglican Communion stands in sound Biblical lineage.

The honesty as well as the validity of tradition need, however, to recall that—it would seem—there was no manual ordaining of Jesus' first disciples. He simply 'called them that they might be with him and that he might send them forth to preach.' Surely that education, that discipleship, sufficed all their need whether for warrant or for wisdom. We might say that the absence of any record of Jesus' 'laying his hands on them' (as he did healing-wise on the sick) is no evidence of the lack of the act.

It is fair to think that the point at issue here had to be taken up into the emergence of the Church when—and only when—the Gospel of its complete commission would have become articulate. Peter, James and John and all the rest were yet raw and *in statu pupillari*, ardent about Jesus but confused about Christ.[2] They were to be 'with him through his trials' (Luke 22. 28) Those 'trials' were also differently theirs—some in their eager zealotry for a political Messiah, others ex-'publicans' drawn out of Roman enlistment, others anxiously tentative in their perplexity. Only post-Gethsemane his and theirs, post-Easter his and theirs, could they emerge into the full fledge of their Gospel and receive their Pentecost. May not all this have been vicariously the only 'laying on of hands' because (a theme to which all here returns) they had known and felt the imprint of the wounded hands of Jesus as now indeed the Christ.

---

[2] It is clear that there were very mixed motives in their perception, or anticipation of his Messiahship. Some were zealots thinking politically, while Matthew and perhaps others had accepted Rome's service as 'publicans'. The Messiahship of Jesus could only ever be an open question until its resolution, within the ministry, via the pattern of redemptive love. Much New Testament scholarship has 'problematized' itself over alleged conspiracy of Messianic 'silence', when the sane reason for Messianic 'reserve' about publicity lay obviously in its avoidance. The issue is further treated in: *God's Wrong is Most of All*, Brighton, 2006, Chapter 6, pp. 61-76.

The Order of the Wounded Hands

May not the same logic explain Paul's insistence in Galatians that 'from no man had he received' his calling *qua* 'apostle'. If, by the Damascus vision-on-the-road and whatever other awareness of Jesus he had known from Stephen or others, he was virtually and belatedly, 'one of the twelve' then he, too, needed no other commission. The general point seems clear that there was no role for ordination until the faith became known and the Church, its institution for witness and ministry, came—by that same token—into urgent being as its human instrument. For it was then—and only then—that, confronted by Rome's angry imperialism and Judaic long-range self-exemption from Messiah-Jesus (despite Jewish originality in sealing it), the faith needed its attested custodians and needed them in an unfailing sequence of 'authority'. 'Are they not all Galileans?' was fit question on the Day of Pentecost. They would need to be much more than 'Galileans' with that accent in their destiny to 'the uttermost parts of the earth'. Harsh tasks of definition, preservation, conservation and 'all the hazards of this life' awaited them in journeys both of road and sea and mind.

In this context of the why and wherefore of their ordination the 'hand' analogy Jesus had used comes readily for note, as in Luke 9.62 about 'putting hand to the plough'. How apt it was for discipleship. For every plough has a furrow, every ministry its field, every hope its fallow ground still untilled. Ploughs are sturdy instruments availing only in rugged hands. They both require and bestow a competence. Like all the other sundry functions of the hand its capacity enlarges by the range of its means, as may a loom, or a spindle or a trumpet or a needle. 'What is that in thy hand?' becomes 'What is that in thy power?' 'Take thou authority'—there is your Piers Ploughman.

> 'And the clay waves break as he goes by
> Only for the soil that stares
> Clear into God's face he cares.
> His eyes are ever on some sign
> To help him plough a perfect line ...'[3]

The constant pre-occupation of the Ordinal with continuity is alert to the danger that hands may be 'taken off ploughs' or these lie abandoned in the middle of the field.

---

[3] John Masefield, *Selected Poems*, ed. John Betjeman, London, 1978, p.46.

Therefore

There are points, as theology more than all else must keep in view, when all metaphor breaks down, all analogy fails. Humankind may be a 'thing of clay' but are not comparably malleable by words or 'turned' to faith like tillage. Yet the image of a plough quitted amid unfinished furrows is a lively sign of ministries foregone, 'authority' relinquished.

It is assumed that 'Holy Orders' are life-long. Yet holding them so incurs a deep issue of fidelity inside them, a private measure of the public urge for continuity of institutional tradition. Can faith in heart and mind ensure, even guarantee, its own security, its steady adherence to its content and its pledge? Is one the same person decades after that initiating exchange of conviction about 'the Word of God' and the trust of ministry? Can one admit of a growing mind if one is thus pledged to a verbal Creed? How is one then open to all the 'winds of change' or to the pressures that faith must undergo in the ever growing burden of a secular indifference to everything most dearly held in the ministerial heart of hearts? How, so stressed, alert, enlist and enable one's lay people in the exercise of their singular ministry as often closer to those inroads into discipline and courage? For the ordained sort has always to be tributary to *all* 'holding the faith in the bond of peace.' Chapter 7 must take this question further.

It might seem that a whole issue of genuine integrity is present in the entire business of ordination, offered and received. That issue only deepens when, as we say, its service is 'stipendiary'. For then a stipend attaches to its discharge so that livelihood is at stake with sincerity of mind around the faith. What then if the sanctuary has the unworthy sanction of some cash motive belonging to its task? Has long tenure of the 'office' to argue some closedness of mind to what may interrogate its sincerity in querying its credal grounds? It is well that the dilemma be firmly faced. For mere longevity will bring 'no discharge'.

Integrity here is had where Paul cries: 'I know whom I have believed and am persuaded that he is able ...' What we have committed is in surer hands than our own. He did not say: 'What I have believed' (as of some scripted formulation); he said: 'Whom'. To be sure, the distinction is not absolute. The 'Whom' can be credally told but only personally followed. Ministry is thus a companionship (are we not constantly 'taking his bread and wine' as guest to host?) in which the private mind can expect to grow, to ripen and mature, and so renew what is a living legacy.'Whom to serve is to reign.' Far from excluding, Christian ministry pre-supposes a growing mind in a nurturing society. 'Riper and stronger in your ministry' is its launching prayer as the Ordinal tells. Thus received and known, continuity is no threat to honesty, only its 'refining fire'. We never come to lectern, pulpit or sanctuary in abeyance of 'the Holy Spirit leading into all truth', as promised for our heeding.

These, our ultimate securities, are all there in the ringing words of the Ordinal: 'Take thou authority ...' said to deacons and to priests; or: 'Receive the Holy Spirit for ...' as in the consecration of bishops. They echo the awareness of the centurion in the Gospel: 'I am a man under authority.' There is thus a hierarchy, a capacity to act via a liability to obey. It is this very quality which is captured in 'the laying on of hands', an authoritative signal out of a past warranting and enabling an ensuing future. Ordination is a token and a gesture within the flux of time where things immediate happen by an ancient pattern and a past employs a present to affirm a future.

But whose, in the ultimate reckoning, are those 'hands'? 'Under whose authority'[4] were episcopal hands 'laid', hands which had themselves been earlier so warranted, renewing their own meaning in this new bequeathing? All, in their sequence, were and are contingent on their *fons et origo*. Must we not realise and feel in all such ordaining the wounded hands of Christ? Are there any other 'holy orders' more apposite than ours thus? Jesus, risen, according to John's narrative, commissioned his disciples, standing among them and 'showing them his hands'. Belonging to 'The Order of the Wounded Hands' is the inner truth of Christian ministry but only because these are the final measure of Christian theology.

For the old cry of one of the Latin Fathers: *Per Necessitatem Christianus*, 'I have no option but to be a man in Christ,' is where the heart of his Church beats. The ringing apostolic formula 'God was in Christ' has to mean that 'Christ was in God', that 'the crown of thorns' belonged with 'the majesty of high', that only the Christian God had wounds at human hands, that only God so-Messiahed could be known as undertaking the burden of the wrong His creation had incurred from us, His human theme of will and love.

---

[4] Matthew 8. 9. On continuity see further Chapter 8.

Therefore

'God as Messiahed' may seem an odd neologism here. Yet how close it comes to the old Hebraic concept of a divine 'agency', a 'servant-son', an 'anointed means in place' at once adequately divine (in terms of what the role must mean) and adequately human and historic (for what earth's wilful wrongness must exact of 'burden' as of 'sorrows'). How might what, on every count, was divinely due from God in self-consistency within a wanted creation, be actively achieved and by what costly means?

This insistent Messianic question had a diversity of answers—political, martial, ascetic-essene, ethnic and esoteric, through the long Hebraic waiting. What it would need to embrace had always been latent inside the ministry of Jesus, not to say the mixed motives of his disciples. In that very ministry it deepened toward a final crisis of decision where, in Gethsemane, it was identified in and as 'the cup my Father gives.' That decision, finding and taking via the love that suffers, the only sufficient pathway of redemption, proved to be *de facto* in truth how 'God was Messiahed in Jesus and the Cross'. Hence the clarion theme 'God was in Christ reconciling the world.' That, being thus *de facto*, the disciples came to know it *de jure* was the very inauguration of the Church. To 'learn the Christ' this way was to reach 'the knowledge—in this love—of God' and have it as 'the keeping of their hearts and minds'. Such was the sequel to the wounded hands of Jesus in their 'layed-ness' on his thus recruited community. For, even of old, it had always been assumed that 'Messiah' would have collective meaning once the historic identity was known.

Such is the utter distinctiveness of God by His Christian criteria. They are criteria only necessarily distinctive in also readily acknowledging dimensions of theology elsewhere that are pre-supposed in a differing integrity. These are a created order, meant for human trust and care, a mission in prophethoods for guidance in that trust and, with these, a meaning about history which must exclude Asian faiths. They dissolve such meanings, while still finding a compassion whose ethical self-disciplines we can readily acclaim.

It must immediately follow that a Christian ministry, bidden by those 'wounded hands', should find itself drawn to the antecedent faith and people of its Messianic norm in Jesus as the Christ, 'Gentile' inclusion could only mean that it served an inclusive reach. Within it, however, would abide a special priority of kinship with a 'first people of God' from whom its own self-awareness had derived.

By a logic, less of debt than of retro-active contrast, it must also know itself bound into serving relevance to Islam.[5] The magnetism Islam has for the Christian mind lies both in its deep positives about a good creation and a human tenure of trust inside it and yet also in how rigorously it denies to divine sovereignty a suffering Lordship vis-à-vis that human scene. Could these undertake a human world in creation with such generous intention, and not register how far that purpose miscarried at our hands? Could Islam's deep positives ever co-exist with its heavy negativity concerning that divine Cross the Christian faith identified as crucial to all else? It was a story of mutual co-conviction concerning the divine will 'to have us humans be', a single enabling fiat: 'Let there be' and a humankind fully commissioned into a dominion/*khilafah* or tenancy-in-trust, upon this singular, us-inviting, us-accommodating globe. The two faiths were one in all the consequential sanctions for technology, carrying the same ecological liabilities for the care of their one planet. They could even concur in the realisation that this Creator-pioneer of our trusteeship, would duly guide us in its discharge by the benison of prophet-messengers serially sent for our education and our mindfulness in discipline.

Islam was even capable of perceiving that prophet-told education as discharging a divine duty, any default in which would have left its Allah culpable of dire negligence of a divine duty towards our wayward history. For, otherwise, we would be left to the self-dooming devices of our *Jahiliyyah*.[6] Any such logic concerning divine obligation—Christianity said—must surely undertake a more than educative role towards the astrayness of the human scene, its inner rebellion against its own calling. The Qur'an was well aware of how dire that rebellion is—witness the urgency of its negation of all false

---

[5] Meaning retro-active in the sense that Islam eventuated six centuries after Christianity, and many Muslims esteem it as having bye-passed the 'redemptive' Christology, which Christian faith reached within Semitic monotheism, by reverting to the early dispensation of 'law and rule'—though without Judaic ethnicism. Thus the relation of Christian ministry with Islam is different both historically and theologically from its relation to Judaism.

[6] *Jahiliyyah* or 'wilful ignorance' is the Qur'an's term for the state in which Arabian society lay prior to the 'knowledge' brought by Islam. It has the double-sense of 'not knowing' and of the social 'uncouthness' or 'wildness' that follows from it. The crucial passage about Allah's 'obligation' is Surah 4. 165. See further: *The Qur'an and the West—Some Minding Between*, London, 2006, Chapter 12, pp. 173-91.

worships, all acts of usurpation, explicit in the very notion of *shirk* and the *mushrikun*. For, truly, the Qur'an's paramount concern for divine 'unity' was never about mere number, about pagan multiplicity. What mattered that these were many was never about arithmetic: it was about defiance. *Tawhid*, 'the making of God One' on our part, was a theme not of 'counting out' but of dethroning. It was an urgent active mission of an ardent monotheism, not a numbers game about atheisms.

All of this had to be indeed attractive to the Christian mind as a fascinating territory of relating ministry both in welcome where it cared and anxiety where it lacked. This vision long ante-dated the time when more recent aspects of Islam came into prominence politically and the 'Islam and the West' syndrome took centre stage. There were times in the nineteen-twenties, after the demise of the historic Caliphate, when some 'disintegration' of Islam, quite other than its resilience, occupied concerns around it.

Irrespective of all political vicissitudes, but not inattentive to them, the vocation of Christian theology has always been with the possible persuasion of the Islamic mind, on its own deep premises, towards receiving into its splendid acclamation of Allah's Lordship some Christian perception of its costliness. What does it matter? cynics will ask. Why should it ever qualify to be a life-long yearning? Surely because a truly suffering divine sovereignty is the only clue, the only urge, to its human reproduction in the earthly scene—a reproduction that has both the warrant and the motive, there in the divine example. The Christian conviction is that only so can our human readiness for love and its errands, for compassion and its cost, suffice amid the cruel realities of the world we know. Others, to their honour, may think to be sufficient of themselves, 'waiting for a Godot who never comes.' Such optimism lives only with an insufficient realism.

It is not as though the Christian case for the self-evidence of God in Christ and Christ crucified need be utterly incompatible with the recurrent cry of Islam, *Allahu akbar*, depending on where and how that cry is heard.[7] All turns on what *akbar* means. There is a hint of some mutually compatible meanings around this 'greatness'. By the Qur'an—in Surah 17. 111—Muslims are bidden: *kabbirhu takbiran*

---

[7] From the *adhan* in call to prayer preferably, rather than in violent take-over of an aircraft as perpetrators burst to the flight deck and the planes plunged into doom. Context will always identify theology.

(using what grammarians call the 'absolute accusative' where the verb supplies the noun):'Make Him greatly great.' So there are more worthy and less worthy measures of 'greatness'. We need to discriminate this *kabir* word and *akbar* with its implied comparisons, what quality it denotes, what dimensions it intends. Truly, not mere mass, or might, or violence, or tyranny, or sheer magnitude, but—surely—something more like magnanimity. Why not love in the wealth of self-expending goodness, capacious to comprehend all that needs it? All such words as 'royal', 'majestic', 'sovereign', 'divine', turn on the question of their true referent, their defining measure. With no clue to these *Allah akbar* will be merely vacuous, tediously teasing or even grimly menacing as in sundry recent usages where only threat and anger carry and its ensign is a clenched fist.

All that could be at stake in an Ordinal's 'Therefore' towards Islam belongs more fully here to Chapter 5. Its instinct is to ponder the Quran's *Al-Rahman al-Rahim*, those two defining adjectives of the *Fatihah*, renewed in all Islamic prayer and the *adhan* to it. There is an inner progress of meaning—the essential 'property of mercy' of *Al-Rahman* and its operative expression, *Al-Rahim*, thus—'merciful Lord of mercy'.[8] This ringing cry invites the query 'How? where? with what credentials?' How will it relate to that basic lesson of theology, the one that learns to say: 'He does what He does that He may be who He is?' Islam learns who Allah is in the reality of our creation and this habitable place of our custodial life, in the benison of prophetic guidance of our minds as to our dignity and of our wills in its exercise and of ultimate accountability in a 'Last Day', the ever real monitor of conscience. These are all seconded by a given regime of habituation and of solidarity via 'the Five Pillars' of *Dar al-Islam*. Such is what a poet called 'the mercy of his means' as bestowed by Allah upon Muslims via their *islam*.[9] For

---

[8] For there is a clear progression in the two derivatives from common root between what 'is' as a quality and how it moves as a 'deed'. The frequent translation 'the merciful, the compassionate' leaves the single root verb and could well belong to either term, whereas, in effect *Al-Rahman* becomes a virtual noun (as elsewhere in the Qur'an) which *Al-Rahim* then 'describes'. This takes in English the shape of 'merciful' *(him)* Lord of mercy *(man)*.

[9] It is urgent to make this distinction, one which the Qur'an observes in its 'sorting by city' of its 114 Surahs, because the Hijrah from Mecca to Medina brought a comprehensive distinction in idiom and content. Meccan themes continued but now with the sanction, no longer of *balagh*, or preachment alone, but of armed struggle in its name—a struggle which radically altered the shape of its appeal and, therewith, the mind-set of its actors. Readers, too, move in a different world they immediately sense. See pp. 85-86.

all the intolerance of its finality, it surely calls for a due appreciation from outside Islam.

The urgent question remains about the mercifulness of this mercy, its measure of the burden of our human wrongness, and how far we can ever say with Isaiah: it 'has carried our sorrows.'

We can perhaps best approach what belongs here by way of the *lex talionis* in human affairs and how might divine 'greatness' mercifully over-ride it in forgiveness? The question may seem a new departure but is entirely germane to all the foregoing, and crucial to any Christian 'therefore' in life.

For there is no doubt that the law of retaliation is the curse of the human story and the steady pre-occupation of the power factor in history. Avenging goes on like a spiralling agent of grief as long as one act ensures its like again against the first party. Only when such vindictiveness is foregone is there a different kind of matching—that of love in hope, in the stead of anger in revenge. Only so is any *status quo ante* viable with all its benediction of recovered peace.

The Qur'an, however, in its Medinan dimension,[10] is totally committed, as are the Decalogue and the Talmud, to the law of retaliation. 'Permission is given to fight' those who attack you, even where there is always a doubt about who initiates the exchange. Even the supreme precept of Surah 5.32, citing that of the Talmud, exempts 'manslaughter' and corruption from its rubric:

> 'Whoso-ever killeth a human being (for other than these reasons) it shall be as if he had killed all mankind and he who saves a single life it shall be as if he had saved all mankind.'

This exemption hides an enormous paradox. On its own showing, any killing violates the sanctity of every life alive and yet that inherent universal sanctity is fit for private violation. We thus, in retaliation, disown our own precious mortal tenure. Feuding, that takes life for life, denies—both ways—the life it takes. Only in not setting life against life do we vindicate what all life is.

Against the Judaic, Islamic instinct for a legitimacy in retaliation goes the ringing New Testament warning: 'Let not the sun go down upon your wrath.' (Ephesians 4.26) Let the setting sun see your

---

[10] See further Chapter 5 and preceding note.

vengeance subside into its reverent glow. 'Sufficient with the day is its evil thing.' Only when we can—and do—absorb, do we not perpetuate. Could there, theologically, be a more thoroughly Islamic principle than that of Paul urging: 'Leave room for the judgement of God'?

There have doubtless been endless occasions of vengeance in the history of Christendom but they have neither echo nor warrant in the New Testament. The Muslim problem here is that they have proud occasion in the Medinan segment of the Qur'an and are thus perpetuated by recital in the mind-set of the faith.

By contrast, there is no doubt where the Pauline ethics of the New Testament in epistolary education of the Church derived their rubric. It was from the teaching and pattern of Jesus himself in what we know as 'the Sermon on the Mount'. There 'retaliation' was to be of the order of 'feeding a foe' and, of 'wine in the wound and the pence at the inn'. For Jesus was no imperial Constantine, wielding a power-persuasion to his faith. Abolition of 'an eye for an eye, a tooth for a tooth, a limb for a limb and a life for a life' was complete. Nor did he tolerate the old Mosaic plea that *lex talionis* in the Decalogue was somehow benign, in that it lay a curb on excessive impulse. Only 'one for eye', not 'ten for one' was lawful. It is clear enough that this need for a curb attested that the 'vengeance-impulse' runs deep and gathers pace. There lies also the logic for its total rescinding. For, at the outset, there is an aggression and thence the victim as vulnerable. But all vulnerability, not least when transacted, asks for the vicarious. The sequence 'vulnerable/vicarious' is always this way, if the 'vicarious' be available for it, as once on the Jericho road, as evermore in the Cross of Jesus. The *lex talionis* bears witness to its own futility. To suffer *from* means to suffer *with* (whence otherwise the passion to avenge). Each present occasion to suffer *for*, should heart and conscience so discern and act.

It is here that we reach the radical distinction between the ethics and theology of the New Testament and those of Judaism and the Qur'an. It is that 'as in heaven, so on earth' of the Lord's Prayer. For (if we may so speak) it has to do with the very character of God, with the nature of Allah. If we can perceive and comprehend the vulnerable/vicarious dual situation as belonging in the very being of God, then we have the ultimate sanction—and only so—for its emulation on earth. That reasoning 'if' takes the Christian to what can be identified in the crucifixion of Jesus as the divine incidence of the Christhood that was always Biblically the open question around divine sovereignty.

Through the garden of Gethsemane we discern the 'Man, where are you?' from the garden of original creation. This is how and where the Lord seeks and finds us. The Cross is 'the place of the divine Name'—to borrow an old Hebraic usage. There we read the utmost vulnerability of the divine to man. It is divine in the very quality of its compassion: human in the factors, moral, political, social, and personal, which in their evil coalition have symbolically and directly led to it. The drama of 'Him there' on that rising knoll beside the city wall centres, as in one experience, the wrong-doing of the world in history and, answeringly, the vulnerability of God in being there supremely vicarious.

By this light, the prayer 'Father, forgive them ...' is no remote, even forlorn petition, but instead a confidently single mind within the divine. 'Father' was the intimate relational word, alike expectant and receptive. It was this apostolic sense of the Cross which gave shape to the term 'God in Christ', 'God this way' in the Christ where He is known to be so. Hence again that primal credal clause 'Christ Jesus Lord', the unison of this Jesus, via this history and all its antecedents, from the Christ in God. All is then understood as truth through personality, as the history of redemption, inaugurated as the incarnation of the divine word. All was what God had to say in the language of dramatically legible event. All was a forgiveness, not in *non lex talionis* terms or negated by retaliatory deed but had only by vicarious action. Such 'bearing' apart, there is no 'bearing away'.

It must surely follow that any ordination into the trust of this meaning should discern 'the wounded hands' in its authority. 'Holy Orders' are to be in no illusion about the force of that adjective in their Christian origin. For only so do they hear and speak 'the Word'. Only so do they serve the ministry of sacramental 'bread and wine'. We note in Chapter 4, via the Letter to Hebrews, how the *hiereus* word is employed only there in Christian context and refers to its exercise by Christ ('our great high priest') and of Jewish temple hierarchy whom the Letter uses in its education of its readers.[11]

Elsewhere throughout, the pastoral, not exclusively ritual, word *presbuteros* suggests the initially pragmatic shaping of the Christian

---

[11] *Hiereus* is the strictly 'ritual' word, though it underlies our English 'Hierarchy'. The English 'priest' derives from *presbuteros*.

ministry. This 'Word and sacrament' must be held closely in one, so that what is 'offered' to God in sacrament is not 'pleading' that which else He would not recognise but celebrating before Him, and with one another, where He is ever known for Who He is. 'Wounded hands' ordain no less, no other.

II

But what, many will be asking, of the public sphere, the social order where collectives and vested interests are engaged? What of the regulatory, the legal and punitive which, like some highway code, wield sanctions which ensure liberty and security? These have their place, punitive indeed but not retaliatory, restraining but not vindictive, as a sort of *lex necessitatis*, such as Abraham Lincoln knew in his 'malice towards none'.

It remains evident that the power in politics, the reach of laws and governings, are capable only of a modicum of justice and its fruits, given the very nature of these auspices. There always persists beyond them—and, if need be, despite them—the tasks of reconciliation. That modicum is urgent and vital but its very partiality as incomplete blunts its competence in the final analysis. So there is always room for the art of peace-making which only the vicarious can practice in the entail of the vulnerable. The evil, as exemplified last century by Nazism and Fascism, requires to be resisted and condemned—manifestly a costly operation. Such war against such barbarity exacts the 'blood and sweat and tears' in its evil-bearing so that its very onus in violence finds it also vicarious. For those strident evils made a whole world intensely vulnerable. Then the necessity of victory demanded all the more a repudiation of vindictiveness. When law and power and war have done their best, but ever partial, corrective, immense tasks of the forgiving will and active compassion still remain.

The situation is surely captured in Paul's injunction, echoing Jesus in its double shape: 'Be not overcome of evil: overcome evil with good.' (Romans 12. 21) Where the negative ends, the positive belongs, knowing the open questions power-wielding always leaves behind. Is not that summary explicit again in the Lord's Prayer paraphrase discussed elsewhere here: 'Do not bring us where evil over-masters us but deliver us from the evil.'

Therefore

It follows that any Christian ministry within 'the wounded hands' is for the sort of victory over retaliatory enmities forever exemplified and fulfilled in the words and the Passion of Jesus which it is vital to understand as the very 'art of God being God' in human time and terms and place. There the redemptive meaning stands fully revelatory, as the sure motif of ministry in its name.[12]

III

What we have come to know as 'dialogue' is plainly in this non-retaliatory tradition in that it seeks mutual comprehension and takes even necessary controversy into expectant hope. It brings a will to listen: it looks for a listening in return. It is a sort of non-*retalionis* of the heart, a resolve not to keep its convictions as a kind of inner monologue but, like conciliation, to covet mutual acceptance. Such was the theme of the favoured Pauline word *sunistesin*, or 'commend'—what he says God is doing in Christ (Romans 5. 8) and which Christian faith is doing concerning that doing of God. The root idea is the invitation: 'Let us establish *(istemi)* together *(sun)*.' The faith of the other is in some sense potential of acceptance and even its 'contraries' will need to be in the reckoning of any 'commendation' of what, of necessity, disputes them. The attitude of 'dialogue' has to be that nothing about the other is to be ignored as present or disesteemed as irrelevant. Our dogmas have to be credentials we 'present', not demands we impose. If this sense of things on the one side evokes a like posture on the other, then something like a mental non-retaliation has supervened and the first big hurdle taken. The love of Christ has nothing to lose and everything to gain by such an eventuation and something crucial has happened to Islam or Judaism or any other inner orthodoxy. Controversy is temperamentally disarmed in order that it may be more searchingly addressed. As explored here elsewhere the benefits can be great in respect of how faiths handle their scriptures and for all right esteem and practice of religious authority.[13] Even when ideas, themes or accents come into focus that can only be

---

[12] The point is further developed in the following chapter—'Messiah' in 'redemptive' followers in his image—the corporate that was always to follow the singular.

[13] The place of 'dialogue' belongs also in Chapter 7: 'All Your Cares and Studies'.

deplored, the lament of Jesus over Jerusalem exemplifies the set of soul that must ensue. 'Thou that killest the prophets, how often would I have gathered thy children ...' If there is a 'grieving of the Holy Spirit' (Ephesians 4. 30) a Christian ministry cannot expect to escape it. Dialogue is no mere 'negotiation', some trading of ideas. It has to be an existential commendation of discipleship, fulfilling an honest will to learn its own sincerity through venture in the open world, lest it be only 'a fugitive faith'. Where-ever the venture takes it in the wideness of the world 'the Order of the Wounded Hands' should never travel in any other terms.

Chapter 4
WHERE MOST INDEBTED MOST FULFILLED: JUDAICA

I

That Christianity is through and through indebted to things Hebraic is evident enough in its very name. For *Ho Christos* in Greek is the 'Messiah', 'the anointed one', of the long travail and tradition of the Jewish story. The shape of that hope, the divine answer to the sharp question of human history, could only have stemmed from the Hebraic lineage that gave it being as 'the desire of nations' and the plea of the ages. The Christian faith and church are totally beholden to the Hebrew Scriptures for their *fons et origo*, the tuition and ancestry without which they could never have known themselves.

Yet it is no less true that they are utterly fulfilled and realised[1] in what they necessarily did with their heritage. The two dimensions of Christian identity need each other in what had essentially to 'quarrel' with its matrix and, yet doing so, to make its benison good in the sequence it gave to it.

This, to be clarified anon, is no language of 'supersession' as something happening to Judaism but, instead, of something imperative in the 'becoming' of Christianity as both debt and difference. The distinctiveness of Christianity which radically separates it from Judaism is no more and none other than grateful expression of its debt to it.

This bald 'statement of intent' in this chapter must take on flesh and blood in what follows and dialogue admit of passion. To be sure, it leads into heavy and often emotive tasks of interrelation, stressed as these are by the current history of Zionism and the reality—or

---

[1] 'Realised' in the strict sense of being 'made real', or 'achieved', rather than of being in awareness.

allegation—of Anti-semitism.[2] One great asset is that frank dialogue invites a clear detection of genuine irreconcilables that emerge in loyal converse and of how they bear on the welcome affinities to be fully shared. This task means the Christian *cums* and *contras* in three exacting areas—Judaic now, Islamic in Chapter 5 and contemporary alienation from or disavowal of theism *per se* in Chapter 6. In all three territories 'the wounded hands' would take us as where we are in love and duty bound to go.

II

Given the crucial debt of Christian faith to Jewry's Messianic theme, it is necessary to define the Christian place it has—as grasped in the first two chapters—and explore its deep origins in Hebrew tradition. Its antecedents lie in four inter-locking dimensions of the Biblical mind in the Hebrew Tanakh. Each needs the others to be what it is and it is vital to note that the first three are, in measure, constituents of all human identities. It is the intensity, and the distinctiveness of the fourth Judaically, which argue their essential Jewishness.

Together they comprise a deep sense of corporate identity. This is rooted in the bond of ancestry and posterity. Together these require and enjoy a lively sense of territorial destiny which is bonded into tribal history. All three marry with a sharp awareness of the seriousness of human sin and the reach of human wrong.

Inhering in all four and warranting their truth there stand the sure sovereignty and demanding holiness of Yahweh 'most high'.[3]

---

[2] It is a sad, misguided current habit in which any legitimate criticism of Israeli policy is promptly nullified by dismissal—or worse—as Anti-semitic prejudice. When this happens, Israel is completely exonerated. On this showing, the great prophets of Israel from Amos on must be the supreme Anti-semitic folk of all. Their conscience about statehood was not to be silenced. It is melancholy in long and recent local history, how the State—no less than separatist groups—can think only of perpetual retaliation, inevitably tending to the tragic non-resolution of their desperate impasse. See also note 32 below. On the subterfuge: 'Moral charge against Israel equals Anti-semitism', there is a lucid analysis in Michael Prior, *A Living Stone: Selected Essays*, London, 2006, pp. 265-272.

[3] Either corroborates the other, in that the claims of the 'rule' of God require the 'sin awareness' of the Levitical system with its 'atoning' of public and personal guilt. The psalmist in Psalm 51, for example, sees his evil done against another as essentially against Yahweh. Divine Lordship demands inter-human penitence and 'sin-offering'. Society is not ruled by what mere humans think they can allow, but by the righteousness of God.

There are large issues for scholarship about the dating—and indeed the vicissitudes—of this people-mind-shape, how and whence it emerged to know itself and through what historical hazards and trials it arrived to be what it became. How far, for example, did the facts of Abraham, could we finally learn them, match the role his 'legend' came to play in ensuring the link with the land via Moses and Joshua? How formative was the experience of Egypt in the positives of the Joseph saga as well as in the oppressives spurring exodus?[4]

Verdicts here will doubtless remain contentious among scholars. What matters—as kindredly in other faiths—is 'the things most surely believed among us' who believe and live them.

Seeing how far and how deeply and how long these four dimensions of Jewry and its Judaism[5] inevitably engendered an isolation in, and from among, the nations at large, it is urgent to insist that the same triad of people, place and past, tribe, territory and time; birth-love, land-love, story-love characterises all and sundry alike, every-who in every-where. In respect of these defining descriptives there can be no exclusifying singularity. Memory, ancestry, posterity, a language to tell them, a culture to house them—these are universal denominators of all human experience. To think them exceptional requires to know them common. It is climates, fertilities, agronomies, geographies that discriminate between habitats and their inhabitants. To read one's own with a theological self-assurance is to incur—in profound irony—a sort of countering apartheid from the rest of humans. Has it not been the tragic irony of the Judaic that it has incurred, through long centuries, just this dark experience of sharply exchanged differentials, whereby history's most insistently 'chosen' people have been its most bitterly persecuted people?

Yet, costly irony though it be, it was this assuredly distinctive identity where alone a Messianic realism could find origin, a realism about God and history, about wrong and its redemption, only conceivable, whether as hope or fact, in a society which knew, as Jewry did, the seriousness of sin and the moral sovereignty of God. No 'new testament' would be possible of reach outside the matrix of an 'old'. Yet the very 'reaching of the new' must pay its debt in breaking from

---

[4] Did not Freud argue that he found Egyptian factors real in the 'monotheism of Moses'?
[5] Strictly one should not be speaking of 'Judaism' prior to the Rabbis' reform after the Fall of Jerusalem and the forfeiture of the Temple ritual.

what made the 'old'—by its own logic—illogical in its confinement of inclusive things.[6] Was there not somehow inherent in the quality of being Jewish a necessity to concede, as Christianity rejoiced to do, its universal relevance? Can any identity truly be itself in peace and hope and not consent to 'belong with mankind'?

It is clear throughout the Hebrew Tanakh how a lively consciousness of 'the nations' ('Gentiles') coincided with the very precept of a 'chosen race'. At the Exodus there was 'spoil to be had of the Egyptians'—doubtless to alleviate the bitter pain of tyranny endured. There were things to be possessed even from their tormentors. Down the centuries there was the steady realisation that they were not alone in the world and that, in the neutrality of the natural order, there was 'a wealth of nations', even as there was 'balm in Gilead'. In his day of sharpening vision, Amos could even trace an 'exodus' of other peoples as the hallmark of their history (9. 7). Hosea, citing the very vocation of Moses in Exodus 3. 14, could warn his generation from a Yahweh saying: 'I am not the "I AM" you think I am.'[7] Return from exile under the grace and favour of the Persian Cyrus prompted a warmer perspective for cultures non-Judaic. The splendid universalism of an Isaiah, affirmed by many a psalmist, could then extend a common and deeply sacramental humanism from within the ancient grace and favour of Yahweh, still essentially 'the God of His people'.

Thus there remained an abiding ambivalence. Any 'towards them' about 'the Gentiles' was conditioned by the perception that for their very sake the distinction from them was vital. Only via a people that remained 'apart'[8] could their ministry 'bless the nations.' Thus vocation *per se* was the guarantee of its own perpetuation. Their 'mission' could never be shared, since they held the copyright, so that 'being not of us' was the rubric about 'hearing from us'. The 'benediction' was not a fellowship joined but a witness given. Hence, abidingly, as the Song of Zachariah had it, the steady juncture of 'thy

---

[6] This Judaic confinement not only—as noted—of nature's equal hand of 'rain on the just and unjust' and the equal feasibility of its processes—farm, orchard, garden, workshop, hospital—without reference to religious allegiance, but also of vocation with truth possession. Mission in Christ could be to and by all and every people in inclusive benediction of the world.

[7] See the clear echo in Hosea 1. 9 of Exodus 3. 10, explaining *Lo Ammi*, 'Not My people'.

[8] The leading historian of Jewry, David Vital employs the traditional phrase and traces its long and costly meaning in *A People Apart: The Jews in Europe, 1789-1939*, Oxford, 1999.

people Israel' and 'the hand of our enemies' and 'them that hate us.'[9] Focus on the Messianic theme will help illuminate how the Christian perception and possession of it enabled the inclusion of 'the Gentiles' in the service of the faith as well as in its 'means of grace', whence 'their repentance unto life' also translated into authentic apostolate to the world, alongside a Jewish one.

III

The sure clue to why and how this radical development from the Judaic into the Christian transpired lies in the founding theme whereby the Cross of Jesus, in its whole context of ministry, was perceived and received as the meaning of Messiah—the utmost about God in the utmost about the world.[10] The faith that had been answered in 'the print of the nails' could learn of 'the Lamb in the midst of the Throne'. The God 'who does what He does that He may be who He is' in creation had likewise been known in the appropriately divine action of our human redemption. The ancient faith of Israel translated itself, in Jewish hands, into the theme of the embracing arms of one crucified, humanly inclusive in being redemptively divine. In all embrace there is both cost and reach. It is 'the one known human signature', the 'cross' gesture we make when the body upright throws out arms, whether in weariness or joy in the shape of all embrace—'one line athwart another line'. So it was alike in fact and symbol in the dying of Christ. The early Church called it *ekpetasis*.

The unison of fact and faith here as the consensus conviction of the New Testament in both Gospels and Letters turns squarely on the entire ministry of Jesus as prelude to its climax in death. In that ministry the Messianic theme was deeply embedded in 'the Son of Man'

---

[9] The long loyalty of Christian Liturgy (Morning Prayer) to this Song, despite this sad preoccupation it has for 'them that hate us,' is striking tribute to its care for Hebrew roots, despite the tension involved with its nearer precept: 'Love your enemies.'

[10] It is sometimes right for theological thought to reach for 'neologism' to register its meanings. 'Utmost' here sees in the crucifying of Jesus—qualitatively—'the sin of the world', and in divinely undertaking it as 'God in Christ' the 'utmost' concerning divine 'capacity'. See further below and my *God's Wrong is Most of All: Divine Capacity*, Brighton, 2006.

language as of 'one begotten'.[11] Any case—as sometimes made—for its absence only attests its presence, when we appreciate how the reasons for non-publicity lay precisely in the ever open question of how 'Messiah' would or could eventuate, notions being so disparate.

When, beyond the disciples' dark experience after Gethsemane, they realised Messiahship in the very contours of the suffering Jesus their decision was truly revolutionary. Never before, it would seem, had the seemingly tragic and the authentically Messianic been so discerned and confessed. Yet there were deeply Jewish perspectives which, if only in retrospect, had the meaning 'on hold' until the double event of fact and faith could recognise how they had come to pass.

Being 'Messiah' was, if more, no less than the age-long pattern of divine 'employ' of human means for divine ends. There was never divine purpose which did not need its Joseph or its Moses, its Amos or its Jeremiah. Prophethoods, in summons to the vineyard of the Lord, His in-planted people, were central to mediation of the divine word, the service of the divine will. Significantly, alike in the parable and in the history, the employed had suffered in and from their errands. That hard dimension must be taken further later. Here it suffices that divine ends take human means. Messiahship is of the same order but supremely so.

Further, deep in the Jewish tradition, in line with the 'burden' (i.e. 'task') of 'his servants the prophets', was—from Exodus onwards—the theme of Yahweh 'bearing His people'. Was not the entire narrative of Israel's human murmuring frailty a story also of divine patience in the odyssey into Canaan? Thus Isaiah reflecting centuries later sings:

'He bare them and carried them all the days of old.'

This because

'... in all their affliction, He was afflicted and the angel of His presence saved them.'

---

[11] The meaning of 'Son of Man' is the source of long scholarly discourse but at least 'identity' with the human realm is its obvious meaning so that 'the Son of Man has nowhere to lay his head' *could* indicate simply a general human homelessness in 'this transitory world'. The 'Son' language, as in 'only begotten' surely indicates a divine agency so close as if to have been 'born' (as a 'mission') of 'a Father's mind'. 'Only' has no mere connotation of number but of utter congruity—a 'One-liness' in equation with 'fulfilment'.

This solicitude of Yahweh for His people's well-being marries with the vocation whereby they, as a 'people' are to be, supremely and corporately, the servants of the divine will in the world by the 'witness' of their very being. There is thus what might be called a *unio sympathetica* between the mind of Yahweh and the destiny of His people. There is no mistaking the costliness to Him of the partnership of His 'people-agency'. Historians and psalmists alike from their number are eloquent of the harmony-discord of this inter-woven saga. We should not be somehow querying the depth of this relation by the usage 'the angel of His presence', if the theological reservation this implies is assumed to cancel the reality. Faith is only thinking with a due deference for the mystery involved. By the same token—as the Church came to believe—is it not a privilege other nations might at least covet to enjoy, even if the Hebraic shape of it allowed no such aspiration?

One of the surest exponents in the 20th century of this theme of 'divine pathos' as he called it was Rabbi Abraham Heschel in sundry writings and notably in *The Prophets*.[12]

He saw in Hebrew 'election' and 'covenant' the deep token of how the being of Yahweh was 'transitive', going across to humanity in intimate relation, setting all life under divine perspective. Somehow (Heschel was loathe to engage in explicit 'dialogue' as unfitting the sublimity of its concerns) this intimacy with Israel lay both within a divine prerogative of particularity and yet prefigured its truth for all, seeing that creation and the natural order told it so inclusively. Thus Heschel 'resolved' the Jewry/Christian issue as 'abiding in a deep tension', approving John Donne's 'No man is an island', but insisting that 'Anti-semitism is Anti-Christianity.'[13] Divine pathos was to be understood in its first Biblical form with a pained reproach for how its second Biblical form had perceived and confessed its presence in the shape of 'Jesus crucified', and how its new disciples had so far purloined the Hebrew'. Scriptures as their own.

There was a deeply kindred theme, however, in Heschel's language of 'man standing under God's concern' and how 'divine ethos does not operate without divine pathos.'[14] Here Hebraic 'seriousness of

---

[12] Abraham J Heschel, *The Prophets*, New York, 1962. It begins: 'This book is about some of the most disturbing people who have ever lived.'

[13] Abraham J Heschel, Inaugural Lecture, Union Theological Seminary, New York, 1965: 'No Religion is an Island'. See also my *Troubled by Truth*, Edinburgh, 1991, pp.108-126.

[14] *The Prophets*, loc. cit., p. 218.

sin' matches the utter necessity of grace in the Christian Gospel. God via creation and 'election' is party to a human mutuality where He is understood in terms of how He acts. The whole of Israel's story is seen as 'God's experience', and this is no 'humiliation' of Yahweh. On the contrary, offering a reading of Psalm 18. 35: 'When you humble me you make me great' he argues as of God, 'You show me how great You are by Your humbling of Yourself.'

How close Heschel comes to the New Testament theme of divine *kenosis* suggesting for Christian theology that Paul, in the supremely Christian *confessio* of Philippians 2. 5-11, spoke from his entire Jewish soul. Suffering belongs with the very being of God. Had such divine pathos not been read on high concerning the plight of slaves in Egypt? So was Moses assured at the burning bush:

> 'I have surely seen the affliction of my people which are in Egypt and have heard their cry ... for I know their sorrows ... I am come down to deliver ...' (Exodus 3. 7-8)

The ensuing Exodus journey Heschel calls 'the itinerary of God'. He sees, notably Hosea, but all the prophets responding to divine pathos in their own costly sympathy. Theirs is 'a whole way of being', 'a fellow feeling with God', feeling 'divine pathos as one feels one's own state of soul.' 'A divine concern becomes a human passion ... fulfilment of transcendence ... an identity between the private and the divine.'[15]

Unwittingly (?) how close Heschel's perception of prophethood comes to Christian reception of 'the Word made flesh', of 'God in Incarnate Christ'. 'Prophecy consists', he writes, 'of a revelation of God and a co-revelation of Man.'[16] It may be this closeness which explains why, by and large, Rabbi Heschel, for all his deep Talmudic learning and godly Jewish roots, was hardly *persona grata* in orthodox Hebrew circles, despite the eminence of the Jewish Seminaries he served in the USA.

That circumstance might argue a certain reluctance to invoke him Christianly, were his *unio sympathetica* not so clear and precious to the deep mind of the New Testament. His witness to what he received

---

[15] *Ibid*. See 'The Philosophy of Pathos', pp. 247-267, and pp. 307-10, and p. 319.
[16] *Ibid*., pp. 366 and 419.

as the very soul of things Biblical encourages a Christian, against the odds, to believe in a genuine unity of Old and New Testaments, though Heschel always refrained from exploring it dialogically.[17] How near he comes to what that second Testament made, in fulfilment of its great indebtedness. Perhaps Rabbi Heschel's sense of 'divine pathos' would have us live in positive capacity of heart, without requiring that church or synagogue should otherwise converge their minds. How close Heschel comes in his great theme to the kindred conclusion of James Hastings, commenting on the significance of Jeremiah:

> 'Prophecy had already taught its truths, its last effort was to reveal itself in a life.'

For, with the same motif, John Skinner who cites Hastings, says of the same Jeremiah:

> 'He breaks through the limitations of the strictly prophetic consciousness, and moves out into the larger filial communion with God.'[18]

IV

Through divine 'agency', to people destiny, to prophetic suffering in its name, the Hebraic tradition we have reviewed is clearly the setting and index for the discerning decision the early Church took in thereby founding itself. That decision had other Jewish precedents to which we must return with the help of that haunting phrase: 'the prosperity of His servant'. Meanwhile, there are two urgent questions. First, what is this doing with divine transcendence? and secondly what of the Davidic theme in all Biblical Messianism, the necessary role of the power-order?

The former is a question many theists and apophatic theologies and certainly Islamic ones will press to ask. The answer crudely must

---

[17] That 'unity' has often been under strain given—*inter alia*—the impossible discontinuity between the *lex talionis* in many a psalm and chronicle and its abolition in the Sermons of Jesus and the Letters of Paul.

[18] John Skinner, *Prophecy and Religion: Studies in the Life of Jeremiah*, Cambridge, ed.1961, p. 16.

be: 'Nothing that transcendence has not already done of itself—in the will to create, the granting of human 'dominion' and legislating for it in divine law. All these mean a divine stake (Heschel's 'concern') already 'transcendenting' transcendence by dint of human relevance. Transcendence belongs to Sovereignty, not to an absentee.

As for the Davidic, the 'Son of David' cry in Hebrew anticipation, did it not follow directly from the centrality of those defining dimensions of people, land and rule by which post-Joshua Israel knew itself? As such it could never belong with any supra-national, extra-territorial righteousness, unless in submission to David-style monarchy. It was only a Messiahship according to Jesus that, could admit of faith-mission (only) 'into all the world'.[19]

Whatever its merit in owning the necessarily political factor in human 'law and order', its polity did not long endure despite the 'promise' of an everlastingness. That pledge could only be realised in other Messianic terms. Exile and dispersion supervened, to be only feebly countered under Ezra/Nehemiah and the Hasmoneans. Then Rome via Titus and Hadrian perpetuated Jewish 'exile' from land and rule until the emergence of the State of Israel in a 20th century.

It has followed—certain versions of Zionism apart—that a deep disenchantment about Messiahship and Messiahs has ensued in the mind and soul of Jewry. There are those who imply that it never really had the centrality which Christian reading gave to it. Perhaps it was that very reading which kindled a calculated disinterest in its vistas of hope. Bar Kockhbah's Revolt in the second century had gone the way of that of Zealotry in the first. Sundry other Galilean pretenders earned only dismal failure. 'Next year in Jerusalem' may have echoed the aspirations of abiding dismay but perceived no way to make it good, The utter disaster of Shabbatai Zvi, with all its bizarre credulity and high intent, proved only a gesture of futility with dire warnings of insanity in mob hysteria in the frenzy to which the hope of 'Messiah' was liable.

That seventeenth century tragedy did not in itself lead to abandonment of the idea it traded but the realities of Jewish distress turned it more and more into a pious dream, if one never to be

---

[19] Inasmuch as only a 'suffering Messiah' could embrace all peoples in an inclusive redemption, whereas Messiahships, via 'power' would, thereby, be based on national, territorial or ethnic instincts, saving their own and subduing others.

relinquished. Could it be that contemporary disavowal—in effect—of Messianism belongs with the power-political form it was assumed to need and adopt? That assumption duly stemmed from the land-and-people nexus so central to the Judaic, Biblical saga. If so, perhaps it was Messiahship according to Jesus via the discerning of the early Church that could avail to 'prosper' in a world-wide realism by means of its own idiom?

In any event, the Messianic theme—in the words of its leading analyst, Gershom Scholem—became one of 'perpetual futurism'. He writes:

> 'Utopian elements in the Messianic idea had to be simply a hope that was projected on to the distant future, an affirmation of faith that corresponded to no real experience.'

And:

> 'The Messianic idea has compelled a life lived in deferment in which nothing can be done definitively.'[20]

The role is one no individual can accomplish, no event can transact or fulfil.

The Jerusalem sage, Martin Buber, shares the same disassociation of the idea from the historical:

> 'Messianic self-disclosure is the disruption of the Messiahship ... it stands or falls with its seclusion.'[21]

'He' or 'it' can only be a figure of hope. Messiah never 'comes' so that he may always be awaited. Hope allegedly realised is the hope itself betrayed. Buber rooted this dictum deeply in Jewish experience of historic tragedy.

> 'The world's redemption did not become a fact nineteen centuries ago. We are still living in a world that is not redeemed. We are still looking forward to the real redemption and each of us is called

---

[20] Gershom Scholem, *The Messianic idea in Israel and Other Essays*, New York, 1971, p. 57 and p. 35.

[21] Martin Buber, *Mamre: Essays in Religion*, trans. Greta Hort, Oxford, 1946, p. 18f. 'At no definite point in history has a Saviour appeared, so that a new redeemed history began with him.'

to do his part in the work of redeeming the world. Israel is the community which retains this purely Messianic experience.'[22]

He adds further:

'Standing bound and shackled in the pillory of humanity, we demonstrate with the bloody body of our people the unredeemedness of the world ... We have been the sin-offering of humanity ... Unredemption begins with us ... our distinctive gift to mankind.'[23]

There are points here to which we must return but the same rejection of any 'realised Messiahship' runs more widely, if less ardently, than in Martin Buber. Thus A A Cohen writes:

'To say that Jesus is not the Messiah is to say that history is not yet redeemed for us ... For we await God's instructions in his own time and in a form coherent with our past and consistent with the future our past has shaped.'[24]

Jacob Neusner, a prolific authority in this context enquires:

'Does Judaism present a Messianism and may we, therefore, speak of the Messianic idea or doctrine of Judaism? The answer is a qualified negative to yield a flat No!'

For Judaism, Messianism is 'left like the rubble after the building has been completed.'[25] Elsewhere he argues for an eschatology that has no place for a historical Messiah.[26]

---

[22] See Martin Buber, *The Origin and Meaning of Hasidism*, n.d. 'To forego hiddenness is to suspend Messiahship. Messianic self-disclosure is a contradiction in terms', pp. 109-110. Also *Mamre, op. cit.*, note 21.

[23] Martin Buber, quoted in *Jewish Frontier*, Vol. xv, 1948, by Ernst Simon, p. 26.

[24] A A Cohen, *The Myth of the Judeo-Christian Tradition*, New York, 1970, p. 109. He adds: 'The redemption of the world is a chimera ...', p. 162, and 'The Jew is an expert in unfulfilled time', p. xx.

[25] Jacob Neusner, in, see *Judaism and their Messiahs at the Turn of the Christian Era*, ed., J Neusner, W S Green and E S Fredricks, Cambridge, 1987, p. 14. He does, however, recognise (the point made here earlier) that 'Israeli Scriptures, emphasising historical narrative as a mode of theological explanation, lead us to expect Judaism to evolve as a deeply Messianic religion.' P. 265.

[26] Eschatology always has to take over when any historical teleology fails or is displaced. An Israel without the blood-rites of the Temple after AD 70 subsumed its hopes into being itself Yahweh's law-abiding community.

In similar vein, and discounting Christian Messiah as the Christ, Yeshayahu Leibowitz warns:

> 'Consider the consequences for Judaism of every historical development in which Messianic, redemption became central. Such situations brought forth Christianity, led to Sabbatianism ... and in our day this focus has become a stumbling-block.'[27]

'Realised Messiahship', in Christian or any other form that is not sheer hope for a future, is thus for these exponents of Judaism now, a contradiction in terms. 'The Messiah who comes, the Messiah of the present, is invariably the false Messiah.'[28] We are left to hope without fact, faith in the absence of event.

Could it be that this avowed rejection on the part of these voices of 'the Messianic concrete' as ever Jewish stems from the failure of the Davidic idea and the fact that the Messianic idea in essence was then, and since, power-political? Here we must return to the Messianic measures of the Lord's Prayer noted in Chapter 2 and to another matter of its translation. This one has to do with that *peirasmos* we pray to be spared—never 'temptation' in the popular current sense, but the pre-Messiah 'time of trial' as feared by Galileans and others in Jesus' day.

'Time of trial' meant what were dreaded as the Messianic 'woes' of the last days. For any historico-political, David-style Messiah, wrong and evil would have to be at a maximum when he supervened to end them. For if they persisted after his alleged triumph in their defeat, Messiah would be quite disqualified, a futile laughing-stock. Men would still be noting bitterly 'the unredeemedness of the world'. The prelude to the Messianic finale would thus be a horrendous climax some might not wish to see.

Such is the moral dilemma of any Messianism which is historico-political. Hence the modern Jewish 'case-against' we have cited. History will always produce an ambiguous result just as law can only ever achieve a modicum of justice. Praying the Lord's Prayer now or then can only mean: 'Do not bring us where "living the evil of time at its worst" proves too much for us, be such as to overwhelm us,

---

[27] Yeshayahu Leibowitz, *Judaism, Human Values and the Jewish State*, Cambridge, Mass., 1992, p. 111. He does not notice Rabbi Heschel, but, as if rejecting him, he observes: 'Judaisim avoids pathos' (p. 13). But see Introduction, pp. xxxiii–xxxiv.

[28] *Ibid.*, p. 72.

but deliver us from the evil.' The two clauses: 'Do not ... but ...' follow hard on each other.

It is the *quantitative* measure explicit in the Davidic, the historical, the—if need be—violent which ensures that time will frustrate it and history baulk it. What then else?

V

It must and will be a *qualitative* Messianic act which, being no less in history, is in no way subjunctive to history in the nugating terms Jewish experience has come to argue. What is qualitatively Messianic happening once and for all stands and abides as representatively in time and place to energise all other time and place. This Biblical Messianism was held from doing by virtue of its inalienable tie to Hebrew covenant and promise. Was not that Messiah an *Aberglaube* as German would say, a going further from existing belief in creation, providence, election and vocation to justice in all these as into a dream?

We might then identify without arrogance, pretentiousness or guile, 'the redeemedness of the world'—redeemedness in terms of what redemption takes as for ever exemplified in a Gethsemane, in a Cross that could translate into 'the Lamb in the midst of the throne', the love-insignia of the sovereignty of God. We are back here, gratefully, with the verdict earlier quoted about 'the one perfect sacrament of that power by which, in the end and in the whole, all evil is redeemed.' There is no reason in history why history should not contain the inclusive occasion of that by which history's own supreme anxiety is answered and its ultimate burden healed. Further history will never overtake it with proofs of its discredit as ever final—the fate which, as we have seen, waylaid all quantitative Messiahships which wanted it 'all in a moment',[29] a 'moment' which later history would promptly unravel.

A Messiah in the quality of Jesus' garden of agony would always await and enjoy discipleships in its emulation. Was it not always assumed by all Messiahships that, however 'Personal' the great 'achiever', he would always need incorporation later in his followers. 'I and those whom God has given me.'[30]

---

[29] Cf. the prayer, in the *tefilla*: 'Let all wickedness perish in a moment.'
[30] Hebrews 2. 13 citing Isaiah 8. 18. 'Behold I and the children whom God has given me.'

His and their efficacy as 'Messiah(s)' lay in that *praotes* and *epieites*—'the meekness and gentleness of Christ', or as Matthew 11.29 has it:'Learn of me that I am …'[31] in close association with 'the yoke', as steady symbol of a task that partners with a meaning. Only such qualities repudiate, as Gethsemane did, the law of retaliation, that *lex talionis* to which the Judaic and Islamic are so wedded, which has long been the curse and blight of human history, the tragic perpetuator of conflict and enmity.[32] Its renunciation—forever costly in that the vengeance it yields was congenial—is where redemption always begins. What does not 'get its own back' has hope to 'get the other back' to something like the *status quo ante*, but enriched in the forgiving/forgiven experience. Thus we are 'not overcome of evil only in overcoming evil with (our) good.' The wrong is not condoned, still less ignored, but 'absorbed' so that its—otherwise—entail is 'disentailed'. It begins to be clear that 'Messiah' could never feasibly be other than a bearing and forbearing—and so, in turn, a suffering figure, and that, not as some sorry victimised idea but in the concreteness and the particularity of a historical encounter with wrong. Such Gethsemane and its sequel were.

Our sundry Jewish witnesses were right in their perception that a Messiah in their traditional terms, could never 'come' and therefore, could only be awaited. Jesus crucified in the saving economy of God in grace both justified them in waiting and—in waiting no longer. For what is that 'hope' to which we can give no content of expectation? Can what conceptually 'happens' hope not also factually 'happen' as its realisation? Can we anticipate and not describe? Maybe 'a realised Messiahship' could be a fulfilment of terms.[33]

---

[31] The Greek is indicating that the Christ has to be learned from him rather than simply about him, with 'imitation' in mind. See further on the Letter to the Hebrews. Was this not also the sense of Paul's '… that I may know him and the fellowship of his suffering'?

[32] From 'the Lord at war with Amalek from generation to generation …' to the malign Treaty of Versailles, to perpetual retaliation provoking steady return between Israel and retaliatory Palestinian violence.

[33] Yet there is great Jewish fidelity in the will only to hope. The New Testament had great 'hope' in the *Parousia* but had to learn to forego its immediate fulfilment. Even so, what is set to be duly realised interminably must have an identity that might have been concretely realised—and realised as a spur to what it left to others.

VI

It is clear how radical was—and is—Judaic disavowal of this 'realised Messiahship' according to Christianity and, therefore, how deep the divide between them. 'Happening'—in the one case allowed, in the other disallowed—turned on a crucial distinction between 'happenings', either as 'only once' things or 'once and for ever' things. Christian Eucharist' was of the second order in the 'once-and-for-all' and 'here, now and ever' Christ. It only had the 'quantity' (i.e. 'content') of event in having also its 'quality'. The redeemedness of the world could have a real 'when' only in having its authentic 'where'. Redemption would be known for what it 'took' by the measure of what it did and how. As such it could be trusted as divine in God's own kind. This 'fact and faith'—to return to the earlier coupling of things in the Ordinal—belonged with 'the print of the nails', and came from 'the wounded hands'.

Other aspects here have to follow below. Meanwhile, it is urgent to perceive, despite all stake between the Judaic and the Christian, how both share alike the truth of 'Messiah' as incorporating community. The several writers we have noted who disallow fact and opt only for hope appreciate, no less that the hope summons them to act here and now. It means no folding of the hands in listless regret. A Messiah we will never identify in history can still be our monitor, our spur and goad in an existence which, precisely in eluding him, recruits us. Despite never 'possessing him here and now—as Christians believe to do (hence their glad Eucharist)—he, as incentive, possesses us.

Thus Y Leibowitz sets down 'the austere demand of God, in the world as it is,' is for Jewish fidelity to Yahweh and His Torah, as the only 'Messiah' there could ever be.[34] This, citing Psalm 103. 20, he describes as requiring 'great fortitude'. Likewise, André Neher excludes divine 'intervention', so that 'mankind may be free'—free to fulfil a wholly human responsibility, which argues and 'necessitates the silence of God'.

> 'It is the human society itself which, since Sinai, has held in its hands the silent keys of its own fortunes.'[35]

---

[34] Leibowitz, op. cit. See p. 108. 'Ye that excel in strength.'
[35] André Neher, The Exile of the Word, trans D Maesal, Philadelphia, 1981, p. 188. God created man to be 'the guardian and sovereign of a free zone of liberty'. 'Man', here is inclusive so that the 'free zone' in Neher is one he sees 'secular people' can also appreciate with Jewry. Yet this 'clue' to us and things stems only from the Hebraic source. 'Human' means Jewish.

For Jacob Neusner also Jewish 'sanctification for eternity' by Torah obedience 'displaces' any historical Messiah. There is an ambivalence here when he writes:

> 'The sages were careful not to take history into the proving ground of theology ... Israeli Scriptures, emphasising historical narrative as a mode of theological explanation leads us to expect Judaism to evolve as a deeply Messianic religion.'[36]

That it did, indeed, do so we have earlier argued. Why then need a Christian 'theology through history, meaning through event', be the less warranted? 'Christ our Passover' might unite them both. Even so, his emphasis is firmly on Torah fidelity as the only Messianic dimension now.

We can surely plead, then, that—with or without any Messianic event in the New Testament sense of 'God in Christ' as history 'on proving ground'—there is enough affinity here for a mutuality of Jew and Christian in being 'a community of obedience'. Christian 'Holy Orders' as mandate to ministry stand within 'the Messiah in God'. Whether synagogue or church more aptly read the shape it has and bring the will it claims remains the open question.

With that conclusion it is sad to find John Pawlikowski wanting to divert Christian theology altogether away from the Messianic theme and suggest instead a 'Christology of divine/human sympathy'.[37] His aim is to alleviate the issue of alleged 'supersession' of things Judaic by things Christian. By present argument there is no 'supersession' but only a differing presence as 'Messianic community'. On either part it has to be a devotion in the here and now to that which never has been, nor can be 'realised', and that which having been 'realised' and 'defined' yet awaits—in its very strength—our part in its on-going. The contrast cannot be denied: it need not be an apartheid of wills or hearts.

Pawlikowski's plea has failed to see how divine *unio sympathetica* is itself the origin of a divine Messiah. We need to cling the more

---

[36] J Neusner. See note 26. But 'the framers of the Mishnah avoided the Messiah myth.'

[37] John Pawlikowski, *Jesus and the Theology of Israel*, 1989, p. 79f. He sees 'understanding the ultimate significance of the Christ-event, not as fulfilment of Jewish Messianic awareness, but as proclamation of a new depth in the understanding of divine/human bonding' (p. 73). Does this leave Jewry still 'awaiting in hope' but without taking in the significance of that new bonding'? And where does all this leave Zionism?

The Order of the Wounded Hands

to its Jewish roots, seeing that 'embarrassment' is a poor motive for theology, least of all given Christian indebtedness to all things Jewish. If we understand divine *kenosis* aright there can be no Christology without the full measure of the Cross, whatever then be what he calls 'the perduring features of the permanent Jewish covenant'. Can it not 'perdure' in the interiority of the Jewish mind and will, while the 'Self-giving of God in Christ' fulfils it in newly inclusive terms?

For surely these in now embracing all nations as 'peoples of God' matter profoundly—and for Jewry's own sake—as, now, their 'share-ability' with 'Gentiles'? There never was or could be 'supersession' as long as Jewry holds to what is inherently its self-identification.[38] Christian theology is not well pursued in terms of how it might mitigate what others take from its *confessio*, if they have done so wrongly. The New Testament does not 'supersede' except in its uncompromising witness to a divine grace which is inclusive for the faith of each and all as—by these presents—one humanity.

VII

Some Christian theologians in the twentieth century gave currency to a theory known as 'the two covenant God' which has found wide favour in inter-faith circles but was and is altogether treacherous to the New Testament. Its founding spirit would seem to have been James Parkes, an ordained protagonist of renewed Zion and a disqualifier of any essential Palestinian tenure in its 'promised land'.[39] Broadly his thesis ran that the Christian Gospel of 'God in Christ' was God's mercy to 'the Gentiles' in which Jewry did not and need not participate since they were already there by dint of birth under the 'old' covenant. This

---

[38] Cf. Leibowitz, *op. cit.*, note 26. 'I know of no way to faith other than faith itself ... I do not regard religious faith as a conclusion. It is an evaluative decision that one makes ... it does not result from any information one has acquired but is a commitment to which one binds oneself ... It is a conative element of consciousness' (p. 37). In such terms Christianity will not 'supersede' that Jewish 'faith in faith' concerning 'chosen-ness' and 'covenant', but it will bear unrepentant witness to the sheer inclusiveness of all peoples in the divine will, alike in creation and in grace.

[39] For full bibliography of James Parkes, his career and thinking see my *Troubled by Truth: Life Studies in Inter-Concern*, Edinburgh, 1991, pp. 91-107. He has won over many hearts, including the renowned Reinhold Niebuhr and Bishop Richard Harries. His position is regarded by many as mandatory for the Council of Christians and Jews, as somehow implicit in its *raison d'être*.

quite ignored the 'no more Gentiles but ...' cry of the Gospel, a *de jure* abolition of that radical distinction whereby 'we are all the children of God through faith in the Christ in Jesus.' (Ephesians 2. 19, Galatians 3. 26) There is no 'two covenant' proposal in John 1. 12f concerning 'authority to become and be people of God through faith in Christ'. Such was the assurance which mandated the expanding of the faith which, as noted earlier, was the very origin of the New Testament as the document of Gospels and Letters which it became.

The Parkes' theory also ignored the crucial role an apostolic Jewry had itself played in that world-wideness of the faith. Barnabas, as a Greek, may have had a vital role but only as junior partner to Paul, the entire significance of whose Damascus road experience it quite ignored. There was also Peter, according to the only 'Gentile' writer Luke, sharing in the 'Gentile' inclusion as the prime 'original' disciple to whom the great pledge had been given by Jesus.[40]

By its ultimate logic the 'two covenant' notion was proposing— in effect—'a church without Jews', surely a sequence they should have wanted to abjure, ominously near as it potentially was to the theme in Nazism of 'a world without Jews'. Further it made renegades of all Jews who ventured to 'belong' themselves with the Christhood of Jesus as honestly fulfilling their own *raison d'être*. To such 'renegades' the Church has been endlessly in debt.

There was also the unresolved issue of 'the law' and whether bare 'command and prohibition' could translate into divine righteousness of heart without the crucial role of pardon in the thrust of grace. Paul did not wrestle in vain with his 'when I would do good evil is present with me.' What of heed to his cry: 'O wretched man that I am. Who will deliver me?' in 'the works of law'. For these were inside the burden. In that yearning he was one with many a psalmist, so that his answer in Christ belonged proleptically where Hebrew psalms had truly been. The writers in Psalm 15, 51, 69 and 139 were all the time asking themselves whether they were 'already there', because, in 'their fathers' they had been at Sinai.

Thus meanings profoundly Christian were elided in the James Parkes' world, in meaning to mitigate Jewish/Christian relations but doing so in such disloyalty to either faith. Nor had the theory lived in the anguish of the Book of Job, that strangely Biblical/unBiblical figure,

---

[40] Peter of course was 'brought' by brother Andrew. But see Matthew 16. 13 to 28.

a 'man of Uz' not of Judea, who probed so tellingly all that remains so 'enquirable' between God and man.

Had the mind of James Parkes and his kindred spirits missed the fine point of Abigail's strategy with King David about 'being bound in the bundle of life'? (I Samuel 25. 29) as a truth all ways. Thus the enormity of the Holocaust was only finally ended at the price of death on the Normandy beaches, in the tragedy at Arnhem and the breaching of the Rhine or by the role a Stalingrad had in the final defeat of Hitler's realm of evil. History allows no respite from human inter-indebtedness and Jewishness is no exception, tragically unequal as the stakes may be. 'Pro-Semitism' can only fully be an inclusive humanism, a 'benediction' across all nations.

By this token too it is clear how James Parkes missed the logic of Jesus' ministry also. However we think to resolve the scholars' preoccupation with: 'Did Jesus intend the Church?' (of which the New Testament has no doubt) we may not ignore—the Cross apart—the accents in his teaching There was the ethnic 'neutrality' of so many of his parables—'a certain man ...','what man of you'—we do not stay to ask: 'But was he Jew or Gentile?' When he did otherwise he opted for the hated 'Samaritans'. En route to Judaic Jerusalem he 'must needs go through Samaria', so that later, in his obedience, his apostles must needs cross that Mediterranean. 'Your heavenly Father knows ... forgives ...? was not restrictive. The highly Hebraic first petitions—as we saw—of the Lord's Prayer were prefaced with 'Our Father'. Restrictive greeting he disowned as contrary to how *teleios* his heavenly Father was with 'rain on the just and on the unjust'.

Moreover, his directives about 'meats', and bans and 'cups' and cleansings passed into the vocabulary of the apostles to ensure the currency of the liberty he had himself enjoined. The ethics of Paul to the Romans (e.g. Chapter 14) or the character of love in 1 Corinthians 13 would be inconceivable without those 'Beatitudes'. 'Let not the sun go down upon your wrath' is one with 'forgive us as we forgive.' Thus the imprint of the teaching Jesus, as well as of the suffering Christ, was stamped on the New Testament Church. It could never have been so had it been a community of 'Gentiles' only.

Furthermore, on Parkes' ground, there would have been no urgent point in the perennial concern of the apostles, in the letters and the pastoral nurture, for the ethical standards of erstwhile pagans, had there not been an inclusivity with Jews. What pains the Church took with a moral as well as a 'believing' conversion, seeing how far the ethic of Torah went with it and could so far have been in jeopardy inside it. That was a lively element in the misgiving of all Jewry around any 'pearls before swine' analogy about 'those Gentiles'. It was vital that such sceptical Jews on the frontier as observers should be assured that, if 'Gentiles' were 'converted' into Christ, they were also 'convertible' to what mattered about Sinai. A 'two covenant' Church where 'Gentiles' were left to their own devices would have had no occasion for such solicitude.

Thus, in the same context, that theory altogether sets aside the debates and finding of the first great 'Synod of Jerusalem', where—according to Luke in Acts 15—this whole issue of 'Gentile' inclusion was addressed. The significance of 'it seemed good to the Holy Spirit and us' was both in that they were freely admissible and admitted and were ritually admonished on moral points. From this and from much else, including the work of the genius with the Letter to the Hebrews, it is clear that the Church found itself truly in finding its 'Gentiles' and releasing all their potential to the future.

When, sadly and *de facto*, the Church became a largely 'Gentile' entity the reason was not 'ideological' but circumstantial, as Jewry opted away in fear for ongoing Judaic identity following the Fall of Jerusalem and surrender of the Temple ritual. A Jewry retreating into the synagogue and 'the bond of the Law' could hardly stay open-minded or open-willed about the newly inclusive identity their pioneers had learned to love. Even then, they engineered no 'two covenant' theory to alleviate their dismay or exonerate their erring ones, Rather, they fortified themselves in their own immutable single covenant and let the malefactors go their way into condign reproach and bitter disavowal. The 'two covenant theory' is at once a grievous distortion of New Testament faith and life and all in all a sorry way of palliating the Christian guilt of Anti-semitism. That guilt has to seek forgiveness from within Jewry in the costly terms of its own comprehension of the God of all the world's redemption. Those terms would not allow the abeyance of a Christian practice of the same inclusion, whether vis-à-vis synagogue, mosque, temple or gurdwara.[41]

---

[41] That 'whosoever will may come' is not a principle the Church can ever presume to rescind.

VIII

What, then finally, of Christians 'the more indebted the more fulfilled' in their Hebraic heritage? It is evident enough that there are, in interfaith, exclusions we must require if there are to be 'inclusions' for which we must be ready. One will be the 'exclusion' from a worship of deity either as a callous tyranny or as a jesting gambler. We believe categorically in the purposiveness of a good creation and, for that reason in the heinous seriousness of human wrong. Both the Bible owes to its Hebraic ground. Both came blessedly to further fruition in Christian faith. Both gave rise to the Messianic hope as a confidence in divine Self-consistency, in respect alike of that good creation and that enigma of its human history.

Due fulfilment, it must follow, of that confidence might look (both would need to be 'in history') either for a quantitative Messianism achieving once and for all the deed esteemed in terms, for example, of Psalm 72.[42] Or it could see itself requiring a qualitative Messiahship where 'what it took'—as in the Cross—would be in deed and fact enacted as what would have need of, and leave room for, the perpetuation of its once for all dramatic reality in a redeeming community to which it must give rise. The Christian Eucharist in 'the body and the blood' contrives to bring into one that onus and that event, neither authentic in the absence of the other. The redemptive, where they find its trusting, lives must make redemptive—not as his in the wideness of the world but within the personhood which, on every count of love and knowledge, they owe to him.

Perhaps the surest way to see that fulfilment of heritage is to set it gratefully inside the most characteristic activity of its Hebraic mentor, namely the priestly system of Levitical ritual and the Temple worship. This, precisely, is what the writer of the Letter to the Hebrews contrived to do. It studies 'debt and fulfilment' alike and enables the

---

If, with Rabbi Heschel, 'Anti-semitism is anti-Christianity', Christian faith's accessibility to Jewry can be in no doubt. It is the gentleness which must belong to it that takes in what, its Christ apart, must altogether disqualify. But neither Christ nor the centuries could argue its being disowned. There can be neither 'special targeting' nor deliberate barring in the reach of mission.

[42] Early Bible annotators thought that David sang it 'for Solomon' with its wondrous picture of universal, age-long peace. 'All nations shall serve him' (v. 11) but in what terms as 'subjects'? 'All nations call him blessed,' but He is still 'the Lord God of Israel'. (v. 17 and v. 18)

Christian the more wisely to cry: *Introibo ad altare Dei* as meaning the Christ-event in story and in sacrament.

If, as seems likely, Hebrews was written prior to the Fall of Jerusalem in 70 when the Temple ritual ceased,[43] it belongs to the first generation of Christian dispersion and witnesses to its presence in capital cities, whether Rome (cf. 'those in Italy' [13. 84]) or Alexandria or Ephesus, while its attribution to Paul attests the authority it carried. The fine style of its Greek, however, seems to preclude a Pauline origin except in general terms. Addressed to *Hebraioi* (not *Judaioi*) it indicates a deeply Jewish element in that dispersion. Thus its guiding concern is to 'translate' or 'transfuse' or 'subsume' the Christian Messiah-Jesus into the symbol and structure of the Levitical priesthood, insofar as this venture in 'transmutation' is feasible, by employing both contrast and analogy. The aim and desire are tribute enough to a ruling sense of debt only understood as deep fulfilment.

Its whole case, we might say, turns on that vexed word 'sacrifice'. Readily used of animals ritually slain on altars in total 'victimisation', it only incongruously fits the deliberate, conscious 'obedience', which the Letter stresses as the Messianic quality achieved in Jesus crucified.[44]

About that self-giving there was nothing artificial, arbitrary, ritualist or contrived. All lay within a 'Sonship' fully reciprocal to a Father's will. It might well be argued that the whole attempt to integrate the way it was with Jesus into the way it was in the regime of Moses and Aaron could only be commended as, in time and place, a necessary effort after *in situ* interpretation. As such, it justifies the puzzle and query we now incur over that elusive figure of Melchisedek.[45] We need patience with an *argumentum ad homines*.

---

[43] Its argument might be said to have more relevance in that situation. Nevertheless, the Temple ritual did not suddenly fall from view and the sense of its loss would keep the Letter's expository goal intact. There is no doubt that its atmosphere about courage, tenacity, tolerance of enmity and ready 'bearing of Christ's reproach' reflects the travail of the lengthening years around AD 70 and beyond.

[44] The word, prominent in Romans also, belongs squarely with the 'Father/Son' relation—the will that ordains and the will that fulfils in the *kenosis* that is both divine and human. Hence the refrain elsewhere about 'the prosperity of His servant' with its strong irony around a 'fulfilment' that was utterly costly. There was never such 'obedience' in immolated animals.

[45] That Abraham was 'in fee' to him and that he long preceded Moses and Sinai and, hence, the law of the Decalogue. But who was 'the Most High God' (?) other than Yahweh—yet to be so known. Should a Canaanite deity have a 'priest' somehow anticipatory of the New Testament? See, further, p. 77.

The Order of the Wounded Hands

The play on two Greek words in 5. 8 *emathen epathen*—'he learned in that he suffered'—brings the surest *argumentum ad nos* in current time and place. With its echo of Matthew 11. 29 and perhaps also of Herodotus and certainly of many a psalm in the Wisdom literature,[46] it comprehends the entire ministry and Passion of Jesus as a 'learning' of the Messiah role. Thus it fits the incarnational truth of the Gospel narrative as yielding the experience, creatively incurred by Jesus in its course from baptism to Gethsemane, from which he progressively discerned what Messiahship must exact. It was about the world as it demonstrated itself to him in a gathering rejection of his meaning, the freedom to love God which he affirmed, the quality of God as 'Abba, Father', the mandatoriness of forgiveness, and the place of conscience within law. Thus his ministry, in setting forth in word and deed the economy of God, kindled what Hebrews calls (12. 3) 'the contradiction of sinners'.

Increasingly, it emerged for him as what had to be 'taken'—not via the *lex talionis* other 'Messiahships' would have assumed in 'taking it on', but rather, as divine 'obedience' said, 'taken up' in an 'enduring' by which the evil in it would be 'overcome by good'. The discerning of this vocation led into Gethsemane where the pattern culminated in the drama of 'the cup he could not pass,' where *lex talionis* was nullified beyond the kiss of Judas in the travail of the Cross. There and then, a representative of that Messianic zealotry, realising the contrasting 'kingdom' of Jesus, pleaded to belong in it, with his: 'Lord, remember me.'

It was this 'learning in suffering' in the ministry of Jesus and its climax which the writer in Hebrews proposed to set forth in the idiom of an Aaronic priesthood. So far removed as this Christ was from such ritual contrived devices, the enterprise much surely seem, to deeper minds a quite incongruous proceeding. The 'sin of the world' was never there in those rituals, only procedurally the sins of Israel. Those would be ever repetitious, since their efficacy was only ceremonial. The 'compassion' of the High Priest was of a very different order from that of an incarnate 'Word'. The 'virtue' of Calvary had no parallel in the innocence of helpless beasts. They could not 'take away sin', since

---

[46] See Ecclesiasticus 51. 23-27 where 'Wisdom' invites 'the uninstructed' to 'bend your neck to the yoke' and 'see ... how light are my labours.' The word *chrestos* ('easy') is applied to God in Luke 6. 35, Romans 2. 4 and 1 Peter 2. 3 in the sense of 'kind' or 'gentle'. For Herodotus, see 1. 207.

they had never 'taken sin up' in the living meaning of its incidence in human society.

'The sum of the whole matter', as the Preacher might have said, lay in the fact that 'the blood of his sacrifice is his own' (9.12 and 13.12). 'Blood', that mystery of what courses through the veins, courses through the verses of this Epistle, even as it flowed so copiously on altars of holocaust in their Jerusalem. In its fascination is the very principle of life. The writer could recruit the blood of Abel (12. 24), victim of the first fratricide, but transcends such 'lesser things' in the non-retaliatory 'innocence' of Jesus.

How should we read the seeming absence of the Christian Eucharist in this Letter to the Hebrews, unless we find it implied in 'assembling together' (10. 25) where 'bread and wine' are not specified? Perhaps it is meant in 13. 15: 'Let us offer the sacrifice of praise to God continually,' with its echo of Leviticus 7.12.

Here perhaps the lore of Melchizedek—he who 'brought forth bread and wine' in converse with Abram returning from a military campaign. They were 'bloodless' tokens that, in the mind of Hebrews here could better 'sacramentalise' 'the body and the blood' of this Messiah in Christ. For the measure of his 'sacrifice' lay in no ritual 'shedding of blood', but only in the engagement of his ministry and his dying with the 'sin of the world'. 'Bread and wine', in their bloodless-ness, are still the giving of their elemental selves in wheat and grape into the final sacrament of God's hospitality to man, begun indeed in creation and the order of nature but altogether realised in this 'Christ of God'.[47]

Thus, despite what might seem the embarrassments now of its chosen milieu of atonement ritual, the Letter to the Hebrews mediates by the very force of contrast the *sui generis* character of its Gospel. Analogies always have to be invoked in the terms in which they can avail. These here do so as index both to grateful debt and large fulfilment. That ancient 'day of atonement' adumbrated in its own terms the 'necessity, within the being of God for the Cross of Christ in our sort of world—if, that is, we were ever to know what 'the sort of God' must be.[48]

---

[47] Hence 'bread and wine' as sacraments both of creation and redemption, as developed further in Chapter 7.
[48] As, in three places the Qur'an has it, we must have 'a right to esteem about God.' Can that be unless in vital relation to the human as the world tells it? 'Adumbrate' means here 'To represent through shadow'.

Only so, in *unio sympathetica* do we read those sundry 'betters' in this Letter—'better than angels', 'better than Aaron and Moses', 'better sacrifices', 'better things'. Yet 'better' looks back as well as forward. What far excels as almost to disown comparison nevertheless relates with what it transcends. The Messianic hope in Israel would not have known why its ultimate realisation need have been so radically different had it not first learned in the first primitive terms the infinite holiness of God and the dark seriousness of human sin.

So it could be, and so it was that Messiahship in Jesus stood and was known to stand, in the very circumstance that—its quality apart—must totally disqualify it. The old Law laid its curse on death by hanging under felony. What should have vetoed forever the faith of a 'Christ crucified' became its sure credential. That it did so in such confidence and urgency in the aftermath of Good Friday and the utmost dereliction of disciples has to be its enduring authenticity, as it is also the meaning of the Resurrection.

Emathen epathen, 'he learned in that he suffered.' 'In that he suffered, we learned.' In the 'taking of his yoke' we learned—as of a narrative in history—the theology of the love of God. The 'weary and the heavy-laden' of the invitation to learn were not only those still hungry for its comprehension. They were those who had no mind for its description of themselves and were the more absent from 'rest unto their souls'.

To these in their post-biblical non-Biblical world the 'Order of the Wounded Hands' relates as prey for their scepticisms and minder of their fears. There are no atheisms that can elude the reach of its care. This in Chapter 6. Meanwhile, there is the non-Messianic theism of the Qur'an and Islam.[49]

How far these first century reckonings are from the grim present of Israeli Zion thus early in the twenty-first—and yet how close. We are still deep in the seriousness of sin, still travailing under *lex talionis*, still the more ravaged by denial of the single humanity which might rein in the pride of nations. The singularity of any identity is truly

---

[49] While Muslim Tradition has an eschatological role for Jesus, the Qur'an sees his frequent title there, *al-masih*, as one 'anointed' to the task of 'messenger'. It does not carry all that the term in Hebrew owes to the concepts of 'election' and 'sacred history' we have examined which gave it rise. The Qur'an disallows the Cross of Jesus both as 'real' event and as ever 'redemptive' in the economy of God. See further, *Jesus and the Muslim*, London, 1985, Oxford, 1999.

'privileged' only in such inclusive neighbourhood, regional and global, as the original covenant of nature assumed and that of grace confirms. Therein, let all interiorise the prerogative of their own uniqueness.

Chapter 5
WHERE MOST EXCLUDED MOST ENGAGED: ISLAMICA

A Diapason Christian Theology

I

The idea of borrowing from one discipline to another may well seem suspect, if its logic is not carefully explored. Here the musical term concerning 'all the tones and notes in one' and, 'the stops on the organ that extend through the whole compass of 'the instrument,'[1] may seem quite at odds with the familiar exclusion by Islam of the salient themes of New Testament faith—the divine Incarnation, Christ's Passion as man's redemption and the ensuing credal confession of divine Unity in 'Father, Son and Holy Spirit'. Yet, as we must see, there are few areas where the Christian 'laying on of hands' has a more testing sequel than in the world of the mosque. It is one that engrosses all things Christian even when most explicitly disowning them. It is urgent to keep both measures of that paradox in mind.

The diapason theme was approved by the poet John Dryden when he wrote:

'Through all the compass of the notes it ran
The Diapason closing full in Man.'[2]

He is in harmony with Francis Quarles earlier in the same seventeenth century declaring:

---

[1] *The Oxford English Dictionary*. The term becomes inapt for the point of its use here, when it adds: 'The consonance of the highest and lowest notes of the musical scale'.
[2] John Dryden, *The Poems*, ed. John Sargeaunt, Oxford, 1935, p. 195. 'A Song for St. Cecilia's Day, November 22nd, 1687'.

'There is none that can read God aright unless he first spell Man.'³

We need both writers here. For what we must call 'a human necessity in God' and 'a human necessity for God' is basic for any Judeo/Christian/Islamic theology.

Seeing how this is so may well begin with the question: Why is the *Shahadah* of Islam so sharply negative—that *la*, as grammarians call it, of 'absolute' negation. It is a nominal sentence without an 'is'. 'There does not exist ...', 'there cannot ever be', any deity 'except Allah'. Here is the supreme negation, making clear that 'the unity of God' is not essentially about number. It is about usurpation. It matters more that Allah is never challenged by a rival(s) than that pseudo-gods be not multiplied and plurality merely offend by number.⁴

Hence that insistent *Allahu akbar*, asserting in the positive the urgent negation of the *la ilah*, another nominal sentence in no need to worry about some 'is', as if to reinforce the utterly categorical. 'God (is) great!' is the sure exclamation of Islam—not 'greater than', not *Allahu al-akbar*, 'the greatest', which might imply, even as superlative, some other ever remotely capable of entering into comparison with the totally incomparable.

Yet precisely because Allah has this entirely incontestable sovereignty as *Rabb al-'Alamin*, its truth needs to be endlessly affirmed since, by a strange paradox, it *is* contested—by idolatries that persist, by blasphemies that deny, by *jahiliyyahs* that ignore, by obduracies that disown. The Allah who is for ever 'the One', *Al-Ahad*, has to be 'held' so, 'made' so, across all the human scene. He has to be known, told—may

---

³ There is deep wisdom in this saying—the human as where a theological grammar might 'spell' its theology—as there is in many other of *Divine Emblems*, the major work of Francis Quarles (1592-1644), a Cambridge poet, lawyer and philosopher.

⁴ This point about the essential 'negativity' with which the Islamic Creed must begin is emphatic also in the root meaning of *Shirk*, the cardinal 'wrong' in the view of the Qur'an. For the *mushrik* is one who alienates from Allah alone—and to some pseudo-deity—the worship, reliance, trust, piety and devotion humanly due to God alone. 'Association' as a possible translation of *Shirk* risks the essential truth of Allah's perpetual 'association' with us as Creator, Giver of our *khilafah* as 'trustees' of this world, and as Judge and final destiny in *Al-Akhirah*. Yet Allah must imperiously be 'dissociated' from all that is falsely thought divine, whether by a crude paganism or a contemporary 'worship' of nation, creed, greed, money, an 'ism', or the state. 'Falsely' here obviates any inclusion of the Christian reading of 'God in Christ' as ever in the category of *Shirk*.

we even say?—allowed to be the who He is. The Oneness has to preside, reign, rule, govern and so be, *de jure* and *de facto*. Neglect, ignorance, stupidity or defiance must never trespass on this divine right of Allah to be, and to be so known, acknowledged, revered and obeyed. There is this sublime intolerance about Islam in assiduous care for the total human submission in due cognisance of God.

The urgency this has in every instinct of Islam and Muslims dwells in two facts—one that it must happen, the other that it may not, that 'the God who is' has somehow also 'to be let be'. Here is the whole point of the Qur'an, the entire mission of 'the messenger'. 'Let Allah be Allah' could be said to be the single cry of Islam. The great affirmation needs the great optative, seeing that this way a subjunctive is involved.[5] 'The diapason closes full in man,' seeing there is this human necessity in God for awe, wonder, praise and tribute, as these are reciprocal in being the divine necessity from man.[6]

In this sense, and in this sense alone, we have to conclude that there is vulnerability in the being of God. The thought ought to be, and would be, unthinkable to Muslims, were it not implicit in their whole vocation. God as 'vulnerable' has ever been a central Christian understanding—thanks to how we learn to measure 'God in Christ'. We need patience to appreciate the place it occupies, by paradox, in the very categorical shape of Islamic theism. When Shakespeare writes of 'an insurrection in the state of man',[7] is not the most heinous form of this 'the insurrection against God' which is the essence of idolatries, in wilful refusal or 'denial of the one right worship'?

II

There is then, the human necessity for God of a right esteeming worship[8] explicit in the divine necessity from man of that right theology,

---

[5] Using terms out of grammar; 'optative'—that which is sought or desired, the 'so that' of a process: 'subjunctive' that something is at stake, at issue.

[6] It was surely this that Quarles and Dryden had in mind as the latter's 'diapason closing full in man', divine reality through all the human notes sounding in the human story.

[7] William Shakespeare, *Julius Caesar*, Act 2, Scene. 1, lines 67-69. Brutus broods on his inner struggle between duty and conspiracy.

[8] The allusion is to where the Qur'an three times reproaches its first audience as 'not reckoning with the reality of God in true measure of His worth of meaning and truth'. See Surahs 6. 91, 22. 74 and 39. 67.

alike in mind and soul. If this seems innovative language that, too, is a necessity against the circumlocutions of controversy.

How then should thought and faith proceed in reckoning thus with Allah as 'vulnerable' on 'earth' and so also 'as in heaven'? What might the divine response require, with what strategy might it proceed? At once we realise how any measures, messengers, prophethoods, guidance-sending, scriptures-affording concede, by their very nature, the theme of deity with human things at stake. There must needs be the 'envoy', some 'from' and 'to' relating God and man, some textual mission into time and language, some active token in time and place of divine concern in its human reach. All such came into the purview and the ken of Semitic tradition and are explicit in Hebrew, Christian and Islamic text. All these see a divine engagement in and with the human scene, however variously they prefigure it, via ethnicity, history, words with meanings, or events which signify.

Nowhere, perhaps, has the New Testament/Quranic incidence of such 'enterprise that enters for us,' been more sharply presented and contrasted than in the deeply-probing writer, the Chicago Islamicist, Marshall Hodgson. In the aptly entitled *The Venture of Islam*, he wrote:

> 'For Christians, being based in revelation means being in response to redemptive love as it is confronted through the presence of a divine-human life and the sacramental fellowship of which that life is the source. For Muslims, being based in revelation means being in response to total moral challenge as it is confronted by an explicit divine message handed on through a loyal human community.'[9]

While Hodgson sees these two as implying moral norms in close resemblance, he finds their explicit groundings to be in total, mutually exclusifying contrast.

Whether this is so can perhaps await a further 'confronting'—to use his term—with at least in common the 'venture' of the divine

---

[9] Marshall G S Hodgson's three volumed *The Venture of Conscience and History in a World of Civilization*, was published in Chicago 1974. The extract here is taken from Edmund Burke in a digest of it entitled: *Rethinking World History*, Cambridge, 1993, p. 80. The place of conscience (the word *damir* does not occur in the Qur'an) is a striking feature of what Marshall here calls 'total moral message as ... explicit in divine message'.

into the human concerning the liabilities of either in the other. Thus far the Meccan *balagh* of an envoy contrasts in content, but not wholly in intent, with 'Word made flesh'. For either constitute a divine-human eventuality, initiated from God as moved by vulnerability to man and to answer and defeat the 'insurrection'.

Precisely in having that character and purpose, the venture incurs a renewed expression of the incipient insurgence. This should be no surprise. The strategy that addresses an obduracy is set to learn its nature further, to re-experience its malice, unless and until it is—as Islam would say—subdued, or—as Christians would say—redeemed. The New Testament parable of the 'vineyard of the Lord of hosts' tells it all, incorporating as it does the entire theology of creation under human aegis, being known here as 'This Sacramental Earth', with coinciding Biblical/Quranic insights.

But, by the same token, those envoys requiring and exhorting the tenants to yield what is due to the Lord, encounter their rejection. For the tenants conspire to become usurpers of the vineyard as their own, free of all divine constraint. Such is the very temper of idolatry in its nature as sin.[10] History tells in the experience of the envoys the wilful shape of our rebellion against God. The Bible and the Qur'an, alike in their disparate mirrors of the human scene, converge on this dark phenomenon—the vocational hazard of all messengers of God. The tribulations of Muhammad in Mecca at the hands of the Quraish, of Allah via him in their *zulm*,[11] are parallel, in their differing context, with the scorning of an Amos and the anguish of a Jeremiah. 'O Jerusalem that killest the prophets' cried Jesus in full and sudden view of the city from the Mount of Olives, brooding on 'the things that belonged to her peace.' The envoys, it is clear, simply learn the reality of the situation it is their task to retrieve. As is often the case with law also, they endure the pain of the problem inherent in their mission.

---

[10] The tenants want to read their tenure as their own property, making them liable nowhere beyond themselves. Such 'self-centring, God-eliding' is the very nature of idolatry, the crucial 'absenting' (actively) of God, living as the Qur'an has it *min duni-Illahi*, 'to the exclusion of God'.

[11] *Via* in the sense that their antipathy to Allah (in Muhammad's term's as God alone, not—as they might have allowed—in a co-existence with gods and goddesses sundry) was the point of incidence of their repudiation of Him. Thus—in measure—the enmity to 'message' was enmity to 'message-source'. God, supremely the Lawgiver, could not be, or seem, immune from the reception of His law-bringer unless He were repudiating His law. 'Messengers' could not be His agency and He negligent of what it underwent.

The frequent re-assurances to Muhammad during the Meccan period of this 'to be expected' about the hostilities he underwent, the reminders about other prophets, the steady and explicit approvals of his status and validity[12]—all underline the reality of his 'valleys of shadows' where even death in failure might intervene. 'Unvulnerable prophet' would always be a contradiction in terms, unless impossibly 'out of this world'. Envoy to grief is one with envoy to earth. The ample evidence of this situation in Muhammad's *Rasuliyyah* is writ large across the Meccan surahs—that steady *yaquluna* ('they are saying') of gibe, or charge, or calumny, or threat, with the responding *fa qul* ('so say') of rebuttal and patience, so that the *mise-en-scène* enters into the very texture of the Book, or the many occasions when recruits were few or tardy and the point where some were constrained to migrate across the Red Sea into Ethiopia. A climax of distress came when Khadijah died and a venture to Al-Ta'if failed. It was out of this nadir of his fortunes that the case for Hijrah emerged in sequel to the interest of a group away in Yathrib with the promise of sanctuary.

It is general now to read the Hijrah as a conscious plan to complete Islam via the further dimension of political statehood in a calculated unison of one Islamic mission in 'mercy to the worlds'.[13] Yet, in actual incidence, it would seem to have been a pragmatic decision taken *in situ* and—it appears—in the absence of any explicit directive present in the Qur'an.[14] What is not in doubt is that it profoundly altered both the ethos and the history of Islam. For it rescinded the firm Quranic injunction repeated six times in Surahs 6. 99, 13. 40, 24. 53, 29. 18, 36. 17 and 42. 48: 'Your sole liability, Muhammad, is the message you bring' or, lit. 'There is not laid upon you except the *balagh*, the theme you have to tell.' That continued, no doubt, but under a quite different sanction, to be, at length, no longer a task of persuasion but of power-suasion which at least some would finally experience as 'coercion', if only cumulatively such. Muhammad himself became a

---

[12] Such as 'You are on a noble undertaking' or '... of eminent standing' (Surah 68. 4) or the commendations in Surahs 25. 30-31, and 94. 1-4. For an example of the 'comfort' about 'earlier prophets likewise', see 51, 51-53.

[13] See, at random, for example: Qazi Ashfaq Ahmad, *Words that Moved the World: How to Study the Qur'an*, Leicester, 1999, p. 136 '... an opportunity to build a society and a state according to the ideals of Islam'.

[14] Surahs 5 and 24 are ascribed to Medina, the other four are Mecca. The *balagh*, indeed, did not cease or falter but it now 'meant' differently as entailed into a political and martial context.

different identity in his repute and undertaking (that *khuluq* of Surah 68. 4). There came a subtle shift in the temper and pre-occupations of the Scripture. In pre-Hijrah Mecca there had been no 'hypocrites', *munafiqun*—faiths under duress do not attract them. The *fitnah* that had first been the testing 'persecution' the faithful endured became *in media res* the urge to avoid the wounds and death and orphan-making of combat, to be finally the trying 'sedition' against success at the hands of ill-will and treachery. The Qur'an becomes busy with booty, ransom and what it calls the *awzar* or toils of war. (47. 4)

This far-reaching change in the entire ethos of Islam seems at least to qualify, if not withdraw, the precept in Surah 6. 105: 'I have not made you a warder over them,' and the ruling of 76. 24 much earlier: 'Await with patience what your Lord determines' (unless we read the Hijrah as what the bidding had in mind), or the attitude Muhammad had when he told the Quraish: 'God is all the witness I need between me and you.' (Surah 29.52)

III

That sentiment in 29. 52 is deeply important in the sequence of the argument here in mind. For we are studying the response, even the policy, of Allah vis-à-vis the vulnerability we see He incurs via the persons of his 'messengers'. If their adversities are in some sense His, being undergone in His Name and for His words' sake, then the transition from persuasion to a power-realm is Allah's also in being thus Muhammad's.

Allah's way of relying on a verbal envoy translates into enablement of a power-seeker becoming steadily a power-wielder. Something then quite radical is involved (to cite three earlier verses about 'esteeming Allah') in relation to the criteria of our theology, our reading of the divine mind and character as will. From the human side of 'believing', there comes now a double dimension to the obedience men bring, from that of faith alone as to truth, to that also of belligerence in its establishment. Islam itself becomes a history of two cities, one yet disparate. Recourse to power conveys religion beyond persuasion as its only proper means, which had emphatically been the case pre-Hijrah. It is clear from the *Sirah* that there were varying degrees of reluctance around the capitulation of Mecca in 630, as well as ongoing tensions between early-time adherents and very late-time ones.[15]

That the quest for hegemony, via Badr, Uhud, other encounters and the steady attrition by which neutrality or antipathy were overcome essentially altered the self-awareness of Islam, even as it changed Yathrib as a haven into Medina as the Prophet's bastion and then his citadel.

Correspondingly, this sequence brings to the fore the ever ambiguous role of power in the service of ethics and the integrity of religion as faith and piety. It thus constitutes a necessarily salient theme for honest inter-faith converse. Or, differently phrased, ought truth to be ever content to remain vulnerable in alliance with the vulnerability of God? Perhaps it has to abstain from power aegis in hegemonic control, in order to be authentically its truthful self.[16] This will in no way absolve it from political liability, rather it will immerse it in even deeper obligation in a ministry of active conscience and of all the wisdom it has to bring to the direction and hallowing of society at large. These will be more religiously deployed by virtue of reliance entirely on their persuasive and exemplifying capacities—resources which may well be atrophied, compromised or disabled by the naked power factor of the state and law.

Thus it must be said that the indispensable political duty and role of religion will be more religiously at work when they are not politically occupying the seats of power. These, in traditional (and Medinan) Islamic terms, have long been the religiously instrumental Caliphate and the legal Shari'ah-sovereignty of Islamic law.

The deep reason why this point must be made goes back to the human caliphate itself inside (that diapason!) the entire theology of a creation, from a divine Creator who willed for it a human dominion which in turn required the directive prophethoods which made it,

---

[15] Tensions, it is right to note, were inherent, in any case, with Muhammad's sudden passing, given the solitary role he filled and its dual shape as both 'religions and political'. The matter of 'succession' was the more critical through accessions to Islam having been shared across both dimensions, and occurring at different points in time and degrees of 'faith' content, as between *Ansar* and *Muhajirun* and family diversities within them at both Mecca and Medina. The dangerous and violent features of the years between 632 and 680, with intrigues and rivalries are witness to how troubled was the legacy of the twofold theme of the *Sirah*.

[16] Seeing that, otherwise, its being accepted in heart and mind will not be by measure of its worth alone but by the constraint its bearers bring. Likewise, the accepting self will be less than exclusively committed to it—thanks to e.g. mere prudence, or safety, or cowardice, or fear.

by their ministry of words, a strenuous entrustment set physically to be known and received as a moral sphere of liability, with nature the accessible auspices as always under God. This divine/human mutuality, in its awesome sequence, led further—we are saying—into the impasse in human terms of resistant wrong as necessarily impugning the sovereignty of God. If that sovereignty were thought to respond by assigning power to resolve it to the very humans whose evil had engendered it, would not the irony be complete? Such, surely, must be the ultimate case against the political order as the adequate guarantor and agent of any moral one? Is not this the more so, if and when the religious task within the ethical realm is held to be politically discharged?

There are two further reasons inside this case for religious faith having relevance outside, beyond and even against the sphere of political power. The first is that power-solutions to human wrong are always partial and inconclusive. The second is that all power exercise develops its own moral prejudice making it never 'right with itself within itself alone'.[17] The two reasons are closely inter-twined. The simplicity—if we may so speak—of the mind within Islam's transition from Mecca to Medina may well find this reasoning both uncongenial and pretentious as of one scaling 'the heights of some great argument to unjustify the way of God with men'. For did not the power-vocation of the Medinan Muhammad prove eminently sound and right? That history must be explored below.

In any event, wider history everywhere seems to have us conclude that powered solutions to human guilt, wrong, evil, sin—while necessarily corrective, contributory to a sane and safe society—remain always partial and incomplete. There is a radical difference between what can be requited as 'crime' and what is still there *qua* 'sin'. Retribution may assuage resentment and constraints serve liberties but only a modicum of justice is attainable, only a measure of retrieval to be had. Such are the dicta of time itself. Law may 'require that which is past;' it cannot re-instate it. A 'remainder', whether of 'envy, hatred or malice' or a host of other factors, persist awaiting only the moral ministries of forgiveness, of compassion, of love and of hope, which the politics of law and power can never afford but only delegate beyond itself, where faith must undertake them.

---

[17] 'Prejudice' in the strict sense that its way of reacting to all situations is slanted to its own concerns as 'power', rather than exclusively to the truth-trust it holds. Power tends always to hold itself self-justified in order to be secure against its own forfeiture.

We might explore this case re power's partiality by reference to that *lex talionis* examined elsewhere.[18] As a law of limits, 'one for one', it can be seen as salutary, even benign. Yet when life is taken for life does not the law's legitimation of revenge (to that limit) leave its own principle open to 'a taking on again of life for the life taken'? If one should exclude retaliation on retaliation, why not in the first case and forego—rather than merely limit—revenge? Some will counter:'No, for that limited retaliation vindicates a rule of law, protects society both from wild avenging and from unrequited wrong.'Yet only a legal fiction about 'feuding curbing' has the wrong 'undone'. After the due retaliation two victims remain and two 'hurts' essentially unhealed. The device is legal, artificial and contrived, no more. The situation has been only legally, not morally, addressed. The crime requital proves no sin-solution.

It is in many other realms that experience indicates the incompleteness of what law and power can achieve inside a would-be just society. That 'would-be' has need of larger, costlier resources for which it must look to some religious ministry of truth and love.

It will look in vain if that religious order is itself the virtual or actual 'disposer' of power or single ground of the power structure. The corruptibility of power is notorious in human history. Its organs develop their vested interests of steady self-perpetuation or of insidious erosions of their due criteria as ever 'on behalf of God'. Any Constantine will likely be self-serving in the more vigorously serving the Church. So tragically proved to be the case when he turned a Christianity into a Christendom. *Allahu akbar* as a power-cry is liable to be an *Islamu akbar* turning a theme of worship into an announcement of aggression across a human frontier.

We have seen how, post-Hijrah, something radical transpired to reshape the original Islam of genuine faith-discipleship into a differently self-minded structure of conflict-told community. How far does the second embarrass the first? Need we ever suspect it does, since the quarrel is just? But can the justice in the quarrel fulfil itself this way?

As some Shi'ah historians have read it, there was a deep presence of this 'embarrassment' around politicised religion. They detect it in the strange hesitancy with which, it would seem, Husain, Muhammad's last surviving grandson, came to the expedition which

---

[18] Lex talionis recurs throughout. See especially pp. 35, 47f. and 67. Cf. also pp. 7, 21, 34, 76, 104f. and 154.

concluded so tragically at Karbala'. It was a diffidence about being thoroughly robust that dismayed his ardent followers, illustrated by his lingerings en route and his oddly unforthright leadership at the climax. Was it that he sensed that the political engagement was on behalf of a sacred cause which might seem to be defiled by the means it used? The cause indeed was just. The Umayyads were promise-breaking usurpers of the holy Caliphate, deriders of the Imamate within it and cursing from their pulpits all the 'partisans of 'Ali'. The long delayed foray into Iraq from distant Mecca/Medina carried all the mystique of those *Haramain* and their Muhammad. Were they rightly to be vindicated in their suffered wrongs by the means in hand of blood and wounds and slaughter?

Whether or not those historians have the theme aright, it suffices that it can be raised. Is there something perhaps inherently 'irreligious' in the passions and the pursuit of power? What, we might retaliate, did Husain in fact achieve, except a legend of martyrdom and the consolations of a liturgy of self-pre-occupying grief? Had he really been the kin of the grandfather at Badr and at Uhud, that resolute subduer of his native city? History anyway, it would seem, produces few power-diffident Husains, unless it be Lears and emperors resigning in final weariness from the illusions of power.

At all events, the religious persuasives of power, the sanction they bring to the currencies of belief, often resolve into dissuasives from authentic faith, if and when they distort the human mind and enslave the human will. Moreover, when faiths seek and employ the sinews of power they contribute significantly to the engendering of schism. Issues of doctrine arising on doctrinal grounds must covet political cover if the one party wields it. Reformed Christianity under threat of 'Catholic' powers required and acquired the sponsoring of 'Protestant' Electors. Elizabeth and her Church of England will need each other because both live with a Philip launching Spanish Armadas against each of them. Religion suffers yet deeper divisiveness because power factors aid and abet it. Only the likes of Islamic Sufism escape this tyranny by a wholly wholesome 'inner *jihad*', or with John Bunyan outlast what power imposes on their suffering soul.

Did it not prove this tragic way in the sequel to Muhammad's death? Whatever theological case the priority alleged of 'Ali, in the context of 'rightly guided Caliphs' and beyond, needed and attained, the impulse was political. The Prophet could have no successor in that office. But this religious status urgently needed immediate succession in the Medinan order of rule. Islam had been made inherently political by that first Hijrah and all subsequent theological thinking, Sufism excepted, remained conditioned by it. The question currently must, therefore, be can it ever be de-politicised or, rather, re-politicised in right and still feasibly religious terms?

These pages reach this question by other routes—via authority, 'manners' with it and the temper of its scholarship. What Islamic factors are there by which an *argumentum* might proceed?[19] For they will need to be Islamic ones, not commendations from aliens to the ethos of Islam. Yet they will call for the whole diapason of theology as Christianity would reach for them, the way that—with gentleness—one faith may focus meaning for another as neither inimical nor domineering.

Through the whole orbit and time-theme of Semitic theological faith runs the divine stake in humankind. It perceives a creation by divine intent and that intent critically vested in a human creaturehood charged with its possession, its fulfilment and its cherishing—all in the sacramental terms explored in Scriptures.[20] In all its contours this plainly constitutes a divine/human enterprise—the divine part that of risk and venture and purposive intent, the human part one of due and grateful and reverent alliance with that intent.

It follows, for all Semitic theisms, that this perception of our human meaning, responding collectively to the divine challenge of Surah 7. 172: 'Am I not your Lord?' with a resounding Yea ...! We so aver,' abides as the true reading of the universe as affording, uniquely, it would seem, this singular planet as our common habitat. This is our Hebraic, Christian, Islamic rebuttal of the atheisms that ignore, dispute, or dismiss its theme, whether out of sheer discourtesy, or lethargy, or intellectual demur. It is not, on our part, any anathema of the 'secular', except only when 'secularity'—a sadly ambiguous term—means just this refusal of a good and pro-human creation. It is deeply on the side of that 'secular' which can only soundly be the taking up of the human

---

[19] In the Latin sense of the word. as a 'proving of a truth or establishing of a case', rather than a quarrel in words.

[20] Where the Qur'an's telling of this *khilafah* is seen in its close identity with Biblical 'dominion', and likewise equipped with the art of praise and tutored by prophet-tuition into the gratitude proper to the skills that manage and exploit it, it tells a common front in the most urgent, moral, ecological—and therefore sacramental—crisis of the global scene here and now.

task of 'being at the world by dint of being in it' in creaturely response to its resources as ready to our hands and responsive to our wits. For the 'secular' this way is the only feasible locating of the 'sacred' and the 'sacramental'.

It follows again that this entire scenario, this divine intent through human means and meaning, is highly critical, a keenly precious enterprise, an 'as in heaven so on earth' regime through mutuality.[21] In both realms it becomes a theme of 'guidance' *(huda)*, given and received. Creaturehood needs—and receives—prophethood: the Creator must become the Script supplier by a 'scripture' enshrining the pattern of His venture, the rubrics of His liturgy, the hymn-sheet of His praise—these being clearly entailed in the intent about a duly divine-human society.[22] Such criteria for it, mediated to human mind by 'revelation' *(wahy)*, bear witness to the human dignity in that they would be pointless to puppets. They are also an index to the nature of God, seeing that the creation alone might be ambiguously read, whereas divine agency, 'sending the human to the human', would be using 'a native language'.[23] We are back with the scenario we have reviewed.

Thus our reading of humanity within creation is seconded by the directing phenomenon of Scriptures, God is the yet more evidently purposive enterpriser in taking this verbal and educative relation to our human imperium and thereby further confirming to us our liable custody of this good earth. Allah as thus verbally 'with us' the more solemnises our dominion.

---

[21] The phrase in the Lord's Prayer (see further pp. 33-35, 65-66) is apt to borrow here—the more so for the Prayer's reference to *peirasmos*, or 'trial, where the human seeks deliverance from the demonic where in *media res* either confronts the other—the world where heavenly business is at earthly stake.

[22] Some in Islam would think 'society' too strong a word, given the sharp emphasis on divine 'otherness', or 'exaltation' above and beyond all human relevance. There were urgent reasons for this in Muhammad's immediate world, with an inveterate idolatry forever 'associating' pseudo-worships with random phenomena which a true theism knew as all assured in Allah alone. The present, scientific cast of mind, with its technologies subduing nature ever more needs the more to learn to consecrate such competence, which means to read it as a trust in which God is intimately involved.

[23] Is not any 'sacred language', ostensibly 'telling' God or 'telling His will', a resort to the 'vernacular'. Whatever is thus verbal (however differently had by *Tanzil* or Incarnation) has God 'in cognisance of man, to bring man into cognisance of God'. Thus it is insisted in the Qur'an that it is 'an Arabic Qur'an'—that, among Arabs, was the requisite of its intelligibility. All that 'a native language' means, connotes and conveys for the human mind and psyche is thus central to all divine 'verbalism', His 'scripturising' policy with words.

But according to the husbandmen parable, it will not suffice. What then? There is a passage in Shakespeare's *Richard II*, in which old John of Gaunt is talking with a bereaved widow about her will for revenge. He refers to the royal murderer in terms which—as we have seen—also describe all of us humans. He tells the woman:

> 'God's is the quarrel, for God's substitute
> His deputy, anointed in his sight,
> Hath caused this death ...'

Her pointed reaction to a counsel of patience is to cry:

'Call it not patience, Gaunt, it is despair.'[24]

Are we not heading for a similar situation in the parable?—messengers killed (see Surah 2. 87), 'God's quarrel', no less, with the vineyard only the logic of His benison in willing it and us, into being at creation. His stake in the orchard means also His stake in the proxy suffering of His messengers. What, then, about the 'quarrel' that is inseparable from the enterprise? How is it further pressed, if 'patience' only implies futility and, therefore, despair?[25]

The instinct in reply of Judaism and Islam—and many forms of Christendom—wedded to their *leges talionis* is to take 'God's quarrel' on themselves. The political regime takes over, its active 'impatience' is its antidote to 'despair'. We have seen how this supervenes in Hebrew Davidism, in Islam's Medinan shape and—for all its measure of secularity—the power-complex of current Zionism creating and holding its Israel by politico-martial prowess in the name of 'covenant under Yahweh'.

The divine human drama thus passes the fertile trust of the vineyard and—thence—the verbal appealing to the vineyard men into

---

[24] William Shakespeare, *Richard II*, Act 1, Scene 2, lines 37-39 and 29. Have not the Semitic theisms been all too ready to take on 'God's quarrel' and make it their own? Then comes the bane of all political religion, so tempted.

[25] It might seem that this 'patience' of the Lord as belonging with the suffering of those He sends, is contradicted by the nemesis on the usurpers with which the Parable ends. Not so, when read in the light of Luke 13. 34. The parable's tactic is to invite the hearers to pronounce their own verdict (Matthew 20. 40-41, with which Mark and Luke are consistent). There *is* a nemesis—witness the Fall of Jerusalem. Divine suffering is not incompatible with divine justice. Moreover, the Lord is still looking for 'a people bringing forth the fruits'.

the ultimate stage, and strategy, of the political regime which was the third temptation of Jesus and Messiahship. It has long been widely assumed to be legitimate and sufficient. We have noted (footnote 25) how, indeed, in parable, a divine nemesis overtakes the guilty. In that context there may be place for some human regime as executant.

We do not well, however, to think that politics with arms can duly take over 'God's quarrel'. The vineyard parable has always to be read along with Jesus' lament over Jerusalem with which it is intimately connected.

> 'O Jerusalem that kills the Prophets, how often would I have gathered thy children under my wings, but you would not.' (Luke 13. 34)

What Abraham Heschel earlier called 'divine pathos' abides, if sometimes through always beyond, the political aegis with its always blundering, always ambiguous relation to justice and to 'the peace of God'. It is clear that such divine solicitude for our human vocation in the earth transcends the feasibility of what may be achieved by the sundry *Dars*, *Hizbs*, or Zions, of political governance and the power order.

It is not that these have no place in the structure of society: it is that the divine purpose with us has willed to be uncompulsive, non-coercive, inherently compassionate on God's part, genuinely responsible on ours. By this necessity in the very nature of God, ours can only be a consenting will, an *islam* we freely yield. How, else, would there have been a defining creation in our trust? How else an educative scripturising of our minds? How else the ever non-combative docility of the messengers who brought the texts for our reading wills? Is not the very naming of Islam, as this *islam*, witness—not to a divine compulsiveness—but to human willingness. It follows that the political/martial order in His Name can never be more than regulatory, contributory and partial, leaving the ultimate task undone. What must be understood from the parable as the divine quest, even yearning, will never be satisfied that way. 'Religion with Allah', as the Qur'an's wording has it (Surah 3. 19) is answering divine expectation, 'as in heaven so on earth'. That divine intent can only be in equivocal case if in jeopardy to the realm of the political—not the old jeopardy from unheeding hearers but from the entanglements of the recruited politics and power. Faith-hegemony, religio-political regime, will be inadequate measure of any divine strategy with the venture of humanity. This is so on two counts. Governance is necessary yet governance is faulted inside its very necessity. A strategy from God holding it requisite must find it wanting.

The requisite aspect derives from how religious faith will always bear liability for rule and order, law and ethics by a responsibility of conscience for a state's guidance and motivation (where Scriptures come again into the equation) rather than an exclusive hegemony it directly wields.[26] Faith, this way, will be more genuinely religious than in the direct assertion of power. Prior to the Prophet of Islam the great prophets of the Biblical tradition always bravely addressed the corridors of power. They never walked within them or were seated on their thrones. Only in not being courtiers were they truly critics and guides.

As argued elsewhere Islam in post-Hijrah terms, took the reins of power, while in pre-Hijrah terms existing only as 'divine word'. That decision remains embedded in their conviction as being the rightly religious form shaping the creation's mandate to humankind—unless it now think back to its first Meccan form as *balagh* alone. This is a crucial issue for Islam's present hijrah into a non-Islamic diaspora in the world, where it can only peaceably exist and participate in Meccan terms of witnessing presence—happily without the Meccan style persecution then.[27]

It is this conscience-told role of religious faith which must operate against the pretentious Islam of the political monopoly tradition. The choice is deeply at issue in the present world-scene, with minority elements present across all establishments and even uniform states having obligations internationally.[28] A genuine co-existence of faiths has become mandatory for any faith at all.

---

[26] Such conscience may perhaps be informed and practised in that temper of 'love at risk with its intent' which is the crucial theme of Christ's Passion as it is—as here argued—of the creation itself as God's 'intent' with humankind. Such 'pity', in any Blakean sense, will then draw the powers that be away from tyranny, greed, callousness and hate, towards gentleness and peace. See here below.

[27] Plainly there was no tolerance for Islam in that Meccan cradle of its origin. In Islam's western 'diaspora' there is every occasion for Muslims to participate with and out of their concepts, insofar as such liberty is not jeopardised by those Muslims who see their only jihadist role as subversive of the liberty they find and then use destructively.

[28] On any equal principle of mutual rights. Co-existence, if anywhere, demands to obtain everywhere and be honoured across all frontiers.

The Order of the Wounded Hands

If, then, on both grounds (a) of partiality and (b) of dire entanglement, any alleged divine strategy the coercive way faces a frustration comparable to that which confronted words alone, what then for the divine purpose? Has politicised religion anywhere effectively succeeded? There is no re-assuring answer. Constantine distorted Christianity in the counter-emergence of Christendom. In the sundry shapes of that Christendom, empire-aegis, state-aegis, papal sovereignty, violated the open Gospel in the frustrating possessive of power sponsorship and inter-warring reliance upon rulers. All too often competing doctrines acquired political nexus which in turn exacerbated the schisms that ensued, just as these again entrenched the enmity. Muslims have had cause to ask themselves whether the perfect Islamic society ever existed or disputed when and where it might be identified. Maybe the state of *jahiliyyah* goes on? Has not the invasive, violent form of an actual Zionism darkly denied, or direly postponed, its founding ideals? Faiths cannot sanely or safely consort with 'might and power', not if they stay faithful and, so doing, prove worthy monitors in conscience.

In view of this, the ambivalence of power, its place and non-place in the 'policy' of God, what might ever follow? What further dimension might emerge? A sequence of failure or dubious efficacy has been made evident in rehearsal of the sequence and its logics—creation, creaturely mandate, human trust, revelatory guidance, scriptural maps, and these all passing into regimes of i.e. Judaic Davidism, a Constantinian Christendom, east and west, Holy Roman Empires, *Dar al-Islam*, the political custody of divine design. And these again, unsatisfactory with humankind and unsatisfying with God still holding to that first high intent. 'Are these what should come: or do we look for other?' The question goes to the heart of any 'theodicy', any vindication of God, of a God who will not fail when such 'not-failing' is the only, the whole, meaning of omnipotence.

IV

The diapason in the course of thought seems to be led to the, highest note of all. We seem to be nearing this way where we already were concerning 'the wounded hands', namely that of the vulnerability of God. Any who shrink from it will have awhile to bear with it. Can there be a sense in which all we have surveyed adds up to a divine experience and task of compassion? Certainly across the human scene there are multiplied situations where the only personal reaction to wrong and grief is to 'bear' it (not merely 'with it' but through it) and only so 'bear it away,' absorb in it in the act of forgiveness. These are the Gethsemanes of the world. Must it not be that they only have their origin and ground as the emulation of what obtains in the very competence of God—a competence moved into play by the very waylayings of the human project we have surveyed? John's Letter knows that 'We love because He first loved us.' Initiatives are God's to take, emulations ours. We are not arguing here from man to God, only from God to man. But by that very priority, response on God's part to being realistically vulnerable will mean becoming redemptive. Christian faith alone is the distinctive custodian of this, a suffering theology.

It has, however, a living ancestry in the Hebrew theme, expounded earlier in Chapter 4, of divine pathos.[29] We find it first in the disclosure for the first time to Moses, of the divine 'Name', Yahweh, in the pledge concerning the Hebrew people: 'I have seen their affliction: I know their sorrows, I am come down to deliver.' (Exodus 3. 7-8) The conviction is deepened in Isaiah affirming of this patron sovereignty: 'You made Me your burden-bearer,' the One to 'carry your sins'. (43. 24) If the analogy is in the 'carrying' out of Exodus, it extends to the forbearance of Yahweh through the entire history of the Hebrew people. In undertaking them schematically, Yahweh 'suffered' them essentially.

Any such theology is a far cry from the mind and mood of Islam. It has no place in the diapason of its Qur'an in any form as clear as the Biblical tradition. But could it be what has always been implicit, though never articulate thus far, in those defining Names of Allah: *Al-Rahman al-Rahim* earlier noted (p. 46)? Can these obtain in the human world and not be so?

Divine 'fellow-feeling' this way may have owed its intensity to the distinctive Hebraic concept of 'chosen peoplehood'. 'People-awareness' this way was its matrix—one which the Qur'an disavowed in ethnic terms. But, given the doctrine of creation, the lesson is totally

---

[29] See Rabbi Abraham J Heschel, *The Prophets*, New York, 1962, and, with Bibliography and citation, my *Troubled by Truth*, Edinburgh, 1992, pp. 108-126.

transferable. Each and all have their native bond with the entire creation. There is no 'privatising' ethnicity. Earth-wise Allah has only 'chosen peoples'. The English Rudyard Kipling, enthusing over Sussex, made universal connection when he wrote:

> 'God gave all men all earth to love but since man's heart is small,
> Ordained for each one spot should prove, beloved over all:
> That, as He watched creation's birth
> So we in God-like mood
> Might for our love create our earth, And see that it is good.'[30]

If it needed the ethnic prerogative to generate that sentiment of 'giftedness' by earth, then all nations were blessed in the precedence. For all may share in its benediction if the heart in them is open. A 'divine pathos' embraces all, seeing that the problematics we have traced of all other strategies obtain across all histories.

It was 'God in Christ' and the Christian New Testament that universalised this comprehension of divine grace in a universal reach, so obviating an exclusively ethnic category for its incidence. On its own law-revelatory ground, Islam also de-ethnicised the heritage of creation for inclusive creaturehood. That case has been clear throughout. There is no racial bias in the proclamation of Surah 2. 30 about the bestowal of *khilafah*. There is a universal audience of all generations of every tribe and people answering the 'Am I not your Lord' of Surah 7. 172 with their single, choric Yea! The sharply Arabic nature of the Qur'an is told as being 'a mercy to the worlds'. 'The best of peoples' are to be the most exemplary of law-abiders, such doubtless as Israeli peoplehood always meant to be.

This Christian, universal and inclusive range given to the first perception of 'divine pathos' in the Tanakh clearly in place, it is clear how it utterly fits *both* the human dignity and the divine 'burden' therewith. It altogether suits the dignity. For what could more befit the status of audiences with envoys than a forbearance that reaches into love? It minds the divine commitment in creation in entire

---

[30] Rudyard Kipling, *Definitive Edition of His Verse*, London, 1943, 'Sussex', pp.215-16.

engagement with its tragic narrative. It signifies that the Lord's capacities are, unfailing vis-à-vis their situation.[31]

But is the concept of a 'suffering sovereignty' really admissible to the theologian, or only distantly conceded to the sentimentalist? Judaism allows it only in covenantal limits. Even the Sabbath, as a kindliness from God, belongs only of right to its proper heirs, though arising—as it did—from the 'labour' of creation which had to do with us all.

It is, however, from Islam that the most insistent resistance comes to this whole 'possibility' concerning God. Crying: *Allahu akbar* negates it roundly. 'Exalted be he above all that that ye associate!' and this kind of 'association' with weakness and a suffering compassion most of all.[32] Where it is seen, in Christian terms, to mean 'Incarnation of the Word', and 'the Passion of the Cross' as ever divinely accomplished, the anathema upon it becomes adamant altogether. No loyalty to Allah can discount, degrade, disown Him so.

The diapason has its highest notes to might, power, rule, majesty and reign. These can go no higher than themselves. *Kabbirhu takbiran*, 'Make God greatly great', has the verb intensifying only its own meaning. That meaning governs its explicit range beyond which no mind should venture.[33] 'Let God be—and be the God He is!' To impute the inconceivable is blasphemous.

But if this Muslim insistence is saying: 'Think God only by His own measure' what if 'His own measure' is otherwise? Is not: 'Let God be God' an open-ended cry? What the Qur'an three times called 'the truth of His measure' *(haqqa qadrihi)* has to stand, if we are not to be found forbidding to God what these might need to be—need to be as realistic about ourselves and as adequate concerning His nexus with ourselves. 'Where most excluded' must prove to be 'where most engaged'. Need Islam, by its own proper lights, be so adamant about its vetoes on the founding themes of Christian faith?

---

[31] The thought of divine 'capacity' as, in context, a sounder term than 'omnipotence' is developed in my *God's Wrong is Most of All*, Brighton, 2006—a study of divine 'passion' in 'the Passion of Christ', as response to human guilt and sin.

[32] As the Qur'an has it about 'right esteem of Allah', verdicts as to God will always hinge on the criteria we bring. See the parallel and crucial question around 'being King', the exchange between Pilate and Jesus in John 18. 33f.

[33] The verb in Arabic supplying the kindred noun, for intensity (Surah 47. 111): 'Magnify Him a magnifying', 'Make Him greatly great'. The K B R root is frequent—*Allahu akbar* most of all. The 'greatness of Allah' requires to be steadily asserted.

Consider the meaning of the 'Incarnation of the Word'. Consider it beyond the complexities that have dogged it from the undiscerned term 'begotten',[34] and from the subtle metaphor of 'Sonship to the Father', or those very terms when falsely read as if they meant paternity. Need the import of 'the Word made flesh' be judged so far from the divine initiative perceived for humans in the Qur'an? If, with the Qur'an, we are praying 'Let me never be confounded,' then surely things eternal must engage with times and places temporal. Some status as 'envoy' is indispensable.

There is thus the common theme of 'sending', whether of 'a Son learning by things he suffered', or an 'apostle' who bears a verbal 'book in being'. There is, to be sure, great difference between 'the Word' and 'these words', but what is common is 'communication'. By light of neither faith does God stay 'un-uttered' in the human realm.

Moreover, 'envoy-personality' is engaged. While Muhammad has a strictly verbal role with a *Tanzil* of language, where the 'Book' results on earth from a 'preserved tablet in heaven', his persona is deeply implicated both within and beyond the Qur'an. *Tanzil* itself associates with his reactions, his controversies, his anxieties, his status over all, so that what the Qur'an tells through the incidence in him of *wahy* is not 'text' alone but 'text *in situ*', and—to a degree—text in *Sirah*, in biography.[35] Hence in the *Sirah*, the *asbab al-nuzul*, or 'occasions of revelation', with concrete situations the environs of what we read. There is a sense in which the Qur'an itself is an event, in being thus 'eventful' and the eventful is the 'personal'.

---

[34] Both in New Testament genealogies and in archaic usage, the word can suggest paternity merely, but in technical credal places and in Johannine language the contrast in 'not made' gives 'begotten' a quite other sense. It sets 'the Word made flesh' as not in the natural sequence of 'birth in the physical order ('of blood, of the will of the human') but via a divine initiative. To be sure, this initiative belongs with 'the Fatherhood of God' (hence the Sonship term) but not in any paternity/maternity sequence but in divine intent. 'Not made' of human origins but occurring in the intention of God so that, by birth and life and mortal history, we might have 'the knowing and the loving of God'. A near analogy to 'begotten' in this credal sense would be how authorship 'generates' a text, a dramatist a drama, a musician music—all as 'the self-expression of a self from a self' in the two inhering dimensions of impulse and result.

[35] It is very clear how, throughout the Qur'an, there is this inter-fusion of 'who' and 'how'—of meaning and situation, of Muhammad in word and Muhammad in experience. The point is explored more fully in my *Muhammad in the Qur'an*, London, 2001. It is one of the pressing needs in Muslim *Tafsir* now that the active 'participation' of the Prophet (never 'authorship' but certainly engagement in) should be brought into better focus. For doing so bears heavily on the present need for study about 'finality' from 'as then ...' well 'how now ...?'

On its own showing and by long, reverent tradition, the personal Muhammad is seen to be the inclusive exemplar of what being Muslim means in character and conduct, the referent for how the Qur'an would have us humans be. This is both far, and not so far, from what Christians understand by 'the Word incarnate'.[36] Why Muslims insist to find it 'very far' is less for reasons of divine strategy with humankind than for reasons theological concerning Allah Himself as necessarily immune from human 'hurt'. Yet the different case is exactly the one we are pursuing. If the issue has to be taken into the being of God, that is precisely where Christian faith is ready to locate it. 'He does what He does that He may be who He is' has long been the Christian theme. There we must leave the actuality—and the impossibility alike—of the faith as to 'God in Christ'. It is our measures of the capacity of God that must resolve the issue, not the complexities credal or the dismissives Muslim about 'adoption', duality, idolatry and the rest.[37] Nor must the theme of the 'Word made flesh' be overtaken by disparate perceptions of 'virgin birth' in the two Scriptures.[38] There have been Muslim writers of late ready to concede to Christians what the Johannine Prologue enshrines for them in faith. It is the Passion of Jesus as ever belonging somehow with the being of God that remains the altogether inadmissible, utterly inconceivable, conviction. Will it be for ever pointless to dispute that anathema, a fond and foolish mystery to think ever of sustaining with sanity or commending to Islam?

What persuasion might any such commending to Muslims of the Christian perception of the human tragedy think to offer? Maybe one recourse might be to invoke the single human experience of being 'present here in the body', in this strange, physical, ever mortally tentative tenancy of fleeting time and frail place—as implicitly appealing for a sharing of compassion and kindred sympathy. We might recall for Muslim hearing William Blake's lines:

---

[36] As in previous note, seeing that Christian meanings are so far united with the persona of Jesus in a history.

[37] Since 'adoptionism' was a Christian misreading around the baptism of Jesus, Islam might be forgiven, as well as commended, for disavowing it, in mistaking that it was something the faith never meant. 'Far be it from the Eternal to take to Himself a Son' was at once a right and a superfluous reproach. Incarnation meant (note 34) what belonged entirely from God and not, post-natally, from human source.

[38] For the Qur'an (Surahs 3 and 19) it is a 'sign' of Jesus' rank and 'significance' as 'among God's messengers' with this unique accreditation. For the Gospel it tells the divine intent to dwell among us in our own text of mortal life.

> 'To mercy, pity, peace and love
> All pray in their distress.
> For mercy has a human heart.
> Pity a human face
> And mercy, pity, peace and love
> Is man, his (God's) child and care.'[39]

So much, it must be argued, belongs inside the *khilafah* that makes all human existence mutually accountable both to God and neighbour. No such accountability can, ignore the tragic in its range.

Blake could call those famous four 'virtues of delight', writing, as he was, a plea that 'all must love the human form,' as where 'God is dwelling too'.

Shakespeare's King Lear had taken note of those 'virtues' of Blake when he cried in grimly different context:

> 'All you unpublished virtues of the earth,
> Spring with my tears.'[40]

How far Islam could allow these 'human virtues' to belong inside the divine compassion announced so firmly in the *Bismillah* of *Al-Rahman al-Rahim* is for Muslims to clarify.[41]

It would seem, however, that the instinct of the Muslim mind would always be to disclaim any such 'humanising of Allah' as somehow involving power in frailty and sovereignty in intimacy. Or perhaps, with rejectionists of these dimensions in God like Nietzsche and D H Lawrence, the traditional Muslim shrinks from such register of human pathos and any responsive divine relation akin to 'like as a father pities his children even so ...'

Yet maybe not so. Warrant has been found within Islam for such a conclusion by a reading of Surah 36. 30:

---

[39] A familiar hymn (no. 506 in the English Hymnal 1906). William Blake (1757-1827) used capital letters for each of these four. His argument from these so deeply in human discourse thus deeply within the cognisance of God—subjectively His, because objectively ours within Him. These 'realities' have their ground and origin in evidently having their direction our human way.

[40] William Shakespeare, *King Lear*, Act 4, Scene 4, lines 16-17. Does 'unpublished' imply that they have their impulse in the private heart, aware of being in steady need of them, rather than in trumpeted publicity.

[41] That there is a deliberate progression in the *R H M* root derivatives from 'mercy' as essentially belonging, and 'mercy' as effectively practised, in the divine will. Cf. pp. 46, 97.

'The pity of it in respect of My servants! Never does a messenger come but derision is what they have for him. Have they not realised how many generations before them We have destroyed and these have never come back?'[42]

'Woe be to My servants' is—almost on all sides—the preferred translation. But 'servants' is describing earthlings such as all of us. At and after 'the Day of judgement' they are filled with regret (cf. Surahs 19. 39 and 69. 50). If, thus, there must be the desperate pathos of missed opportunity in the presence of the message, must there not be, antecedently, the same—or deeper—pathos in the *kufr* (69. 50) that was heedless? Does all that is tragic in eschatology (as condemnatory) not argue a condition of heart no less seriously tragic in its mortal incidence? The element of deep 'pity' is there, whether in the bitterness of irreversible 'regret' and 'self-reproach', or as the fact of the once living situation. Can Allah 'necessitate' damnation out of His law and will, and not 'minister' pity in the priority of life in time? Can the one 'necessity' of remorse obtain humanly and be required divinely (as proper to the heedless) and not argue the prior 'necessity' of pity not only for 'the human form divine', but for the 'human form in the wrong'?

The Qur'an would seem to argue that there was sufficient pity in the present giving of the Book and all its 'ministries' as guide, reminder, friend and mentor. But if—as is evident in its rejection—the Book, in those terms, has failed in its intent (a failure told in its being scorned by the heedless) might the will behind the Book not have other resources to expend? Pity in all human realms must needs be versatile and resilient. Is not eschatology all the time making the case for grace even if grace only tells a worthier failure?

In any event, Surah 36. 30 can have the positive reading: 'O the pity of it about My servants', as a cry of divine compassion. It

---

[42] The usual exegesis is certainly for the 'Woe be to ...' reading and seems warranted by the other two usages. For the 'Pity for My servants ...', see Muhammad al-Nuwaihi, *In Quest of an Islamic Humanism: Arabic and Islamic Studies*, ed. A H Green, Cairo, 1984, pp.181-195, esp.191-92: 'The Qur'an is nothing if it is not a suffering identity with creation and humanity. Hence its passion, its chagrin and sorrow for the disobedience and sins of man'. Al-Nuwaihi is arguing from the same context of human heedlessness of 'messengers' as the 'Woe be ...' reading. But what they take to be anger and resentment, he finds to be grief and pain. Any 'regret' dimension is God's rather than—post mortem—men's. Doubtless disputers with him will say: 'This is Islamic humanism, not Islamic theology', which only leaves us with the question: 'Which is Islam?'

must have, if we are to let the whole issue move out of exegesis only and into 'the right esteeming of Allah' for which, as we have seen, the Qur'an pleads. The measure of the human has to be the measure of the divine, both in what the human does against the divine and what it may be held as doing in emulation. The former we have argued just now, the latter takes us to the New Testament dictum: 'We love because He first loved us.' The evident, irrefutable, human capacity for compassion, as derived from God's, is the only sane logic. 'The creature', as Robert Browning knew, 'does not outdo the Creator.' The 'original' had always been with God and only so the argument about 'pity' in either direction, Allah's for us and ours for each other. If the mind of Islam wants to see this mutual pitying told in law and *Dar* and text, so that inter-human debts are paid in these, we are all left with the question—What beyond these when these stay incomplete as answers to our state, our plight and our alliance with the wrong, the *kufr*, they must still engage?

If, with such enquiring theology, we move firmly into history where—we have to ask—might the God be seen to act who will fulfil towards us what our situation cries for? The place, as Christian faith identifies and tells it, is 'God in Christ' reconciling the world through 'the Incarnation and the Passion of Jesus as the Christ'. Eastern Christianity, in a Johannine reading, tends to find this 'salvation' in receiving the divine Christ of Incarnation into emulation in the soul so to restore the divine image by His indwelling grace. Western Christian tradition has set that same meaning, via Pauline/Petrine tuition, in our acceptance into the forgiveness at the Cross of Christ, so that the Passion is the working in us of a 'death to sin and a walk in newness of life', thanks to a liberation into 'pardon and peace'.[43]

Either way, that Christ, alike in sermon, life and Cross, abolished the *lex talionis* with its perennial 'getting our own back' via the entail of wrong and wrongs by which the long human story has been benighted and its sorrows and guilts renewed. Such forbearance, as the Cross of Jesus showed, is tragically costly. But that costliness is the price inherent in what the love that suffers bears—and only so—'bears away'. For the enmity that retaliates has been absorbed into love where it stays, stops and ends. 'Neither is there salvation in any other ...'[44] That

---

[43] Of the theme of 'resurrection' in 'Easter Eucharist' pp. 133-136 below.
[44] The familiar words in Acts 4.12—Peter's famous sermon (according to Luke) is not exclusive.

'our peace' is upon him, through him, because of him, thanks to him, is the utmost meaning—within us his discipled lovers—of the 'man of sorrows' in whom we read the image and the likeness of God.

We are here on Christian ground but only for the sake of its commendation. It has to be loved and told only in its own idiom, running counter as it does to notions of power, status, superiority and coercion.[45] It asks only to be understood. Yet it has properly an imperative will to be present, to be heard, to be heeded and available. For such is its distinctiveness that were it allowed—as Abraham Lincoln might have said—'to perish from the earth' or ever consent to be silent or silenced, a dangerous pride, a dark cynicism and, with them, a desperate forfeiture of meaning could engulf us all.[46] Truly, the diapason 'closes full in man' and what, in its range, is most included in the music of one faith proves unreachable in another's. If 'closing full in man' is right about the 'diapason', must it be that our theologies respond to our understanding of ourselves?

v

But why should it matter in these careful theological terms in the hope that perhaps Muslims may take due note of what a Christian theism holds? We can live and let live—or we could, did not that caveat of Abraham Lincoln about some thing 'not perishing from the earth' not urgently obtain in this context of something about God no less precious than what he saw in Gettysburg. Theological perspectives are no less vital than moral ones. For here they coincide.

Yet what, the realists will ask, about the whole business of power and law and order in the world, which we left behind just now in being so theological about mercy, pity, truth and love as 'human

---

The audience is wholly Jewish and has the Judaic anticipation of 'Messiah' as the conclusive answer from God to where in need we humans are. Peter avers that this singular hope has been caused to happen in Jesus crucified and had interpretation, from within, in the words: 'Father, forgive ...' If we hear that—about our own sinfulness—we 'learn how and where we too are forgiven.'

[45] Hence—as here throughout—an 'Ordination only of the wounded hands'.

[46] 'Dangerous pride' seeing that, without pity, ruthlessness takes over. Cynicism and despair follow if, as Pushkin saw in *Eugene Onegin*, to the pitiless 'all others are but zeros and we ourselves the chosen few.' The many millions of two-legged creatures are only tools for us.' (Chap. 2, Stanza xiv)

virtues of delight' and God's meanings also.[47] It is obvious enough that these can and should obtain in the personal realm where they are duly feasible, making us all—so willing—duly non-retaliatory 'redeemers' in our immediate society. Can this be also so in governments and the powers that be? No—in terms of their necessary exercise of rule and directive and control and so of force. Yes—in that these can and should learn to be non-vindictive, mercy-conscious, in their exercise. There can be a calculated distinction between necessary law and order and what would be punitive in malice or brutal in will.

This will be more due and right in those other extra-political realms of power that belong in culture, custom and all that makes for harshness, on the part of majorities towards-minorities in many areas of their tensions.

Aspects that are harshly retaliatory, as in the *Dhimmi* system, have often entered into areas of life, so that 'otherness' has excited estrangement and estrangement a one-way vindictiveness. The 'secular' factor has been one salutary curb on inter-religious asperities, but faiths need a tuition of themselves by all feasible norms of their own against their innate liability to hostile or bigoted attitudes of mind.

Thus we need to see that the power realm, whether of politics or of society, needs a non-retaliatory ethos no less than the personal, if ever authentic justice is to be done or honest law have writ and right. Indeed, the two will merge into one, inasmuch as powers are exercised in all human offices and a private style hatred or vindictiveness attach to public or social policy when applied in human hands. Much of the incidence of Dhimmitude turned on the local officials who had its imposition in their private sphere. Thus the sins of office align with the sins of concepts. Both do well to learn and allow the practice of those 'four human virtues', and to let their sanction in the very character of God inform their incidence in the realms of earthly power. There is no political realism in ousting them from its sphere or its tasks, unless politics is to be a law unto itself or enthrones *lex talionis* as 'right in its own eyes'. The danger, too, is that culture empowers a dominant faith in sharply qualifying an actual tolerance of others by exercising

---

[47] It may seem odd to invoke here William Blake's 'four virtues of delight' as clue to at least a potential meaning of *Al-Rahman al-Rahim*. For Blake was no friend of 'clerics' or mullahs and their religions. Yet his instinct that these 'virtues' could not be ours, unless God was 'dwelling there also', could be seen as in line with an Islam holding that Allah's is the primacy and priority in all things, *Al-Awwal wa-l-Akhir*, 'the First and the Last'.

a privileged status in vital areas of education, social ideology and also in identity *per se*.

The other side of this equation is the right of minorities, whether in Israel or under Islam, to the human freedoms that admit the four virtues. Then there is hope of creative 'minoritism' with a resilience to undertake its unprivileged or under-privileged condition with courage and zest.[48] Only so can it escape the cult of inhibiting 'martyrdom' and survival by gallantry. Thus faith 'not perishing from the earth' redeems the world by its fidelity. It redeems itself by being undaunted by its own sufferings. 'The whole diapason closing in man' has no room for *lex talionis*.

There is a strange angle on this truth in Palestine/Israel. It lies in the steady de-Arabicisation, the insistent re-Judaisation of Jerusalem as 'the inalienable capital of the Jewish people'. This process has been proceeding apace since the widening in 1967 of its territorial extent, and by the expulsion of Arab residents.

This is, however, accompanied by the strangest irony, namely that the continuing tenure of Islam in Jerusalem—one, short of some madness in chaos, also irreducible—is essentially and only 'religious'. It is those two inalienable shrines anchored on Temple Mount. The circumstances under which they stayed intact in 1967 are a remarkable story.[49] In terms of Islamic ideology, it is a most incongruous and

---

[48] For all the long Christendom tradition in the West, minority status has been the steady experience of Christians elsewhere. In taxing ways the distinction drawn here between political duress and cultural disadvantage was quite overridden. The two became one under the Islamic *dhimmi* system. Where there is, in fact or theory, an 'equal citizenship', deep disparities persist. Minority elements incur suspicion: majorities cherish superiorities. Heavy economic consequences follow of loss and gain, whence social ones of avoidance and reproach. An ambivalence bedevils the notion and practice of human rights. Memories are long and maybe rancorous. Muslims in minority status, whether in India, the West or elsewhere, learn a new dimension of themselves that re-locates them—persecution apart—in their original Mecca, which ought to be no uncongenial thing, i.e. that of finding themselves 'just a religion'. Since, for Christians, the entire New Testament was brought to pass in that condition as 'de-privileged' it need be no hard task to live with that Scripture's norm and quality. For both parties, the task—surely—is to ensure the fact of their presence 'in the earth' by the worth of its continuity.

[49] When, in June 1967, the Israeli forces overran the (then) Jordanian eastern sector of Jerusalem and the Mughrabi warren of streets, fronting on the Western Wall of the Temple Area, there were religious pressures on them to seize also the sacred area. These were resisted by the military command—to their great credit. Israel has had to be satisfied with the great national plaza erected where those streets used to be, a sort of shrine of nationhood. But, for many, the yearning for the Mount abides. While it remains Islamic, there will always be a Muslim presence to compromise and disavow Jewish monopoly of the city.

uncongenial presence by dint of its setting inside Israeli state-power. Islam abides in Jerusalem only in the religious terms of hallowed shrines of memory and faith. Does the situation resemble how Muhammad was allowed to revisit Mecca by permission of its pagan lords as one who did—and did not—belong there? Then, however, he was on the verge of a total recovery of Mecca—a prospect Israel is determined to deny Islam today in the asserted unilateralism of their Jerusalem.

Christianity also has its mother city—its first, not its third, holiest defining symbol in like case. Christian tourism, however inattentive to the local tragedy it will often be, does something to offset the de-Christianisation of the city. To tourism on sundry counts, Israel is hospitable enough. There are deep differences between the two other faiths and Israel's treating with them. For the Islamic mind the irony of Temple Mount, its Dome and memories, is deep and dark. It makes also strange comment on the theme of this chapter of 'where most excluded most engaged'. Where Islam will not rule, it will still venerate, tell its story where regime eludes it.

Surmount the ancient walls—that hill of Zion, that Haram al-Sharif, overlook Gethsemane. Replace the walls—they once housed at their northern end, lately extended by the Romans, the judgement hall of Pilate. These and their imprint on the city are no less an inalienable Jerusalem.[50]

---

[50] Islam's first *Qiblah* and Muhammad's 'Night Journey' to Jerusalem and much else ensure an abiding Islamic sharing of the city as *Al-Quds*. John's graphic narrative (18. 28-40) of the drama of Jesus before Pilate—with the garden and the Passion hard by—mean an indelibly Christian Jerusalem.

Chapter 6
WHERE MOST DISCOUNTED MOST INVOLVED: THE SECULAR AGNOSTIC

I

That the psalmist's joyful cry of fulfilled access to 'the sanctuary of God', which has been our introit here into study of Christian Ordination, could serve for a notorious satire on Christian belief is a ready measure of cynical contemporary banishment of the will and art of Christian worship.

James Joyce's *Ulysses*, 'a most goddamn wonderful book' as Ernest Hemingway found it, opens thus:

> 'Stately, plump Buck Mulligan came from the stairhead, bearing a bowl of lather on which a mirror and a razor lay crossed. A yellow dressing-gown, ungirdled, was sustained gently behind him by the mid-morning air. He held the bowl aloft and intoned: *Introibo ad altare Dei*.'[1]

Peering down the dark winding stairs above which he stood, he called: 'Come up you fearful Jesuit.'

The symbolism of some 'high altar' and a flowing vestment at the elevation of the Host is evident enough of a bitterness in repudiation. In Joyce it stemmed from a savage apprenticeship with 'altar-faith' and education, and he was furnished with voracious reading in religious lore that gave his paganism a subtle edge. His parody of the sanctuary was both wry and cruel, the product of hated nurture in his native Ireland. The opening page continues with sly allusions to 'the genuine Christine, body and soul,' and Mulligan with a 'jowl like a prelate' in the Middle Ages. More recent disownings of the Christian

---
[1] *Ulysses* was first published in Paris in 1922. The passage here is p. 9 of the Penguin Modern Classics ed., London, 1969.

The Order of the Wounded Hands

tradition are less likely to have the sort of aftermath of origins Joyce possessed only to abandon. There have since been longer years of unfamiliarity so that rejection is of an already receding thing. But the nonchalance is similar:

> 'Blind faith. Safe in the arms of kingdom come. Lulls all pain. Wake this time next year.'[2]

Joyce is very free with his urge to blasphemy and tells a readiness that has intensified since his day. But does he not resemble the engineer who is hoist with his own petard? For he needs what he decries in order to decry it. Like enmity, it cannot be, without the reality to which it stands related.[3]

Blasphemy is like a parody which needs an original to give it point at all. We cannot take the force of Joyce's use of Ulysses to model the sordid stream of Bloom's consciousness through a single day in Dublin without reference to what Tennyson could do with the same classic story.[4] The negatives, in photography, belong only with the positives just as the ridiculous is the foil of the sublime. Obviously Joyce needed the Latin Mass to have his blasphemy. It was the necessary target for an Irishman of his time and mood. Only what is 'consecrate' admits of denigration. A liturgical 'use' is apt for popular abuse. The wit of the parodist and the thrust of blasphemy still leave, as an open question, the warrant of the 'holy' they interrogate but do not cancel. Theology will not be gainsaid by atheism: it will be the more explored.

It must be significant that, so often as here with James Joyce, the very incidence of scepticism and irony comes from a religious source. It is because of Beethoven's *Missa Solemnis* that Theodor Adorno finds himself asking: 'What and how may one sing of the absolute without

---

[2] *Ibid.*, p. 82.

[3] Witness the old adage about 'Hoist with his own petard', viz. a device charged with gunpowder fixed to a gate or barrier it was meant to blow up but might well, however, explode against the user thus caught in his own blast. The usage goes back to Shakespeare in *Hamlet*.

[4] In one of the finest of his poems, 'Ulysses', *Poetical Works*, London, 1994 ed., pp. 147-148, where the aged, not 'idle king' resigns his sceptre to Telemachus and resolves to defy old age and lead his followers.' 'Tis not too late to seek a newer world ... Death closes all but something 'ere the end ...' 'Though much is taken much abides', and thus 'That which we are we are. One equal temper of heroic hearts ... strong in will. To strive, to seek, to find and not to yield.' What tawdriness—in contrast—lives in Joyce's miscellaneous voyages and voyeurisms of soul!

deceit?'[5] The music is supremely 'religious' in its theme and only so kindles the misgivings it arouses. Could Matthew Arnold in 'Dover Beach', a threnody on loss of faith, have brooded on

> 'The sea of faith ... retreating ...
> ... down the vast edges drear
> And naked shingles of the world.'

had there not been a wistfulness within to cry:

> 'Ah, love, let us be true
> To one another! for the world which seems
> To lie before us like a land of dreams,
> So various, so beautiful, so new
> Hath really neither joy, nor love, nor light,
> Nor certitude ...'[6]

His verdicts of negation have not completely silenced the positives on which their logic turns. We note that subtle 'really', that querulous 'seems', and how 'love' is both tenderly invoked and bitterly denied. The mood that kindled the poetry has not clinched the case for his lament. To take for metaphor a 'sea' that only 'ebbs' is to be victim to analogy. Doubt always needs to suspect how partial dubiety may become. There must always be 'the grand perhaps' to curb 'the everlasting No!'[7]

---

[5] Theodor Adorno, *Essays on Music*, p. 575, cited by Edward W Said, *On Late Style*, London, 2006, p. 91.
[6] Matthew Arnold, *Poetical Works*, London, 1903, pp. 226-7. Arnold was returning to England from honeymoon in Europe. Did he sense some answer to his near despair when, later, in 'The Scholar Gypsy', he wrote: 'we ...
Vague half-believers of our casual creeds,
Who never deeply felt, nor clearly will'd ... '
Before this strange disease of modern life
With its sick hurry, its palsied hearts, was rife ...'
in contrast with the moral earnestness of 'The Scholar'?, pp. 278 and 279. (Some versions read 'heads o'ertaxed' for 'sick hurry'.)
[7] In Carlyle's celebrated words, setting 'No!' against 'Yes!'

II

Such thoughts, however, can only be a prelude to the intellectual liabilities of any contemporary 'theologians', understanding the term in its fullest sense as 'lovers' of God, alike in mind and heart. For mental purposes, belief and unbelief, faith and unfaith, will always be inter-associates. Neither can retreat into insulation from the other. Thus the Ordinal bids its priests, deacons and bishops no less, to 'seek for Christ's sheep scattered abroad in the midst of this naughty world.' The Church is an entity strange in existing essentially for those who do not yet belong. The whole world, like the traditional bounds of ward or village, is to be its 'parish'.[8] 'Sheep scattered' is archaic as analogy now from a once deeply pastoral world, but there is no question of a wide 'dispersion' from churchly precincts. 'The naughty world', like death, brings many things to nought—a sense of wonder, a will to worship, a capacity for truth in its demand for sincerity markedly among them in the current scene and mostly in the West.

Why, then, are they 'scattered'?[9] In all that is bewildering about the spread of secularity in the strict sense (not of a 'secular state' theme) of 'secularisation' as the recession or abandonment of the sense of God, it is proposed in this chapter to seek answer in six areas of thought and action. This, hopefully, will best serve both the fulfilment of the Ordinal and how, therein, Christian ministry is the more involved precisely where it is most discounted. The vacancy no less than the tenancy of the pew must excite its sympathy and claim its mind.

The first of these reasons for faith in current limbo must surely lie in the miscreant quality of religions themselves. Here Joyce's instinct was cunningly right. The villain of the piece was the spectacle of his native Catholicism, the superstitions with which it connived, the yoke it laid on Irish society. Revulsion is now deep, both inside and beyond Islam, for the image of that faith which some of its activists currently present violently to the non-Islam for which these zealots have a dire and dark hostility. Much of what matters here turns on whether faiths enthrone, or can disown, the law of retaliation. How the faith of the

---

[8] Making good, in fact, the original meaning of *paroikia*—'dwelling anywhere even as a stranger', or 'at home far beyond the village pump', or 'habitation anywhere'.

[9] The Ordinal way well be echoing Matthew 9. 36—Jesus' comment about Galilean listeners as compassion saw them. See stridently, Richard Dawkins, *The God Delusion*, London, 2006.

Qur'an might co-exist inside a religious diversity has been explored in the preceding chapter. It would require it to be again the thing it was in its first and definitive reality in Mecca, prior to the added dimension of retaliatory power and armed force it acquired after its Hijrah to Medina.[10] Then it was only and entirely a religious witness to 'Allah and His apostle', these being still to this day the twin elements in its *Shahadah*, assured in the simplicity of its brevity. There are factors in its current diaspora, where no Medinan-style regime obtains—not the persecution which it long endured in Mecca—that might well contribute to such recovery of its first self for its own sanity and for a Muslim re-assurance to the world at large. And what of Judaism in Israel's belligerence where retaliation rules?

Meanwhile, the menace of a wildly retaliatory Islam contributes darkly to the over-all disdain for, or suspicion of, religions *per se*. For they give a bitter, combative edge to contemporary disavowal of faiths in general. 'We are safer and saner without them,' the protest runs. 'A plague on all their houses,' as nurseries of credulity and organs of obscurantist bigotry. The transcendent, with such custodians or guardians, is brutally thwarted and forfeit in 'the houses of its friends'. Whatever might be the meaning of 'God', is nullified, becomes expendable, merits derisive demise. The clarion cry of the theisms: 'Let God be God' is answered by: 'let that magistracy, that fallacy, that lunacy no longer haunt us.'

Perhaps it is no surprise that religious structures should generate a stridency of voice and tyranny of mind. Perhaps these are the occupational hazards of being, ostensibly, in trust with things absolute. These do not take readily to 'perhaps' and 'peradventure'. To many, they seem in demeaning contrast to the clear empiricism of the sciences. They have sacrosanct Scriptures and deposits of faith and careful, sure transmission of these, without loss or compromise, to waiting generations. Thus their stance is backward-looking where

---

[10] There can be no doubt of the essential priority of the Meccan Islam, radical as the change of character was following the emigration. Though it would appear never to have been divinely commanded, it was a pragmatic development (referred to in the Qur'an as 'they went out and they struggled' in past tense verbs) seizing the opportunity presented by the invitation to sanctuary on the part of elements in Yathrib, as Medina was first named. When it became the base for retaliation against the Quraish a watershed in Islam was passed, which Muslims firmly believed valid and timely. That it happened on behalf of the Meccan mission is not in question nor, by implication, its subordination to that originating quality of Islam.

truth sacredly abides, rather then forward where refining truth awaits. Inherently conservative, in this way their credentials seem to presuppose a submissive will sheltering a closed mind.

Though actually or potentially countered from their own texts, these dissuasive features of their image have powerful counter-sanction in the psychic realm. Leadership, office, expertise, cling to status as the bulwark of validity, so that dogma and custody, liturgy and tenure reinforce each other. This means that religion's custodians, with all the problems around that concept as some elitism (even vis-à-vis their own laity), need a lively respect for the integrity that can belong with sincere scepticisms. This will be the more difficult for Orthodox Judaism and a traditional Islam—the one with its rigorous self-definition over against 'Gentiles', the other with harsh attitudes to unbelievers in its own Qur'an.[11] It is not well for faiths to cultivate and esteem a sharp apartheid in the human context as all 'fundamentalisms' are prone to do to the dismay of many in their own societies.

This very term, so frequent—and disparate—in present scenarios, needs careful reckoning. In one sense, all faiths—being concerned with and for 'ultimacy' whether of 'truth' or moral 'guidance'—are in trust with fundamentals. These, by their very nature, do not admit of equivocation or, in any cheap sense, of negotiation. Yet the very presence of that—and those—which/whom dispute such finality must require that the due religious assurance 'internalise' (i.e. hold within themselves) the authority it claims to wield externally. Thus it will rightly retain its ultimacy as ever in their trust, yet do so in a temper that does not automatically assume that its content has to be absolute elsewhere in those inward terms.

So to assume, by sheer dogmatism, will betray both the nature of the faith concerned and the genuine task of its commendation. A stentorian voice will be no part of proper posture. The temper in which it offers itself will be the mind-test of what it offers. 'This is the word

---

[11] It is this feature of the Qur'an which has made it difficult temperamentally to greet the invitation to dialogue with the proposal thus at least to co-exist. For there are concepts 'out there' about the same theism which they are required to resist and which, therefore, do not merit a patience that might explore them more perceptively or, at best, allow them to be held by the other. This 'hard heart' towards 'unbelievers' sharpened notably after the Hijrah and when physical combat was joined. In Mecca also there was the necessity for an urgent disavowal of its paganism. The issue is perennial between vital 'belief and the disbelief of others. On the Quranic scene, see David E Marshall, *God, Muhammad and the Unbelievers*, Richmond, 1999.

of the Lord' is not in the megaphone of the town-crier. It needs and seeks the inward kindling of conviction.

Faiths, therefore, need in turn a lively cognisance of the impulses that discount and deplore the relevance of religion(s). This must further mean a mind for how far those impulses are aroused by how faiths behave, how far they act as their own worst enemy when critically viewed from outside the citadels and sanctums they contrive for themselves. There are pleas in many a psalm: 'Let *them* be confounded that seek after my soul' which many zealots in faith would readily echo (or, perhaps, 'seek after our truths'). In one psalm, however (69. 6), the direction is reversed. The writer prays: 'Let not those who seek Thee be confounded through me.' How apt is such a prayer in today's world scene! The psalmist was afraid then that the adversities he suffered would suggest to observers that his God had failed him and was so disqualified of deserving any awe from others. Thanks to him the God he had had lost all credence.

Free of that malign 'cause and effect' logic now about adversity, the case is all the other way. Worshippers and witnesses discredit their deity by the 'calamities' they bring on Him, by their arrogance, their self-esteem, their prejudice, their too ready censure of 'the unbelievers', their avidity for suicidal rewards, and their tragic appetite for war.

Much, therefore, in this context will turn on what resilience faiths have, what cognisance of these demands. Can truths be more receptive to the relevance of doubt, more apt like the sciences for integrity of mind? Can theology undertake its Scriptures with adequate attention to history? How will these liabilities figure in the education of their custodians, the posture these adopt in the exercise of authority? The question in religious witness is both what and how, together.

These issues are not only deeply relevant because of the range and urgency of secular alienation as faiths must now realistically face it. They are also vital for two positive reasons. One is the degree to which any faith—if at all—can wisely relate to another in this situation, as entailing on them all. This must await, for Christian purposes, the chapter following. The second reason is simply the wide areas of human need and the incidence of technology in which there must be mutual engagement between believer and agnostic, between secular aegis and religious systems. These must be in concert alike in analysis and remedy, in policy and action. The secular mind may well be stronger on strategy towards endemic poverty, illiteracy, hunger and disease: faiths may think themselves strong on motivation and 'non-weariness in well-doing'. Either has their means of knowing or of doing, but 'the meaning in the means' can be one. The secular is not implicitly high-minded. Greed, exploitation, cunning, fraud and deviousness beset it. These will always need rebuke, exposure, discipline and redemption. But neither are religions free from the dishonesty, the wilful enmity and cowardice that corrupt the ministry they ought otherwise to bring to these evils. Meanwhile, incentives to unbelief are deeply present in the image and impress of religious practices. There is a counter-discounting of 'things most surely believed' and in their 'believing' the more paradoxically to be disowned. 'Let judgement begin at the house of God,' lest 'faith unfaithful keep it falsely true.'[12]

III

This disrepute of religions widespread in the social order, this often militant shape of their secular disavowal, taken here as prime cause of contemporary 'irreligion', has its corollary, as a deterrent from belief. It arises for many from the sheer diversity of religious claims and allegiances. The more we realise our global *mise-en-scène* the more we are primed to query our own identity or, as a kind of rebound, to assert it more aggressively. Identity, in any event, is a curious commodity.[13] There is in vogue now, thanks to writers like Salman Rushdie, a measure of assertive 'hybridization', a cult of 'inbreeding' and 'cross-identity'. This can be deeply confusing, if not alienating, to earnest devotees of their 'true faith'. For such, if anything and everything is credible, compatible, congruent and agreeable, then does anything really mean? This is more miasmic for the private self in the faith-field than the familiar troubles of positivist philosophers over what language can 'say', what words can 'mean'. These troubles do not much disturb those who hold with 'common sense', though we may have to take note of them elsewhere.

---

[12] 1 Peter 4. 17, and Alfred Lord Tennyson, *Poetical Works*, London, ed.1994, p. 523; the poet's paradox concerning 'Sir Lancelot', in 'Idylls of the King: Elaine'.

[13] In both senses of the 'curious' word, i.e. requiring and attracting attention, and being, thereby, intriguing.

The disquiet of believers—and thereby the liabilities of faiths to their faithful—make the more harshly for misgivings about worship and the legitimacy of a creed-in-a-credo. It would seem that 'if anything goes, nothing means' and even the very notion of 'identity'—viable, legitimate, decisive—goes also. And yet when such drastic subversion of identity *per se* occurs, what remains of being human, being here and being alive? A 'me' somehow legitimising place, birth, speech, time and society as due constituents of 'me-ness' seems explicit in existence itself. Shorn of all these valid particulars, who, what, where, whence are we?

The plurality of religious readings of this 'me and mine', seems, to reflective souls, to deter any trust in one unilateral direction. People in any one faith may well concede to co-exist with others in a practical sort of tolerance and in the pursuit of common human goals. Yet such postures argue against any decisive commitment in the singular and suggest a similar effective negligence of how radically doctrines diverge. It becomes problematic thus to co-exist and at the same time to pro-exist—as convictions surely must—for the one allegiance these demand. The issue is particularly acute for office-holders in immediate trust with worship, liturgy, doctrine, law, jurisprudence or discipline.

Living mutually and yet belonging sincerely is for many the more difficult in that plural faiths propose plural claims about which there is no agreed or viable criterion of judgement and no possibility of final verdict. All come with sacrosanct Scriptures presenting different versions of the human crisis and its divine solution. Comparative study may partially align their drift and counsel, but will not resolve the conflict of their authority. It is this situation, for some among the faithful round their Scripture, which may well erode the vital sense of 'given-ness' and the total devotion they ought to bring to it. To sense the competitive situation and to be obligated to concede it readily sets a query around a singular adherence. If warrants for faiths can be many, why need discipleships be mandatory and not selective? The more co-existence is enjoined the less may distinctiveness commend itself or command us.

Doubtless for many, this situation is not felt, out of inertia or the reach of dialogue ideology. Faith is all too often customary and traditional. For others, however, it is answered by a determined counter assertion of singular authority. Muslims will read themselves as immune by Islam's finality from any necessary self-interrogation. Christians may, in apprehension or disquiet, take refuge in an assertive Biblicism that has no room for what it owes to truth and ethics. Others' may take refuge in the unexamined *magisterium* of the Church as assumed to save them from the onus of any 'private judgement'. When these duly settling absolutes are had, perplexities elsewhere are only the more increased. Moreover, there is a lack of integrity in such options unless these 'deciders' are subject to the same responsible assessment as genuine faith itself. This is the less likely if they have been sought as a refuge from that very task.

It follows that when this task is fully faced, the weight of things between divergent sources of authority increases. A Christian, still less clergy in their particular custody of discipleship, can scarcely be indifferent to Islam's firm historical disavowal of, and spiritual veto on, the Cross of Christ as ever being within the divine economy.[14] Or Judaism's self-exemption from Christianity's inclusion of the 'Gentiles' in a single, ultimate peoplehood of God which Jewry itself learned to share—according to the New Testament.

How might gladly co-existing with these contradictions of one's soul-truth consist with mental honesty? It will not do to say that 'doctrine does not matter.' For then devotion goes as well unless both are cancelled together.

Need the cult of 'dialogue' have this enervating effect on honest faith and full devotion? For some it proves so. For others there is an eagerness for the one that has scant concern about the other. Such may take solace in the mere fact of 'truth of' and 'true for' distinction where believing underwrites belief—obviously an impossible solution. What of the conduct that the content generates, the fruit from its roots? Some honest sifting there must surely be.

'Sifting' can discern elements of 'truth of' inside 'truths for' analyses which may be critically welcomed, provided that such discrimination is allowable between adherents and the remaining

---

[14] For this is where Christian faith has always placed it to be, therefore, firmly disallowed. While Surah 4.156 calls into ambiguous query the historical matter of Jesus' 'death', its utmost rejection is on the theological grounds of its impossibility as ever within either the forgiveness or the sovereignty of Allah. All three aspects of veto, are studied in *Jesus and the Muslim*, London, 1985, Oxford, 1999, pp. 166-188.

Where Most Discounted Most Involved: the Secular Agnostic

incompatibles frankly recognised as such.[15] For many, however, patience and insight here are too taxing. The will to enmity remains as deterrent to ierenic venture. Thus the sheer fact of religious diversity kindles widely a too ready surrender to the demise of conviction and the sorry abeyance of ripe devotion.

IV

Nevertheless, the more thus 'discounted' the more is faith 'involved'— involved in the trials of its own resilience, the range of which we must resume in the chapter following. But nowhere is the 'discounted/ involved' formula adopted here more warranted than in the area of the competence and esteem of science with their sequel in the prevailing mind-set of technology, seemingly proclaiming the total triumph of empiricism, man contriving the mastery, so that the God-dimension is elided, whether as a factor in causation, or as a haven of refuge, or as a theme of adoration.

'Discounted' is *le mot juste* inasmuch as this seeming omnicompetence of science has quite superseded the divine dimension and argues the entire elision of God. Indeed, it has registered His demise so that 'the death of God' has been, with 'God's funeral' as well, set formulae of secular philosophy. It had its earlier prognostications in the atheism, for example, of Edward Gibbon—not to say of Thomas Hobbes—but 'the secularisation of the European mind' is credited to the nineteenth century, the century of Charles Darwin and Thomas Huxley.[16]

But 'involved' is no less apt a word for Christian theology. There was indeed, ironically, a certain prompting factor in the long enduring 'sense of order' assumed by medieval Christian theology[17] as divinely

---

[15] Dialogue often produces exactly this situation—'I am ready to recognise that "X" is truth for you, but will never be for me.' While welcome as beyond barren controversy, does this position leave hope and fidelity prematurely so that, in the end, 'tolerance' then forsakes its full task?

[16] See, for example, Owen Chadwick, *The Secularization of the European Mind in the 19th Century*, London, 1976.

[17] Even if still needing, perhaps clumsily, to be 'reconciled, with revelation, this medieval impulse to bring rationality into lively play in areas a later sophistication would despise certainly served to promote and practice the intelligibility available in life and nature to the human mind. Cf. A N Whitehead, *Science and the Modern World*, 1926, Chapter 1. 'The Middle Ages formed one long training of the intellect of western Europe in the sense of order ... by the long dominance of scholastic logic and scholastic divinity', pp. 12-13.

belonging to the natural order and only thence becoming the working rubric of an empirical intelligence seeming, and thinking, to elide it. The point needs to be appreciated in the full irony of its elements, so that science readily talks of data—its perennial 'stock-in-trade', while often ignoring in what their 'given-ness' consists.

For, expressly, there is no chemistry, no biology, no physics, no biology in nature.[18] They are there only as implicit and discoverable. For the order of things that houses them is no chatterer, no idle gossip. She is only a residual empire, where the sciences may be identified and pursued by an attentive, vigilant and persevering custodian, i.e. the human tenant of her wide domain. This intervener in her territory is no creator, no ordainer, no sustainer of their consistency: he is only their dependent, their occupier, their debtor. He yields to what they are: they yield to him the 'dominion' he thus enjoys. Neither they nor he alone stage the scenario, but only both in common in a partnership in which either waits on and waits for—the other.

Moreover, what nature affords to the scrutiny first and then the recruitment of science is strangely neutral, alike to the religion and to the ethics of the scientist.[19] Nature will 'send her rain on the just and on the unjust.' A microphone will be one and the same, *qua* technique, in the hand of a vile propagandist and of complete sincerity. Were it not so, there could be no morality. Quite evidently the moral and spiritual issues of human capacity for the sciences are left to turn on human will alone. The means will never supplant the ends: the ends will always inform, distort or justify the means. The current range and self-enlarging 'dominion' of applied science are sober, irrefutable evidence of how far they are 'involved'—by the very sources of their efficiencies—in the allegedly 'discounted' terms of a theology they too often think to supersede and relegate to pointless limbo. In the very neutrality of their processes, end-wise, they anticipate where theology belongs in any reading of the whole where they are partial.

---

[18] They are only latent there and waiting as such for the identifying, observing, categorizing mind of humankind, bringing the mental discernment their latency awaits.

[19] Structures and systems which minds examine and exploit do not ask as to the intentions, morals or convictions of their 'employers'. Only via such passivity are they 'realised' in life and culture. They are party to a 'dominion' they can only furnish and equip but never usurp.

Where Most Discounted Most Involved: the Secular Agnostic

This is not to say that theology is alone the guardian of the ethical. It is possible for moral philosophy to affirm some 'sovereignty of the good' and see no reason to think that human life is other than wholly self-contained. Yet how 'only self-contained' when life is so evidently 'contained' in things outside the self, as the farmer in the farm, the musician in the music, the engineer in the machine, the technician in the experiment. If we are bold to add: 'the servant in the serving' are we not close to recognising a 'sanctuary' where all is 'ours' to employ and enjoy, accept and appreciate, and thus not 'ours' by source or origin? The subject is only possessed of the object by an invitation to which it must respond, by a bestowal to which it must relate as partnering with debt. By such light, we are far from attending 'God's funeral': we find ourselves guests at 'God's banquet'. 'You spread a table before me' was how a psalmist saw it, speaking of the very landscape as a scene of hospitality.

It is thus that theology is 'involved' in the utmost masteries of the technical sciences, all of which are either occasion for endless gratitude or urgent scrutiny as to their social role. For they belong in and with a context far wider than the laboratory in which they were contrived. There they were complete and fully self-referent in their pursuit: outside there they are liable to areas of reference they could, or must 'discount' in lawfully pursuing their self-containment. It would be right to apply to them the old Latin/Christian principle: *Regnare, servare*. Indebtedness is the hallmark of their achieving, whether to the past of accumulating findings, or to inspired imagination, or—most of all—to the ever dependable, accessible, patient, modest amenability of nature. It would be odd to think to assign to the sciences a mastery that was not also an honoured servitude. Happily many practitioners have not needed theologians to tell them so.

Unhappily, many beneficiaries, far from these, have presumed to think themselves heirs of a world 'come of age', that needs no consecration at their hands. It belongs only to the wiles of exploitation and the 'bias of commodity'.

In the light of this human status in the natural order, the 'involvement' of Christian theology is two fold—to nourish and articulate a sense of wonder and surprise, against the jadedness that goes with bare indulgence and satiety, those other fruits from technological roots. This can come at a later point. Akin to this is to marshal the full meaning of the Christian measure of 'sacrament'. Here the Qur'an can help us, with its dual reading of *ayat* or 'signs' that 'signify' *for* humans *in* nature. These are the sundry phenomena which, as we have argued, arrest and steer investigative science towards its findings. Only so does insight from enquiry develop into technique and control. However, the same *ayat* which 'sign' us that way are also meant to kindle awe and thankfulness—spiritual perception towards consecration at the very point of practical study towards dominion. Thus the field of science is full of the themes of worship, not worship of the items which would be 'idolatry' but of their Originator in the sort of creation which offers them to our creaturely empire of indebtedness.

Such is the sacramental principle by which—if we allow it— 'all that is is holy.' It is one which Christian faith intensifies via 'water' and 'bread and wine' in rite and liturgy. It only does so as belonging to a 'sacramental earth' *in toto*. Then *data* are known as *gratia*. Only by such 'consecration' do we counter the 'bias of commodity' and the rule of greed via the cult of mere possession. We register a basic courtesy towards our being here at all. We can enlist the arts in the glad celebration of what the Qur'an calls 'the bounty of our Lord'.

But the dubious or the cynical will say: 'All this is the *parti pris* of a traditional piety which has not reckoned with how deep and far a radical 'discounting' of its confidence has gone in the march of the secular mind. What is the necessity, this mood will ask, for any divine hypothesis, when purely natural factors are discernible in the coming to be of all that is? Is theology concerning creation not a construct of the human imagination, a fashioning of deity in the image of man and, as such, a solace in the burden of existence? Has the human heart not devised it out of a haunting fear of vacancy or the menace of some rule of chance? Purpose, being necessary to the equanimity of our private selves, we assume it for the universe at large, or at least for the apparent uniqueness of our own planetary abode.

Moreover, there are sufficient explanations discernible to the sundry sciences which account for the habitable earth and our human habitat. Do we not have to concede and conclude that we are here by dint of processes that had no intention that we should be? It may take a certain courage to allow that were never 'divinely meant' but there is a realism and an honesty—some would say an arrival at adulthood—in acknowledging it to be so.

So has often run the case for a secular conclusion about ourselves by which we say, 'We are simply here.'[20]

But how can we mean 'simply' if we have any due capacity for amazement or unless we mean only to assert the obvious? Perhaps this very usage, in its very carelessness, is the clue. The whole issue about what to do concerning it is a theme for choice of ours. Inasmuch as we cannot 'not be' the situation requires a policy, a strategy which, as such, cannot not be purposive by light of some option we take. No option can be devoid of 'meaning' in the taking. Thus, our 'hereness' essentially dictates the effective meaning we ascribe. We may posit meaninglessness: we may not practise it. 'The world is too much with us' to be discounted in its immediacy to our selfhood: why should it be discounted in its totality? There is perhaps a deeper courage in allowing ourselves to belong with the whole.

Moreover, that 'whole' in terms of the universe of current astrophysics presents features remarkably persuasive of its 'destiny', given the incredible chances through which it has survived, the mysterious 'peradventures' which by the narrowest of margins would have irrevocably doomed it. Such case-making, in no way theological in its incentives or its skills, is profoundly 'theological' in its conclusions as about an earth so brought to pass *as if* an intention, coping with massive hazards, had willed it to be the thing it is. To cry, for whatever motive: 'We are simply here' can be no trite dismissal of what is an amazing status. 'Simply' would be the most crass of words. We have no cause to dismiss ourselves, as in no way significant vis-à-vis the universe itself. On every count we have far less reasons to do so in respect of this planet earth, and that earth on our account. Where consciousness belongs is where philosophy and faith come alert for verdict on themselves.

Yet the 'discounting' impulse persists. We fear lest we take ourselves too seriously or with the seriousness which any theology requires. The human dignity is then pretentious, unseemly, we are told. We should take better stock of finitude and stay illusions about the Infinite. The 'findings' of a Charles Darwin are more to be heeded than the phenomenon of a Darwin himself, that assiduous pursuer and

---

[20] As Iris Murdoch does in an oft-quoted passage. See *The Sovereignty of Good*, Oxford, 1970: 'I can see no evidence to suggest that human life is not something self-contained ... Our destiny can be examined but it cannot be justified or totally explained. We are simply here', p. 79. What then, is the point of the word 'destiny'? 'Destiny' is no equivalent of 'condition'.

reader of how 'species' came—and come—to pass. Perspective he may well have changed, but did he, could he, change the plot?

Unless evolution finds itself 'blind', it could well be compatible with a creative will as the means employed. That will still leave us with hard questions such as a theologian finds, like Charles Gore reportedly, on visiting a zoo. Yet the old distinction between 'final' and 'efficient', though as old as Aristotle, still abides. There is what wills an end inside what contrives a means. The one cares for the question Why? the other for the answer How? The first will only lack the second where the item is negligible. Negligibility is never a category to fit the universe, nor yet the earth within it and ourselves upon that earth. The panic that troubled theologians in Darwin's day was precipitate and unnecessary, as were the premonitions of disaster that beset his godly mind over dire results for a Victorian piety. With hindsight, we can see how his evolution could have been taken in theological stride, as no more than the possible pattern of a creative will. To be sure, that would—to its benefit—sift the mind that so concluded and refine its formulae. There would be no room for alarm over some divine demise, but only a more learned version of its strange wonder.

Or, if the 'death of God' syndrome persists and the secular order of the day points to other and numerous issues that complicate all conclusions, perhaps all parties can agree that a 'grand perhaps' remains and that what may never reach agreed consensus may deserve a definitive policy, an exercise of choice, an option of mind by which to live. The 'perhaps' the Qur'an's word *la 'alla* sets all squarely within the competence of mind and will. 'Perhaps you will bring your thought to bear, perhaps you may think yourselves responsible and responsive' amid this realm of 'sign-significance'.

There the whole matter may humanly rest and, resting, hold itself divinely sanctified in so doing, but without pretension or hostility to those who see all otherwise. Truly 'we are simply here' if such be our simplicity. Either way, we cannot do otherwise, contriving to be absentees. Maybe we can conclude that the more we are present to ourselves the less God also will seem an Absentee.

V

Christian faith as a 'construct' to be 'de-constructed' by cosmology and astrophysics and science at large is one thing. What of a New Testament consensus 'de-constructed' from within by its own scholarship trading in endless permutations of analysis—this is quite another and, manifestly, a potent factor in the genesis of faith-misgivings both inside and outside the faith world. The 'scattering' from allegiance we are studying has supposed sanction from the critique of its own documentary warranty. There is no doubt that strong current factors in unbelief, or disabling misgivings about faith and worship, stem from disquieting controversy about their textual bases and origin and authenticity.

For the ordinary believer the matter is exhausting, its *materia academia* inexhaustible. The range, longevity and sheer mass of scholarship devoted to the New Testament must be as voluminous and recondite as that bestowed on any other territory ancient or modern. What C F D Moule calls 'The Birth of the New New Testament'[21] is a story of the well-nigh incredible, given the odds that told against its very possibility with the shape it has, the inner confidence and its accompanying hazards.

Yet it transpired to be, as argued in two earlier chapters, the ultimate sign of its own veracity. Consider the potential negligibility of the preacher Jesus in the torrid world of Roman politics and the seething scene of Jewish zealotry due to erupt three decades later in the Jewish Revolt. Though eternalised in creed, Pilate's tenure quickly passed, why not Jesus with him into the limbo of history's minutiae in the oblivion-consigning flux of years? Why not Jesus, as a condemned felon, also a candidate for such non-fame, like that other itinerant preacher, Hanina Ben Dosa with whom Geza Vermes sought to compare him?[22]

---

[21] C F D Moule, *The Birth of the New Testament*, New York, 1962. He is 'pursuing the genesis of Christian writings' via 'the fact that upon Jesus converged the whole history of Israel in the past and from him deployed the whole future of the people of God', p. 69 and pp. 67-68.

[22] See his several studies: *Jesus the Jew*, London, 1973, *The Religion of Jesus the Jew*, London, 1993, and *Providential Accidents*, London, 1998, *The Changing Faces of Jesus*, London, 2000. His works have been widely translated in European languages. Perhaps the key point at stake is his dismissal, roundly, as 'myth', of the 'Messiah' theme. Everything Christian for him emerged as an 'aberration'—which is to fail to reckon with the whole phenomenon of its emergence and of the text and community to which it gave being.

But it did not happen so. The fact of an active faith became a new fact of the situation, abidingly coupled with its reading of what the original fact had been, the one corroborating the other by an inner necessity between them.

This is not to say that 'believing makes it so' in any and every case, as if what events were held to mean could never be illusory or false. It is to say that, with events so catastrophic in their incidence as the crucifixion of Jesus and the disastrous experience of all his disciples, the emergence of the apostolic Church in sequel deserves to be read with its veracity writ large. What the document purports to tell of Messianic origin and communal sequence witnesses to why the document itself exists. It will be honest to hold that this takes care of the numerous problems that remain and are in no way shelved. Rather they deserve to be 'contained', as so much has legitimately to be in all the things of faith.

There are two reasons why this can be so. The first is that Christian faith must always be a matter of trust with the will rather than infallible truth to the mind. The second reason is that 'Messiah', whether as hope or fact, dream or reality, stands as the crux both of theology and of history. It concerns whether the God-theme of the one is adequate to the human-theme of the other. The good of a purposive creation was crossed by the wrong in human history, and could be proven only in some righting of the wrong. There would have to be 'God—somehow—in a Christ' or no God at all.[23] Or, in the more philosophic vein of Ernst Bloch: 'Messianism must be understood as being the secret of the whole history of religion.'[24]

This sense of what human history demands of any honest and adequate theology must be the ultimate Christian response to the New Testament criticism, however erudite, which discounts it. Scholarship has every right and duty with the minutiae of the text into which it probes but, with the minutiae, it has no liberty to ignore 'the many splendoured thing' which is also in this context 'the many loaded thing'. A Jesus, towards, to, in, through and beyond his Gethsemane with the ensuing text of Church, Gospels, Letters, memory and tradition, cannot

---

[23] The word 'crossed' has both of two meanings; in the way in which 'cross-roads' intersect as 'parallel' lines do not, and in the costliness of what then ensues as that whereby the 'evil is overcome' in the good 'o'ercoming it'.

[24] See *Geist der Utopie*, 1923, p. 246, in K H Miskotte's translation.

well be forfeit to the lore of the Dead Sea Scrolls or some welcome rehabilitation of the Pharisees.[25]

Let all the conjectures, searchings, findings and labours of New Testament critical scholarship have their due place in the intellectual integrity of current Christian studies, whether it be form criticism, or redaction, or pseudepigrapha or the waning of *parousia* or apocryphal writings, or the role of the Canon. The crucial thing in any pastoral context, as here, is the erosion of the will to faith which can ensue among the many who have neither leisure nor skill to cope with these dissuasives of faith, yet feel the impact of their distractions or their implications. Conspiracy theories about what orthodoxy has wilfully concealed or suppressed sow a disquiet which then conspires anew against a will to trust. The situation, for many sounder minds, is not retrieved by invocations of inerrancy or absolutist claims. We may learn in the end to turn from questions we cannot answer to hold with answers we cannot escape. Meanwhile, 'let patience have her perfect work.'

VI

Beyond, yet through, all the foregoing as factors in the enervating of lively faith, textual, doctrinal, intellectual and practical, there may supervene a crippling loss of personal worth or self-identity. Could this explain the plea of that long, alphabetical Psalm 119, where the writer prays: 'Lord, seek thy servant'? What cause is there to pray so, since he is already there, and has the language, and can add: 'I do not forget thy commandments.' Thus he is no renegade and yet he prays to be 'sought for, like a sheep that is lost.' Whatever his setting and his soul-unease, he represents a very modern experience of near futility even in the context of aspiration. The worth of things has somehow lapsed and with it the worth of selfhood. It is hard to recover from a plight which by its very nature disarms the will to its own salvation.

Though the weight of this ennui was familiar enough in many a medieval cloister, it is too often the insignia of the contemporary

---

[25] Important as these are in their own context. In any event what Jesus said of the Pharisees was in no way disparatory. It was, paradoxically about 'exceeding a righteousness', already careful and exacting, by infusing it with a wider compassion and a warmer realism.

'office block' or the corridors of social power and—no less—the playhouses of a banal culture. Does it stem less now from 'what Sophocles heard long ago' of human grief in tragedy, and more from satiety, indulgence, acquisitiveness and boredom? Literature abounds with its malaise. Figures like those in Samuel Beckett are somehow minimally present in the business of living, wearily sceptical of any romantic gestures since empty ones they could only be. Albert Camus' graphically presented Mersault in *L'Étranger* has reached an uncanny atrophy of a deep human feeling, moving in a sort of abeyance of belonging, as if very selfhood had shrivelled away.

These are doubtless extreme examples yet symptomatic of lesser forfeitures of the will to engage, to relate, to participate and live. The factors, no doubt, are varied—sheer routine, rival pressures, the pace of life, emotional insecurity via marital disloyalty, or family tension and the perpetual presence of the cult of the moment. The catalogue is endless, with the public scene so far dominated by the search for entertainment and the flux of the sensational. Or there is the restlessness of a tourism which has 'been there, done that' and never really arrived to possess a wealth and understand a human-ness. Maybe these ills of our restlessness have a mirror held to them in the ready discipline of psychology, aspiring to apply the more exact methods of the physical sciences to the less amenable world of the human psyche in the social scene. Hence the consultant's couch as a novel theatre for introspection and the self-interrogating pre-occupations to which it may, or may not, usefully minister. At least we are thus prompted to be the more self-aware and, perhaps, thereby, the less self-fulfilled as—in less anxious ways—we might have been. Taken too far and into isolation as a theme or inquisition, this process may find us concluding our non-necessity to anything or merely its spectators.

In few writers has this 'self-question' been taken into deeper anxiety than by Franz Kafka, for whose 'heroes' existence affords only agonising doubt of its own reality. There is an alienation in the mind itself which, applied to its burden in the absence of meaning, recoils frustratedly upon itself. The self has no viable reckoning with itself as caught in a clueless maze. Nowhere has the dilemma of selfhood been so direly analysed. Yet the liberal or the romantic instinct which might think to ridicule such morbidity as some sick self-flagellation has to learn some saving will to honesty about its depths. 'Let him that thinketh he flourishes take heed lest he cower.' Only full measure of hopelessness 'stiffens the sinews' of hope.

Whatever the abysmal reaches of the condition told by the Kafkas, the Ionescoes, the Becketts of its literati, the burden was well known in the long monastic tradition of earlier centuries. Monks drew on the Greek word *akedia* and called it 'accidie', a state of spiritual torpor, a sad desuetude of all the arts of worship and the will to praise or prayer. The current secular world has larger, less trained, aptitude for the like abandonment of the structures and habits of religion. It submits more readily to an absenteeism of mind and soul from the forms and disciplines of belief and practice, even while it may retain a wistfulness within that sometimes queries how it might be otherwise.

How then does ministry relate? From where may wisdom be found? The self which is the centre of the situation has, ironically, to be the crux of the salvation, by a sane attack on the negative factors which have induced it and a resolute reach for the positives which can surmount it. It does not lie in a re-assertion of the self, as Byrons and Shelleys would, by passion and a pseudo-zest. Rather, it means a different self-surrender that learns to yield itself into a liberating captivity to that abiding unselfishness which is the love of God. We are thus dispossessed of that which will always enslave us by the tyranny of false desires to be freed into a self-possession ready—and thus readied—to be instrumental. The newly captive liberty will be enlistment into being and belonging, self-grounded, to be sure, but not self-complicit.

This is more than the 'unchartered freedom' of which William Wordsworth wrote, yearning for 'a repose that is always the same.'[26] Rather, it is a 'chartered freedom' bringing an engagement that 'no more may charge its name.'

Thus, both 'selfed and unselfed', we may reach to resist and reverse those sundry factors which have festered into our apathies and discontents, and renew all those faculties of wonder, gratitude and courtesy which foster a wider benediction than our own. We are then no longer on 'the dread watch-tower of man's absolute self'.[27] Rather, in being willingly recruited into the one great 'unselfishness' which is

---

[26] William Wordsworth, *Poetical Works*, ed. E De Selincourt, Vol. iv, Oxford, 1947, p. 85, 'Ode to Duty', lines 38-40.

[27] Samuel Taylor Coleridge in Letter to Wordsworth, 30 May 1815.

the love economy of God, we possess ourselves in the utmost relevance to the world and of the world to ourselves.

The very order of the secular is where it must be proven so. Here, by a strange paradox, is the remedy that answers the poet Gerard Manley Hopkins' self-counsel:

> 'My own more heart let me more have pity on; let
> Me live to my sad hereafter kind,
> Charitable; not live this tormented mind
> With this tormented mind, tormenting yet.'[28]

Except that for his 'sad' we now have 'glad'.

VII

Beyond all the foregoing around the factors in human time and story that prompt the 'discounting' of Christian faith and, therefore, the more involve the Christian ministry, the last, in every sense, is 'the grave and gate of death'—'the undiscovered country' to which all mortality progresses, the last of all our serial 'and thens'.[29]

Here stands the sharp query to the very preciousness of life and, therefore, the crisis in its meaning. Moreover, death is something for ever 'un-experienced' until it supervenes. It is not an event of which life has cognisance, being instead the term of all experience. This makes it the more arresting in its incidence, with its intense loneliness, its eclipse of all we hold most precious and significant, its grim hint of the foreboding

> '... which cannot choose
> But weep to have that which it fears to lose.'[30]

Here is the ultimate 'discounting' of all that counts in human experience What 'recount' then can Christian ministry offer, if we are not to cry extravagantly with John Donne: 'Death be not proud'?[31]

---

[28] Gerard Manley Hopkins, *The Poems*, ed. W H Gardner and N MacKenzie, 1970, p. 68.
[29] 'And then we say' a refrain in one of Philip Larkins' lines, with '... and then the only end of age'. See *Collected Poems*, ed. Anthony Thwaite, 2003, 'Next Please', p. 50, 'Dockery and Son', p. 109.
[30] Shakepeare's Sonnet 64.
[31] John Donne, *The Poems*, ed. H J C Grierson, 1933, Holy Sonnet X, p. 297.

To be sure 'it comes to all equally and makes all equal when it comes.' What of the utter negligibility of the private individual in the vast numberless welter of the populations of the centuries? And what of the harsh incidence of its tedious arrival:

> '... no sudden but a slow-paced evil,
> A long day's dying to augment our pain.'[32]

Somewhere in his novel *Humboldt's Gift*, Saul Bellow proposed two options by which our strategy might palliate the dying problem. The first was to drill oneself slowly into a listless cult of oblivion so that death would spell no great change. You might manage thus to miss its worst, but only by dying never having lived. Or, alternatively, one might so increase the bitterness of life ('Sophocles heard it long ago') so that your actual demise became a welcome release. Death can only be cheated this way by first cheating life itself, akin to how for John Milton, Eve's notion of 'wilful barrenness' was 'reluctance against God'.[33]

Yet is death somehow 'God's reluctance against us'? Life, the world, time, love, truth and hope would for ever give the lie to that. We can only truly read, interpret and handle death in and as the riddle it must be. We belong in a universe which could readily do without us. Yet it has not done so. We must hold on to that. The first 'Let there be ...' was no 'nullity decree'. Should death somehow, at length, annul it or how might its continuity be read? 'We see through a glass darkly' with no clear lens into the *ainigmata*.

We can recall that 23rd Psalm and read its metaphors in Christ or recall, in tune with it, how the Spanish of 'Death Valley' for Hispanic Americans translates as 'the palm of God's hand'. The secularised may well neither heed nor understand.

We must, in inward soul or outward ministry, contain in peace what we cannot explain in word and betake ourselves to the founding Christian truth of the sacrament of the body in the hallowedness of creation and the gift of being here and of being the who's we are. That sacrament is ever given as received, ever only received as given. It is ours to yield in the very terms by which we call it ours. This has

---

[32] John Milton, *Paradise Lost*, Book X, lines 964-65.
[33] *Ibid.*, Book X, lines 1042-45.

been the secret all along, as argued thus far in this chapter and explicit in all else.

It shall be no less so in respect of what some have finely called 'the last curiosity'.[34] That sense of adventure speaks of an invitation to discovery but it hints at a vocation faith can differently recognise as conscious 'offering'. Physical death, thus read, becomes the sacramental sign of a completed sacrifice to God. It is then no merely inevitable event for resignation but, instead, the final episode in the life-pattern of self-offering. Or, as Charles Wesley sang:

> 'Ready for all Thy perfect will
> My acts of faith and love repeat,
> Till death Thine endless. mercies seal
> And make the sacrifice complete.'

'Where is thy sting, O death?' is a question that then falls away. But on every count the living are the more involved as 'redeemers of the present time'.

---

[34] Thus Walter Pater, *The Renaissance: Studies in Art and Poetry*, London, 1910, p. 129, writes of Leonardo da Vinci: '... one who had always been always so desirous of beauty, but desired it also in such precise and definite forms ... looked forward now into the vague land and experienced the last curiosity.' Also M Guyon, *Non-Religion of the Future*, p. 538, has 'Man's last agony and his last pulse of curiosity are one.'

EASTER EUCHARIST: A COLLEGE SERMON

Magdalen College Chapel, Easter Sunday, 16 April 2006

'At the least three times in the year, of which Easter to be one.' So runs the rubric in the 1662 Book of Common Prayer. Frequencies are different now but the abiding link between the Lord's Supper and the festival of Resurrection is foundational, alike in Christian theology and liturgy.

Yet there is surely concerning it a strange yet often unsuspected paradox which it is my concern here to explore—both for its own urgency and for the fact that it opens out for us a deep dimension of this great Festival of a risen Christ.

The paradox is simply implicit in one who says: 'Do this in remembrance of me' yet will shortly be saying: 'Behold I am alive for evermore.' How incongruous they are when we consider them both together! What can be the point of anything in 'memory' of one who assures his disciples: 'I am with you to the end of the world.'

Even apart from the Easter meaning, was not Jesus utterly unforgettable, bound to be abidingly unforgotten? Certainly that was so for immediate disciples for whom the ordaining was first meant, even if, as the Qur'an has it, it would 'be a memorial through all their generations.' Could Peter, John and the rest ever forget those Beatitudes or the entire band not keep endless recollection of the hillside throngs, the lakeside summons, the gathering crisis of his leadership, the tumult of their own motives in believing him—so ambiguously—'Messiah'? The New Testament as a document, the Scriptures that comprise both Gospels and Letters, are eloquent enough concerning how effectively and assiduously Jesus was remembered. For his whole personality is imaged there as cherished and mediated through their vivid sense of him in ardent retrospect. However we resolve the paradox, it is evident enough that the 'Remember' command in the Upper Room has nothing to do with *whether* Jesus would be 'remembered'. We must learn why elsewhere.

Moreover, it is worth noting about 'memory' that means or symbols or rituals designed to ensure it may all too readily fail, if they move the onus from the heart itself. How often have we seen folk gossiping on the steps of some monument with its 'Lest we forget' inscribed upon it when forgetting is precisely what is happening? The device has taken over the task and the task is more easily ignored. Oblivion can overtake anything for lack of insistent will to frustrate its menace. The very urgency of means and tokens of mind-enablement witnesses to what is otherwise our fallibility. Thus 'Do this in remembrance' only avails with our eager consent. How many deeply inattentive Eucharists have we all attended despite the ever present 'mystery of love' and may be, as here, the benediction of the sound of music?

There is an honoured academic precept that when confronting a contradiction, as here and now, you look for a distinction. That Eucharist had never to do with *whether* Jesus would be remembered has us realise that it had everything to do with 'how'. Consider what different devices Jesus might credibly have decreed. He had been phenomenally a teacher, with his: 'But I say to you …' Why not then a ceremonial, public recital of that 'Sermon on the Mount'? Or a re-enacting of his Isaian inaugural pronouncement in the synagogue at Nazareth where his ministry began? Why not these 'in remembrance of him'?

To query them as only dubiously right is in no way to disown the vital significance in Jesus, of the teaching role nor the art of the parables in the education of his disciples. For their nurture into his meanings was no small part of his mission and, so manifestly, of the ultimate wealth of the New Testament as a document. There was to be 'the New Testament in my blood' as 'this cup' for its most definitive location.

Furthermore, the celebration of Jesus it terms of his preaching ministry and reminder of the 'never man spake like this man' tradition could so readily lead to a culture of possessive admiration, even loud applause. The situation then could well have been like the acclaim of Cicero when the thronging Romans flocked into the market-place, saying: 'Wasn't our Cicero great today!' Did not grim young Kierkegaard have us understand that 'Jesus did not come to be admired.' He came to be followed. He sought not fans but disciples. The crucial emphasis would be elsewhere: 'Do this in remembrance of me.' The treasure of the verbal teaching was ever present in the story of the Passion. For nowhere did Jesus teach so tellingly as in Gethsemane. But only in the 'breaking and taking of the bread' would the heart of him and of his words be understood and realised. The Cross would have to be the clue to right remembrance. For not to have the Cross in true focus would mean that everything else would be undone and Jesus might belong in history as either deluded or a malefactor or perhaps even pass out of it for ever. Only where and how he was vindicated would enlist authentic discipleship through all the time ahead. 'Do this in my remembrance.'

But there is another reason why it must—and ever has been—so. It takes us to one of the several meanings of Easter we are liable to miss. It is one which has to do with the deepest of our moral problems. We have it there in the Easter Anthems: 'Reckon ye yourselves dead to sin but alive to God ...' What can the meaning be, or do we pause to ask?

I think it has everything to do with what we may call 'the art of selfhood', a theme, which incidentally, has long been the anxious burden of the Buddhist world. Here we are, all of us, in a selfhood that makes us 'egocentric' factually, me in my body, you in yours. This physical ego-centricity is inescapable as, indeed, the only locus of any non-egocentric living, Here, precisely lurks our moral dilemma, in that self-hood is ever prone to self-preening, self-aggrandising. These vitiate its honest destiny. Yet where can we find answer to our ever acquisitive quality of mind? Clearly, not in somehow opting out unless we mean some proleptic suicide. As Marx had it, to be in the world is to be at the world, or—with Sartre—*en soi* equals *pour soi*. How, then, can we exist actively and essentially?

Note how even humility can be crudely proud and even penitence self-congratulatory. Surely it was not the intention of the parable about the two men in the Temple, to have us cry: 'I thank God that "I am not as this Pharisee."' 'Look at me, standing afar off, beating my breast.' Yet that way our self-esteem will work. What self-absorption there persists even in the hermit's cell.

Albert Camus took this point in *La Chute* and the penitent needing to liken the deceptions of his soul to the concentric canals of his native Amsterdam. Iris Murdoch seeks to make the same point when she has one of her characters opine: 'You can only be good as long as you are good for nothing.' It was her persistent quarrel with religious ethics that she thought Christianity, for example, ever ministering to self-commendation, lustful after the self-esteem law and grace alike must somehow incite, so that no heart could be pure.

Yet selfhood can never 'be' factually and 'not be' morally. Where is any self-liberated me-ness to be found, any 'me' saved from unworthy self-ness?

It is here that we come to the whole meaning of Easter, or rather the 'ethical' among the sundry other meanings—evidential, factual, artistic—an Easter sermon might engage. For the Resurrection as the Easter Anthems sing, yields a paradigm into which we can fit our ego-centric being. 'Reckon yourselves dead to sin and alive unto God through Jesus Christ as Lord.' We can be 'good for nothing and yet everything' by the pattern of the risen Christ. We can 'count ourselves dead' and know ourselves given back to us with no occasion for that clinging shadow. For then we shall be invested in the only unselfish recruiter of selfhood which is the divine kingdom, which takes 'all that a man has' and restores it into only serving hands aware only of a vocation to gratitude. Paul has it in the sequence: 'Not ourselves ...' 'and ourselves ...' (so we are there again but only) '... your servants for Jesus' sake.' We are thus enlisted into a selfhood which requires all its self-esteem to die except as it is garnered into 'perfect freedom'. Faith in the Cross is where we learn by identity: 'Let this mind be in you which was also in Christ.' We make ourselves over to the utterly unselfing, yet self-employing Lordship that is 'alive for evermore'. We are 'lost and found' in the active love of Christ.

The place where all the Christian centuries have done so is here, in 'bread and wine' as we make these our own.

> 'Here with love's perception
> Find we daily bread,
> To His task recruited,
> At His table fed.'

Chapter 7
ALL YOUR CARES AND STUDIES

The charge in the Ordinal for the Ordering of Priests prior to the 'laying on of hands' might well seem daunting in any less heartening context. Here it will be promptly followed by *Veni Creator Spiritus*.

> 'Have always printed in remembrance how great a treasure is committed to your charge. For they are the sheep of Christ which he bought with his death and for whom he shed his blood ...
>
> Wherefore consider with yourselves the end of your ministry toward the children of God ... See that ye never cease your labour, your care and diligence until you have done all that lieth in you, according to your bounden duty ...
>
> Forasmuch, then, as your Office is both of so great an excellency and of so great difficulty, ye see with how great care and study ye ought to apply yourselves ... so that as much as lieth in you, you will apply yourselves wholly to this one thing and draw all your cares and studies this, way ...'

The language betrays its century and that century's Cranmer's pen, but the logic is apostolic. 'All your cares and studies' to be engrossed in one entire self-offering in the ministry of 'Word and Sacrament, in inclusive tasks of mind and total direction of will, the very 'cure of souls'.

If, as reportedly the Table Talk of Martin Luther had it: 'Begin with the wounds of Christ for all understanding of God,' no less must be true about this 'laying on of hands'. If it proceeds as 'liturgy into biography' as the Ordinal intends, then it moves with and from the 'wounded hands of Jesus'. The Ordinal is saying so in its open allusion to 'the Church which he has purchased.' With this 'printed into remembrance',[1] it is well to examine here the personal onus of Christian ministry under the kindred theme of the 'vicarious and the vulnerable', these two that are always coupled where the *lex talionis* has been abrogated. Ministry is 'being on behalf of' and 'being on behalf of' means the cost of what it takes, the bearing it exacts. All means 'offering' as the Ordinal has us know.

The point then in this chapter is to examine how these two characterise the narrative of ministry and do so in three dimensions—the intellectual, moral and inwardly personal. We have seen ample occasion for the exercise of all three in the survey of fields of ministry in the several previous chapters. What is predicatory of 'God in Christ' in Word and Sacrament in commendation into other-faiths territory leaves ample occasion for its servants to be vulnerable from the misunderstandings and prejudices to which their meanings are liable. Thus they are vicarious in carrying the onus of metaphors misread, terms misconstrued and cherished things ignored or despised. The Ordinal told of 'great treasure', doubtless echoing the Pauline language about 'earthen vessels'. Where there is 'treasure' there is also risk, whence the Pastoral Letters came no doubt to warn about 'right handling of the word of truth', and 'needing not to be ashamed' in that regard.[2]

Few things are more precarious than the intellectual trust of Christian doctrine in the 'earthen-ness' of its 'vessels' in vocabulary, its users and its hearers, its 'text' so often like the weaving of a fabric.[3] Such accepting to be liable, with the patient pain it may involve, will keep us close to the temper of the Gospel itself. It will also be a salutary monitor of the mind in coming to the art of what, these days, has come to be known as 'dialogue', though in many ways what it demands of resilience and venture had always been present in what New Testament language likes to call 'commendation of the Word'.

---

[1] The 'print' word, verb or noun, in the Ordinal carries the mind to the narrative of Thomas in John 20 and his will to see 'the print of the nails'.

[2] 1 and 2 Timothy and Titus at a point when the expanding Church had had time to develop qualified servants in its local *mise-en-scène*, urgent for the education and nurture of new believers in an alien culture. For example: 1 Timothy 4. 12-16 and 6. 12-21, with 2 Timothy 2. 15.

[3] As in 'text and textile', the word that gives us 'exegesis' is close to 'weaving' in that things are 'woven' there which wait to be 'drawn out'. This might be analogy for how in John 1. 18 the writer sees in Jesus the 'exegesis' (unfolding) of God. The word was used, in the 'Mystery Religions' of the one who presided over initiating rituals.

II

As a norm, then, of longsuffering 'mediation' of faith, there are two points of note at once concerning dialogue. The first must be that it belongs within the trust of ministry. It cannot honestly be some plunge into a pool of neutrality where notes are compared and ideas exchanged, some 'defending of faith' as if 'faith' was an innocuous 'something' presenting no credentials. Merely as 'faith', it could be Nazism, apartheid, paganism, vulgar patriotism or a mystical evasion of identity. One cannot engage with a cipher. 'Faith' as a term must somehow be 'faith' with identity. Thus dialogue will not well belong with neutrality but belong only within ministry. Its personnel will not well be crying *Introibimus ad altare Dei* as if with their backs towards that sanctuary.

Its pursuit, however, within ministry will not mean that it becomes a subtle form of deceptive recruitment, as if no minds were open and no wills honest. It stays loyal to the 'whoso-ever will' of Jesus himself, thoroughly respecting the integrity of the private heart and of the other 'home of souls' with which it converses. It thus conforms to the principle of the Incarnation, as 'Word made flesh' seeks and finds 'the address of the addressee', the divine the human.

Where—to use a Christian term—the laity of all faiths are more and more in mutual contact in a wide range of current pursuits and endless mobility, some 'expert' attention to the faith-relations they encounter is the more a pastoral obligation from their 'clergy'.

It is significant to remember, in this context, what change has take place in a bare quarter century. Archbishop Michael Ramsey favoured a 'Wider Episcopal Fellowship'—a slogan of his day, but held aloof from inter-faith acts in any direction.[4] One could not proceed from an inter-Christian ecumenicity to some inter-religious one. Of course, depending on the criteria—whether doctrinal or emotional—Canterbury may be no farther from Varanasi than Vatican from George Fox, so that 'covenants towards agreements' are now more readily envisaged and attained.[5]

---

[4] He once observed to me that 'not everything religious is either admirable or desirable.' Disparities and contradictions were too great for there to be any 'ecumene of religions'. For good or ill the readiness to engage in the possibility is more forthcoming now, though the problematics are no less.

[5] Like that between Canterbury and the Al-Azhar University in Cairo from 2003.

In this situation it is important to be alert to misgivings which may arise, so that those perplexed among the faithful are not provoked into taking refuge with reactionary versions of some *magisterium*, whether of the Bible or the Church. There are dogmatists in all religions for whom dialogue is a dangerous irrelevance. Such dubious or hostile minds need to be heeded, since their intransigence is only a measure of what is legitimate in the task. That can hardly be a venture within faith that fails its own faithful in what these think to be their loyalty. Though it may never gain a unanimity it should recruit a consensus.

The point here may take the vexed form of a bid for the abandonment of 'mission'. The issue was noted painfully in Chapter 4. One cannot hold, of faith, what one must withhold. The issue about mission, for ministry, has never been whether, but how. Belief systems cannot abrogate from the common human scene, not stay self-admiring, self-inclosed, inside it. There is an element of tribute to another faith in the impulse to commend the implications one's own might hold for it, whether of stimulus or interrogation. Meanings that are not contrary to courtesy will not be forfeit in its practice. Such is the very nature of commendation.[6] The reality of a faith is staked in its speaking and its heeding honesty with another. Thus, for example, Islam's *Allahu akbar* is heard, discerned and explored in the passion of Jesus as the Christ. If it has been enlarged, it has not been contravened, except in a theme in which it partakes and is transformed.

The original Greek term *proselutos* may signify usefully here. So far from the reproachable thing we now call 'proselytism'; it meant 'one who sought to understand', or 'a stranger coming where he sought to be made at home.' He would 'seek out' where he might 'belong' (or whether). It meant, by our crude colloquialism, being interested in the interesting. Dialogue then can no more be the repudiation of mission than mission can be the manipulation of dialogue, or hospitality fulfil itself by withholding its viands.

---

[6] The Greek word *sunistemi* used frequently by Paul in two Letters has the sense of 'establish together'. It recruits what of ideal or goodwill may be present in the other to elicit the recognition of the truth being offered. It seeks to evoke an ally in the act of communication. Thus it carries over into themes what might acquaint persons with each other when a third party 'introduces' either to the other. Paul 'commends Phoebe ...' in that sense no less than he commends Christ. (Romans 16. 1)

III

That hospitality analogy is the more apt here in that its 'guest' corollary is hardly how any of our Scriptures present themselves as 'givens', even 'absolutes' of authority to which due submission must be brought. The Hebrew Tanakh, the unison Bible, the New Testament, the Qur'an—all these mean to be definitive. They are 'oracles' we must reverently heed, not sources we are free to subject to our will. Each will be thus sacrosanct only to its 'people' as 'people of that Book'. For some, this situation may be non-negotiable. But, with due courtesy to disparate 'possessing of possessions', it is possible to take up what 'text-authority' intends, simply by the warrant of 'contents'. Only on behalf of these does the status matter arise. If then, we go gently to each for 'what gently it says'—the authority with which it says it apart—then both parties can escape the 'absolute' without decrying it. Rather it is honoured in the careful heeding of the reading. With all the Scriptures, if in different measure, we can claim that this is what expressly they ask of us.[7]

Going this way, there are things dialogue can usefully achieve. One, urgently, is rebutting mistaken exclusivisms never soundly understood. An obvious example is the dictum in John 14. 6. 'No man comes to the Father but through me.' This has long been cited as confining all knowledge of God as 'father' to Christian auspices. So read, it has offended many as crude intolerance. But so to read ignores the whole Johannine understanding of what is reciprocal between the Fatherhood of God and the Sonship of Jesus. Thus Johannine theology, for which the fullness of this reality is mediated in how and where and why Jesus was 'the Son of *this* Father', in no way cancels Psalm 103. 13 or Malachi 2. 10 or Isaiah 63. 15. These abide in their reading of providence in nature and in history, compatible, too, with much the Qur'an's emphases on God as *Al-Wahhab, Al-Razzaq,* the bestower/provider.

The whole meaning of the Sonship of Jesus deepens and enlarges those descriptives but does not abrogate them, nor disqualify

---

[7] 'Do they not reflect on the Qur'an,' Surahs 4. 82 and 47. 84 ask, while Biblical summons to 'Hear ...', 'Listen ...', and 'consider ...' are frequent.

their use.[8] Dialogue has justified itself if in this way it can eliminate invalid stumbling blocks and also liberate undetected meanings into vigorous circulation. This is no sleight of hand. It is only a sane handling of a transaction in truth.

There is a similar misreading around the alleged 'intolerance' of Acts 4. 12: 'Neither is there salvation in any other.' Again a vital point needs rescuing. Peter is addressing a solidly Jewish assembly, a people whose supreme and crucial hope is—in whatever guise—the 'Messiah'. Now, Peter tells them, hope has been realised, eventuated, fulfilled in 'Jesus crucified'. It needs intense statement in being seemingly so incongruous. And its claim is valid, seeing that 'only in the love that suffers is evil inclusively redeemed.' 'We have no salvation in any other,' since revenge, retaliation, stoicism, law-enforcement, human striving have never redeemed the world, and never can and never will. Peter speaks true but he does not quench some 'smoking flax' elsewhere that might lead men to his Christ.

In such ways, dialogue may avail to reduce instincts of rejection while, in the very process, elucidating precious truth. In this way it is vicarious towards how folk misunderstand. It is vulnerable in that it bears with a genuine problem. It does not say: 'There it is: take it or leave it: I'm telling you.' It does not shelter like a coward in authority: it lets meaning be liberated.

Sometimes this onus in the task of dialogue has to work in the opposite direction, namely calling fuller attention to familiar assumptions. Thus, for example, it is frequent to hear from Muslims that all divine 'messengers' brought the same message, despite the clear flux of circumstance from Noah via Joseph via Moses to David to Muhammad. To include 'Isa (Jesus) in the series makes discovery sharper still. It may be further argued that, in this light the Qur'an integrates them all in its own finality so—perhaps—we need not look outside it. If this forecloses our will to study outside the Qur'an, what diversity we will forfeit. For example, the parables of Jesus are totally absent from the Islamic text.[9]

---

[8] The entire Johannine tradition (Gospel and Letters) has this refrain: 'To have the Son is to have the Father.' A new depth or criterion of divine 'Fatherhood' is ours in the whole significance of Jesus in Sonship which enriches lesser ones. We might draw a parallel from: 'If you would have the music you must have the musician.' A Beethoven is both, one in his 'music-self' as in his 'music-making'. Likewise with dramatist and drama, poet and poetry.

[9] There is an apparent allusion in Surah 2. 87 to the 'messengers' sent to the keepers of the vineyard: 'Some of them they said were liars and some they put to death.' But that is all. The

They were monumentally ignored, together with the Sermon on the Mount. It will readily be evident that Amos was an utterly different figure from Moses, and Jeremiah from Muhammad. Due care must also be taken to inhabit, when reading, the generation and the locale of spirit in which prophethood occurred. It would be odd to stand under their 'sendings' and not inhabit the places of their 'being sent'. The inclusive idea rides roughshod over acute differences of temper, theme, vocation and character. If their alleged singularity of 'message' means the consistency in the divine mind, that very truth tells of a quality ready for engagement with the flux of history. Thus a salutary 'criticism' of an Islamic theme may still be deeply contributory to its intended meaning. While divine revelation is in way chaotic, it has to be situate in histories.

There are other ways in which the vicarious mind can undertake what dialogue entails of caring patience. These have to with vocabularies both ways and with the necessary metaphors Scriptures must employ. What, for example, might the Qur'an mean by 'desiring the face of God'?[10] Or Christianity by its theme of 'original sin'? Not clearly, the mere sequence of heredity which would violate all theology of a sacramental earth and its 'mandate-to-be'. It has to do with the reality by which, being an 'I' as I am essentially by simply existing, incurs *per se* a will to be a self-serving 'me' unless and until I find that which (never 'unselfing me') leads me to a salvation in which my 'me' finds 'unselfish me-ness'. 'Original sin' is thus the ego-centric situation as both inescapable and inwardly critical. 'In sin has my mother conceived me' can, Christianly, have only this meaning.

Such elucidations prevent truth one way from obscuring or denying its other bearings. It also raises the question whether texts can develop discernible meaning they were not first seen to convey? Either way, we are made to realise that they may not merely be cited as if they were not also to be sifted, within the meaning of the Holy Spirit, at once guide and mentor.

only words in the Qur'an verbatim from the teaching of Jesus are: 'Forgive us our sins.' With such great silences there is hardly the same message. And there is the neglect of the great contrasts in historical circumstance as between Banu Thamud (Nabateans?) and Moses at Sinai, or Muhammad at Mecca. There is also the contrast within the Qur'an between the *mise-en-scène* in the two cities of the *Sirah*. Did Muhammad's message remain the same?

[10] *Ibtigha' Wajh Allah* (Surah 2. 272, cf. 92. 18-31) concerns almsgiving, or paying as in Allah's sight. It has also lent itself to Sufi quest for ecstatic *fana'* or absorption into God. See more fully, *The Mind of the Qur'an*, 1973, pp. 163-181. It is clearly a theme of great potential for inter-faith theology.

Metaphors are a large area of this obligation. There is need to take on how far they can be opaque, even repellent, to the unfamiliar. What, conceivably, could John of Patmos mean by 'the Lamb in the midst of the throne'? 'Lamb' has such a long evolution from Levitical sacrifice, via the *Akedah* of Isaac, the life-long tragedy of Jeremiah in which he reached for this analogy to understand his sufferings, to the evangelist John's introduction of Jesus to the two disciples (John 1. 29). In the course of this long lineage quite radical change has occurred—from arbitrary animal ritual immolation to deep, personal acceptance of vocation at great cost. As for being 'in the midst of the throne' what could that mean but that the Passion of Jesus belongs altogether with the sovereignty of God. 'The midst of the throne' is utterly true and truly apt.

It has to be likewise with 'blood cleansing', which is what normally it does not do, seeing that it stains, and it accuses, or it simply flows. Its arriving to 'cleanse' can only refer to how suffering even unto death can take guilt away by the quality of forgiveness it thus—and only thus—affords to wrong-doing summoned to repentance, as retaliation never could. Of this washing is a well-nigh universal image.

Examples of the potential strangeness to others of familiars to us have been many in three previous chapters. Perhaps here we are only taking stones or boulders out of the highway. Intellectual ministry has to pass to major themes with each frankly setting the agenda for the other, the secular no less than the religious. 'All our cares and studies' carry ministry far beyond the pulpit and the sanctuary but only by first belonging there diligently, the better to think beyond them.

With the clue of ministry as mentally vicarious there must be a case for taking into register the things mirrored in literature, the novel, the drama and the media. This takes us off the ground of dogma—Christian or other—and into a kind of at least initial neutrality, maybe of the sort the 'servant' in Isaiah said he came by.[11]

Here the onus in ministry moves from the great themes of faith and from the potential pitfalls of vocabulary, into the caring art of their service in the personal realm, in 'the cure of souls'. 'To those who are

---

[11] Isaiah 50. 4-9, both as to its place in the context and as to the identity of the 'servant', and of the 'education' to which he referred. There is a 'neutrality' in literature in that it portrays without preaching and thus 'presents for a verdict' without enjoining it. What is 'in season' 'finds' the heart. 'Learn' long had this double sense of 'teach' as well as 'learn'. In the art of ministry they still belong together.

weary', from whatever source, must be the 'word in season'. The term has become proverbial, inasmuch as what the heart needs some other heart must undertake with the timelessness of human 'season'.

We have noted earlier the vital place of this 'learning' theme in the experience of 'Messiah' himself. Is not 'the servant' recalled in the Matthean passage about Jesus' loaded invitation into discipleship—loaded in allusion to a 'yoke', and in its warning against all 'unlowliness of heart'? 'Learn of me' that my Messiahship may be the norm of your discipleship.

In the Isaian passage, the 'servant' only becomes 'as a teacher' by dint of the deep—and for him—harsh learning experience. If both are to be the quality of Christian ministry it must be well taught in the *Zeitgeist* by steady reckoning with clues in literature which that context yields into its education.[12]

Here a Gospel parable holds a powerful hint about inadequacy.

> 'A friend of mine, out of his way, has come unto me and I have nothing to set before him. (Luke 11. 6)

What follows is a story of improvisation, of borrowing from elsewhere (with some loss of face but admirable promptitude) what he sadly lacks within himself. That initial 'has come *unto me*' makes haunting echo of Matthew 11. 28, which said: 'You will find.' Does the story fit what George Herbert once called 'the sweet mediocrity of our native Church'?

What is so telling is that note about 'out of his way'. Had the would-be guest 'turned in for a night' or was he 'off life's road'? All too often in our time the casual is where the crisis is, which nothing casual will satisfy. Then the Gospel has to be a somebody with the wit to respond. Thanks to the meaning of the Incarnation, there is no disembodied Christianity.[13] 'Lend me three loaves' is a plea the Christian minister may well address to the literati whether of the secular world or of other religious culture. Not themselves 'the bread of life', their

---

[12] What self-searchings, for example, are present for Muslims in the novels of Najib Mahfuz or in novels for readers in the West ever since Defoe.

[13] Or, as we might say, its policy is people. 'I in them' was how Christ, according to John, told it. 'Christianity' as a word is a derivative of 'Christian' just as 'Christian' is of 'Christ'.

neutrality, with their realism may, as borrowings can, deliver it via the 'learning' it affords towards 'the season of the words'.[14]

Could this be what that long tradition concerning 'a learned clergy' was always intended to mean?

IV

If so, these mental realms of any 'ordering by wounded hands' must bring their intellectual cares for faith amid a society 'out of its way', into a deeply moral commitment—by light and energy from those realms—to the rigours of the common good. The private aspects of this ethical dimension in personal life must await a third section of this chapter, their claims, however, must be assumed throughout.

What, in short, is the commission of Christian ministry in the weal and woe in the contemporary scene? Its first duty could be clearly to appreciate its own fragility. People no less 'out of their way' in the world, are less likely than the forlorn in the parable to seek out the Church as a friend. The song that enquires: 'Were you there when I needed a neighbour, were you there?' was the Lord himself, not 'the man off the street'.

It is noteworthy in twentieth century literature how even minds aware of intimations of transcendence in their human experience fail, or simply omit, to refer this dimension to any formally Christian frame of reference. The trend was evident enough in the nineteenth century. Wordsworth, for example, with his nature mysticism, was no Thomas Traherne, no Henry Vaughan, marrying his faith closely with any sustained pattern of doctrine or liturgy in which to find its necessary expression.

Any such 'necessity' is implicitly rejected. Rather a studied dissociation from dogma is instinctively preferred. The transcendent is the more truly acknowledged, either in the flow of an intuitive poetry or in a privacy persuading itself that it can disown the crippling vested interests it associates with the 'religious' connection. It is, as it were, itself 'religious' but in an anonymous way.

---

[14] The parable must not be pressed too far, or it becomes misused. Yet how often, in ministry, 'the cupboard is dry' when even secular neighbours can replenish us 'at midnight' if we are enough driven to consult them.

This avoidance of the forms of Christian faith and worship has doubtless been accentuated more recently by perceptions of how inimical to the transcendent religions in general can be by their perverse vulgarity and their oppressive ways, especially—in Western eyes—the frequent image of Islam. 'A plague on all their houses' is readily invoked, so that even faiths genuinely deferential to their own scepticism are equally shunned. Christian ministry, therefore, needs to be alive to its own unwantedness and only wisely relate that unwantedness to the unwantedness of 'God in Christ'. Taking that onus duly is no small part of how its own hands are 'wounded'. 'Holy Orders' only prelude this contemporary situation: they ensure no immunity from it. 'Church Going', as we have noted, can be a very ambiguous thing, curious perhaps about architecture or vaguely impressionable about history or nostalgia for a lingering-past but in no way importunate to 'borrow bread', like the man in the parable.

Thus the will to preach is hugely discounted and those who 'have a gospel to proclaim' do not have a stance that 'lifts the stones out of the highway.' His generation tolerated the wit and the witticisms of G K Chesterton and the charm of the plots he weaved and had even a sneaking admiration for his over-worked gift of paradox, but they had only demure or dismay about his preaching ways. What academic eyebrows C S Lewis raised—for all his academic professionalism—when he stooped to commend 'Mere Christianity' or announced his sequence from atheism into theism and from theism into 'God in Christ'. *Confessio* of that commendatory order—it was assumed—was improperly intrusive into 'English Literature'.

A little reflection, and any lively 'lay' awareness in that vast realm from Shakespeare's Sonnets to Browning's *The Ring and the Book* and beyond quickly register how absurd that attitude. Yet its absurdity measures how an anti-commitment prejudice may go.

This diffidence, less or more, concerning 'religious' allegiance, it might be argued, is genuinely concerned to be 'existential', 'devout' as it were, 'serious' and engaged into 'the mystery of things'. It finds flippancy abhorrent. It represents precisely that 'heart to feel and understand' that informs the origins of Christian faith, the origins we have examined here, as they applied just that quality of 'existential realism' to the significance of Jesus as the Christ and of the verdict about us humans which his ministry and his Passion embraced and illumined in its reach into our dark.

Yet reluctance persists for any 'serious' souls to allow that sequence now or concede its credal and liturgical claim upon their mind and soul.

A salient example of the point at issue here is evident in the phenomenal success of J R R Tolkien and his famous creation of 'Middle Earth' in his *Simarillion* and *Lord of the Rings* and other writings. For there are no discernible avowals of Christianity in them, despite the author's staunch identity with Roman Catholic Christian auspices. His aim seems simply to have been to amuse and entertain and raise no doctrinal question about the 'humane' world he conjures into narrative charm. He is content to engender appreciation of his fantasy world and its intuited values and its imagery, but its actors are nowhere moved to 'borrow' Christian loaves with which to feed the passing reader who, anyway, is not 'out of his way', unless it be in quest of verbal delight.

Thus Tolkien and his appeal witness to this quiet but radical detachment from the web of Christian doctrine for its ethics and its value-world. It leaves the critical reader wistful towards a world it would be 'nice to believe in' if only we could believe it real, whereas we must be content to let it caressingly divert us. One notable feature, re an absent Christianity, is that 'Middle-Earth' evil is simply negative. Hence the absence of all that 'the Passion' has us comprehend. The world is more comforting precisely in being less 'heavily laden'.[15] A doctrinal Christianity knows it has learned to be—and stay—more 'serious' still. But how to commend that necessity to a reluctant or an escapist world?

This feature of Tolkien is the more noteworthy in view of his personal practice of devout Mass attendance. It can hardly be, in one so erudite, what Thomas Mann once described as a romantic feeling for the Roman Catholic Church, dubbing his 'Protestantism' merely 'a culture and not a religion'. Mann saw churches as affording escape

> '... from the seething unrest of some metropolis or other, surrounded suddenly by echoing quiet colored gloom breathed on by the fragrance of centuries.'

---

[15] For fuller discussion, see Brian Rosebury, *Tolkien, A Cultural Phenomenon*, London, 2003, pp. 152-55. 'The experience of transcendent order giving value to the world can no longer be credibly propounded as a datum, but must be glimpsed, as a possibility or a hope, through a persuasive evocation of human experience.' but see also *Reading the Lord of the Rings*, ed. Robert Eaglestone, London, 2005, where Tolkien is cited commenting on his unison of devotion to his Church and his 'non-preaching' stance.

All Your Cares and Studies

If theatricality in the ritual aided that sense of 'comforting superstition', it made for a pseudo form of piety. Yet, with another side of his mind, Mann saw 'kneeling persons traitors to the dignity of mankind ... a refuge receives you where the Cross is raised for prayer.'[16] There is a double irony in this recurrent view, in the contemporary world, of the sanctuary as a refuge and liturgy as a haven, so far from that real 'help from the sanctuary' which knows 'the bread and wine' as 'Messiah's diet' and the place where, by its summons, we 'present ourselves, our souls and bodies to be a living sacrifice,' both rested in the presence and renewed into its obedience. The 'romance' of Holy Communion was never of the soporific order. For we kneel to the transcendent 'mystery' of 'the body and the blood' and to no theatre-born solace which, as Thomas Mann saw it, was to be meekly non-political.

How then does Christian faith, with worship duly 'telling' it in word and symbol, wisely inhabit the political order? Sundry Christendoms have had their long possessive answers, while Islam since Medina, has seen itself as inherently political.

To be sure, we kneel only to God but, in that kneeling bring the political order there with us in terms of what William Blake called 'mental fight' for its sanity, its honesty, its 'godly' discipline—and these fit to take us off our knees.

'Holy Orders in the Church of England', whatever they may face in wider mission, obtain or belong under three highly exacting circumstances and with one supreme principle of faith. The three are the forms and practisers of democracy with complete adult suffrage, electoral process and a party system for the testing of ideas: the symbols of Establishment which at least affirm that the State is no 'absolute', subject to no transcendent reference: and a well-nigh universal and strongly local architectural presence across the whole national landscape. The third doubtless brings many problems, as buildings ever must. It prompts calls for other ways of meeting to escape the utter negligibility for many of ecclesiastical structures. Those monuments of historic faith may even ironically provoke columnists to select 'One Thousand Best Churches', with architecture their only relevance.[17] Even so their presence may still

---

[16] See Hermann Kurzke, *Thomas Mann: A Biography*, London, 2002, p. 243. However, he was ready also to 'kneel before Pope Pius XII and expressly remark how easy and natural this was for him.' (p. 242)

[17] Thus Simon Jerkins in a handsome, much valued survey of striking edifices. He seems not to have registered the isolation of one feature that might identify what was 'best' about churches.

'visit' the mind of 'visitors', as places 'to grow wise in',[18] while their space and location lend themselves to various kinds of local communal usage. Their very presence, given an adequate clergy and 'inner folk', remains a visible sign and sacrament. It is no idle romanticism that an 'Angelus' can still be heard or a steeple appeal to more than 'chasing'.

The second and third return us searchingly to the first. For democracy, with its role for the supposedly autonomous individual, is no sure panacea for the ills, no ready means to the hopes, of a wayward society. For its processes are subject to manipulation by vested interest and its arguments stymied in the ears of the bored. It too often fails to kindle the deference it needs, while—as Martin Buber had it—'the word "I" remains the shibboleth of mankind.'

It labours under the banality of mass communication. It pre-supposes capacities of intelligence, commitment and discipline which it cannot of itself ensure. It can well leave more than half an electorate disinterested in its workings and careless of its fruits. Thus, ironically, it connives among the absentees with the anonymity of the self while purporting to engage it. Democracy is thus what has been called 'the political cognate of romanticism'. Yet what, less open to the blandishments of power, can wisdom propose as a better substitute? How do we save ourselves or society from a cynicism which has its origin in ourselves, aided and abetted by scepticism of the very art of language and the 'voidance' of any 'anthropic principle' honouring our human significance?[19] That 'I came to save the world' (12. 47) on the lips of the Johannine Christ sounds in our present ears as incongruous as it seemed elsewhere.[20]

Meanwhile, our society would seem more and more bent on being entertained, 'trivialised' by a sort of counter act of the trivial.[21] The sane power of sustained attention wanes under the media usage of slick images and brash headlines. Modesty, courtesy, reticence fall

---

[18] The sentiment—wistful or still sceptical—of Philip Larkin's poem 'Church Going'. See *Collected Poems*, ed. Anthony Thwaite, 2003, pp. 56-57. He meant 'Going' not for worship but for a curiosity, that felt many dissuasives.

[19] That principle which perceives a world suited to, and for, human sub-sovereignty within a purposive creation, not a world which confronts us with our own irrelevance even as its 'spectators'.

[20] Was it Ionesco who wrote in an essay that 'My plays do not try to save the world'?

[21] One of those two-way words, like 'brutalise'—often used to describe what 'imperialisms' do to 'natives', when it also reacts to do the same to them. They too are 'brutalised'. So it is with the 'trivial' and those who let it be their diet.

by the wayside, while the easy invocation of 'change' has scant care for the testedness of old tradition.

We witness a penal system weighed down by its prison population and the inadequacies of its own working philosophy. Doubtless the well-springs of human magnanimity abide but they are too often dried or drained away by a compensation culture legally enforced, as if we can no longer 'take' adversity without resentment. There follows a decay of old-style volunteerism in caring for adolescents, as scout-leaders and the like used to do—or teachers reluctant for 'adventure groups' for fear of litigation. We thus allow a mood of inhibition which deters us from well-doing and well-being. We would rather be safe than serving.

What, in this context, of the urge to identify, register and publicly locate paedophiles, while the media and the cult of advertising so far concentrate on pre-occupying people with their sexuality when it had better be a theme of reticent wonder and grateful delight. Society seems restlessly at odds with itself, its sanity and its inward peace, while a certain contempt of the West develops where its sophistications fit uneasily on other cultures, defensively or angrily reacting to its example.

There is a subtle issue also, in the recent pleading for the criminal justice system to concede the right of sufferers to plead in court about the sentencing of the criminals at whose hands they have known deep tragedy. Will this bring into play a potential 'retaliatory' dimension in formal proceedings? What does it imply for long tradition of 'the King's—or the Queen's—peace' so that even, as jurors' oath has it, a squalid drunken brawl was 'the issue drawn between our Sovereign Lord the King and the prisoner at the bar'. This 'royal peace' tradition was only long and painfully achieved.[22] It withdrew all private quarrels, all personal vendettas, into a single resolution. Doubtless it is seemly that the aggrieved should be keenly known as such, but is it not within the competence of judges and of counsel to comprehend all the measures of what confronts them? Does some recrimination lurk in the sufferer joining with the prosecution?

Griefs and aggrievings come so heavily, either from the drug culture and the crime it induces, or from unbridled sexuality. What

---

[22] From the time of Henry II when a royal judiciary travelled to take over where lords and barons had meted out oppressive judgements within their local 'peaces'. The notion of the King's Peace, taking over all men's indictable quarrels has long been a basic concept of English law.

should we think about the upsurge in the demands of homosexuality and the apologia that talks so readily about 'inclusion' and homophobia, without duly reckoning with other aspects of the foundations of society? The debate about its 'given-ness', even its 'vocation', for the genuinely homosexual is already won, but need this mean that it has to be aggressively pursued into disparagement of the heterosexual condition, its inherence in marriage, its readiness for procreation, parenthood and the family? Need homosexuality monopolise that word 'gay' or malign the first 'Lesbians', as if Wordsworth now had no right to his 'pleasure with the daffodils'? Is the sense of social constraints, factors not latent but acquired, not present in *some* arrivals into homosexual practice? Need it invariably be that the dignity of same-sex friendships, with all their commendability, are inevitably supposed to proceed into furtive, bed-seeking, sexual expression?

Here the Christian and, even more conscionably, the priestly mind have need to reckon with the sacramental and the natural in the due hallowing of the body as a realm of wondrous trust. It is something much in dispute. But if 'male and female' means anything, it means that an obvious organic fitness (not some 'awkward' one, like foot-painting artists) is what a sacramental 'minding' requires.[23] For in mankind all humans are mutually involved. Only what is natural is sacramental.

There is, surely, a New Testament parallel available in the vexed question of an 'inclusion' of homosexuality—the ready 'inclusion', that is, of the condition and its genuine physical incidence in personal experience of personhood in the body. The 'condition' as genuine, honest and God-given, should not be in question, still less as being fit for accusation. Such ready inclusion, however, needs—for many—to be firmly distinguished from homosexual practice, most of all if this obtains inside the Christian ministry. For, otherwise, there is a threat to the friendships *per se* which have long been a benediction to society without their taking to bodily indulgence or lusting into bed. For then the hard question emerges as to whether on Christian ground—in that all living is priestly—whether what is not 'natural' can be duly sacramental, if 'the body is the temple of the Holy Spirit.' Or have not all been praying daily, that 'our hearts may be ordered by Thy

---

[23] That analogy has been used to justify what, otherwise, must seem bizarre even if actually feasible. Doubtless the concept of what is 'natural' may not be categorically resolved. There can be less question about what is duly 'sacramental'.

governance to do always what is righteous in Thy sight,' as a purpose about which we are duly caring?

The precedent from apostolic time that can be adduced here avails in the issue of 'idol-meats' in 1 Corinthians 10 and Romans 14. When an idol's name had been invoked over meat was that idol 'legitimated' as such, so that eating the meat involved acknowledgement of the idol? Minds with scruples, or 'idle/idol' fears said Yes, and therefore we must abstain. Idols matter and 'one can't be too careful.'

By contrast, those who thought themselves 'adult' insisted that idols are non-entities, thus their invocation means nothing and all meats are clean. We are free to eat what we will. Had not Jesus also, in a similar non-pagan, Jewish scrupulosity, made all meats 'clean'?

But wait, the scrupulous un-grown-up fellow has a valid point. Idolatry is subtle and pervasive—not merely in the way meat is 'sanctified' but in how society invokes what is other than God alone as their worship, their 'liberty', their defiance, pseudo-deities such as 'us and our folk', power, greed, profit, sex, the state. Unless we are alive to all these evils and wrongs with a critical vigilance we connive with false worship. Conceding this, the liberty-people think again. Moreover, 'endeavouring (strenuous word) to keep the unity of the Spirit in the bond of peace', 'the strong' resolve 'to eat no meat while the world lasts,' or at least until the simpletons 'grow up'. An arguable liberty is forfeit to the common good.

The analogy fits exactly, if we will allow that the scrupulous or the free about homosexual practice (as distinct from condition) are like their counterparts about 'idol meats'. There is the same call to forbear with the 'primitives' in mind, as an imperial style, American liberty dubs it, a will to restrain the notion that we are pioneers of some urgent, brutal education of the whole Church—with its culture-set liabilities of relationship—into a proper mind. Has this stance reviewed its own enormous egoism, its falsification of 'the bond of peace'? The notion of 'pioneer' status that despises any common mind is a heinous self-esteem.

Contrariwise, a group of Nigerian bishops, distancing themselves from Canterbury, describe even the homosexual condition as a 'cancer'. Have they never read how Paul, to the Romans insisted of the other party: 'To his own master he stands or falls'? Who are these 'judging another man's servant'? Can they not concede that his reading of his Lord's will might be sincere? 'The bond of peace' lays its claim on either side. Nor is their point in arguing that the pioneer would be foregoing what some vocation—of superiority—demands of him, or that in scorning some *consensus fidelium* he honours 'the mind of Christ'.

What is noteworthy about both parties in this question is how they are liable, by emotive language, to let some *lex talionis* creep into controversy. The will to be right moves into the will to reject. Issue passes into retaliation, some *nemo impune me lacesset* ('Let nobody ride over me and get away with it') rather than *decus et tutamen* ('Graciously and seemly')—those Latin inscriptions on the rim of the English pound. The parties in their advocacies have not learned to be vulnerable to the points that challenge them and, therefore, are no longer vicarious in shouldering the burden either of truth or unity. Both these treasures—and their unison—have descended into a 'who wins' conflict. Do we not find, at every point, Jesus' supreme abrogation of the *lex talionis* key to the sequential vulnerable/vicarious pattern of relation any duly Christian handling of dialogue and decision must learn to take? It is central to this whole logic that it was the heart of everything 'Messianic' concerning Jesus and of his Gethsemane most of all.

v

Some in Christian tradition, facing a welter of perplexities and the unease they bring, have called for something like a 'counter-culture', a withdrawal into studied contradiction of a wayward world. 'They would be safe where no storms come' as the poet thought monasteries to sing, disowning a world for which they had lost heart. To think of a 'counter-culture' is to forsake the vocation to be vicarious, since it withdraws from the vulnerability of love. To care is to belong. If we would redeem we must relate. In line with the Incarnation of the Lord, we cannot exempt our humanity from what others make of theirs.[24]

Moreover, such withdrawal is likely to provoke a counter to the counter—which was always the problem of the Pharisee, lit. 'the

---

[24] The rubric 'not to condemn but to save' (John 3. 17) is not a total contrast, nor an absolute negative. It means, surely, that rebuke and reproach come in the task and the cost of the 'saving'.

separatist'. 'Malvolio' is the name he gets where 'cakes and ale' are in demand. He 'wishes ill.' So while he symbolises an issue he never joins it. The libertine does not own himself undone: he feels himself justified. Jesus had reproach for the Pharisees, not for their 'righteousness', but for lack of an 'exceeding' of it which might take in the 'publicans'.

Accordingly, the Christian faith of the Incarnation, of 'the Word made flesh' and 'dwelling among us', must inhabit the world these serve. Only so can they ever prove vulnerable or find themselves vicarious. That *to* which the Word comes is that *in* which it is present, the divine to the human, the human for the divine. Such is the very principle of Christhood, when 'and was made man' has 'man' in its full, generic sense where 'male' and 'female' do not isolate but only contrast.

This incarnation principle at the heart of the faith itself has, perforce, to characterize the Church which serves it, as participatory in the living world, incurring, not eluding, its burdens. It may seem trite to say that the business, therefore, of the parish or the chaplaincy is to enable its people to belong, in all forms of their presence, with the tasks of God's love, as faith knows them through the 'God in Christ'. The 'mental fight' goes with what this could mean in the explicit context of profession, role, activity and relation in which they 'have their being' and pursue their meaning within 'the time of life'. Then conduct will be the clue to character and character the evidence of faith, insofar as words also will show reason. The writer in Titus 2. 10 was bold to call this 'adorning the doctrine of God as Saviour', perhaps recalling a psalmist about 'the beauty of the Lord our God', always in line with 'the work of our hands' (Psalm 90. 17) or—as he might have added—'the labour of our minds'.

This is other than what some in the nineteenth century called the 'Work Ethic' where well-doing often arrived at 'doing well'. It is rather the call to a 'Life Sacrament', the cast of mind and set of soul which the Letters of the New Testament steadily enjoined on their readers. 2 Thessalonians 3. 13 dubs it *kalopoieo* and five times in 1 Peter come *agathopoieo* or *agathopoia* and—perhaps with an allusion to Matthew 11. 28—there is a hint of the 'weariness' the 'well-doing' might encounter from within the self or, doubtless, from the ever pressing counter-drag of a pervasive and hostile Roman imperial culture.

That this was no effortless magnanimity but a deliberate sacrament of the self as gathered into the human world underlies the steady element of greeting across the membership the Letters convey. That sense of the personal was the corollary of a costly self-expenditure in the world at large. We should doubtless beware of idealising the New Testament Church revealed in the Epistles, few and selective as they are. Yet there is no mistaking their commitment to Christ as, by the same token, a liability towards the world, its sanity, its peace, its suffering and its hope. There was even a fusion in vocabulary of 'worship/service' in that *logikes latria*, 'logical offering', or 'self/sanctuary', to which Paul in Romans turns from his faith-exegesis as its practical logic in the world at large (Romans 12. 1).

In the contemporary world this New Testament faith/ethic can only mean that 'cares and studies this way' apply whatever of heritage, education, skill, talent, circumstance, wealth or indigence have made of us, to the personal and public world where the Christ already is. Jesus called it 'putting your hand to the plough'. If such is the being of the Christian, such also is the 'order of the wounded hands'. How far this joins issue with mortal time from John Milton's early view

> '... of this dim spot
> Which men call earth, and with low-thoughted care
> Confin'd and pester'd in this pinfold here,
> Strive to keep up a frail and feverish being.'[25]

VI

With this understanding of Christian destiny in human terms what of an individual ministry called to nurture and fulfilment in the open world where politics, the arts, science, the commerce and all things societal proceed? What of it inwardly in the perpetuation of all that Ordinal began? Or, in the language of the Latin world:

> 'O Sacerdos, quid es tu?
> Non es a te, quia de nihilo ... Nihil et omnia.'

John Donne, Dean of St Paul's, an ecclesiastic more apt than many to dramatise himself via pulpit language, pondered the answer

---

[25] John Milton, 'Comus', lines 5-8, 'pinfold' being a "pound" in which to pen stray or distrained cattle or sheep.

in lines he wrote 'To Mr Tilman after he had taken Orders'. Donne knew well to begin with 'hand unto the lowly plough', and to note 'Lay scornings of the Ministry'. 'What bringst thou home with thee?' he asked. 'How is thy mind affected by the vintage?' Was the metaphor right of 'steele toucht with a loadstone'? What of new thoughts, new motions? 'Thou art the same materials as before', he warned. 'Only the stampe is changed.' Was the prosaic Mr Tilman, 'new feather'd with celestiall love' since he, as angels are, is 'bearing God's message'?

The *fortissimo* came in Donne's final climax with its wry concluding line:

> 'What function is so noble as to bee
> Embassadour to God and destinie?
> To open life, to give kingdomes to more
> Than kings give dignities: to keepe heaven's doore?
> Maries prerogative was to beare Christ, so
> 'Tis preachers to convey him, for they doe
> As angels out of clouds, from pulpits speake,
> To bless the poore beneath, the lame, the weake.'[26]

'The poore neath the pulpit' indeed! Donne's world—and his loftiness—are no longer ours.

'This thy coronation', he had told this Tilman, borrowing the odd imagery of a new king's head on new coinage, when only the usual substance is there under the new face. Oddly, yet duly—perhaps beyond his own subtle knowing—Donne captures the theme of the person and the office, the self and the status, the 'I' who is and the role 'I' serves. Since they cannot be parted, how readily they may compete, so that 'office' ministers to 'self', the selfhood usurps the deacon, priest or bishop. How to be and not to be is the abiding theme, to be *qua* mandated, not to be by virtue of an un-self-conscious humility, innocent of the clinging pride which the very incidence of authority might induce.

Thus 'cares and studies all this way'—earlier pondered in their intellectual and social focus vis-à-vis the laity and the world—have their deepest liability in the privacy of the heart.

---

[26] *The Poems of John Donne*, ed. H J C Grierson, Oxford, 1933, pp. 319-21.

This must be why the criteria of ordained ministry must be rigorously met in full self-discipline. As and when practising homosexual clergy are sure that theirs is an honest sacrament of the body, there is still a 'care and study' about how their menage fits and serves the charge of ministry. Within many a marriage there may be 'journeying oft' in some far-flung episcopate or cure which bring acute loneliness and, with it too, a discipline of chastity. The mentality that argues 'If we can we may and if we may we will' has no place at 'the laying on of hands', or 'the vows then made for me' seeing they were them made by me. The mood of easy indulgence which makes for the alcoholic has no part in perfecting ministry in the sight of God. This is no 'holier than thou' posture but no more than what a high athleticism is to the athlete and in line with Paul's use of that analogy. Likewise in every other theme of self-negotiation.

Robert Browning's Bishop Blougram was well aware of how readily the very doctrine in his *confessio* might consciously be drawn into a licence to deceive. He became the casuist of his own self-congratulation, 'drawing comfortable breath'. He more than suspects his own sincerity yet clings to his episcopal tenure:

> '... now folk kneel
> And kiss my hand—of course the Church's hand.
> Thus am I made, this life is best for me
> And thus that it should be I have procured ...'[27]

Blougram, it would seem, had the cunning and the nonchalance about his calling that enabled many a pluralist in careless times to slacken in their cures.

Article 26 of the Church of England might assure itself that 'the Unworthiness of the Minister ... hinders not the effectiveness of the Sacrament' but the ruling at least told a misgiving that it might be wrong. For it drew attention to how intimately office and person belonged together. Thus the more ornate and, as it were, dramatised the ritual, the more self-conscious the fusion of the two became. Likewise the potential self-congratulation of the pulpit could be no less compromising of a 'purity of heart'. It is well *Introibo ad altare Dei*—be it preaching 'the Word of the Cross' or the ordering of 'bread and wine'

---

[27] Robert Browning, *The Poetical Works*, Oxford, 1905, pp. 437-448.

in Communion—should be ever prefaced by the threefold plea where 'all hearts are open, all desires known and no secrets hid.'

'Perfectly to love, worthily to magnify' leads us into what the poet called 'His Easter in us'.[28] And we, with that 'Easter in us', ever with the likes of William Blake when he cried: 'I behold London, a human, awful wonder of God.'

---

[28] Gerard Manley Hopkins, *The Poems*, ed. W H Gardner and N H MacKenzie, Oxford, 1970, p. 63, Stanza 35 of 'The Wreck of the Deutschland'; 'Let him easter in us, be a dayspring in the dimness of us.'

Chapter 8
THE OBEDIENCE OF TIME

I

Thomas De Quincey, with the perspectives of his opium addiction, ends his *Suspiria de Profundis*:

> 'Death we can face: but knowing, as some of us do, what is human life, which of us is it that without shuddering could (if consciously we were summoned) face the hour of birth?'[1]

The poet Thomas Traherne would not have agreed.[2] For him birth was hailed as a privilege and greeted as a prize. In any event we are not consulted. Deacons, priests and bishops, their Ordinal and long tradition assume, are taking on a life that is for life. Short of something catastrophic, it is like marriage—a pledging 'till death do us part,' this me and this ministry. Though in this way a 'birth into a life', it is firmly prior-consulted.

> 'Do you think that you are truly called according to the will of our Lord Jesus Christ ... to the Ministry of the Church?'

preceded by:

> 'Do you trust that you are inwardly moved by the Holy Spirit to take upon you this Office and Ministration, to serve God for the promoting of his glory, and in the edifying of his people?'

---

[1] Thomas De Quincey, *Confessions of An English Opium-Eater and Other Writings*, Oxford World Classics, 1985, pp. 180-81.

[2] By contrast Traherne anticipates birth and with retrospective gladness in 'Salutation' wonders about 'where he was before he was,' exulting in what has come to pass in giving him being. See *Centuries. Poems and Thanksgivings*, ed. H M Margoliouth, Oxford, 1936. Vol. ii, p. 6.

These personal questions have necessarily followed the public ones about being 'duly qualified'.

The Ordinal is thus asking for a commitment into time at a solemn time of commitment. 'Shudder' would be a curious word to coin at such a point. 'Daunting' it might be, in view of such a pledgedness to the years. What might they hold? As De Quincey had earlier written in *Suspiria*: 'In today already walks tomorrow.'[3] What may it 'walk away with'? Personal faith has its vicissitudes, likewise also does doctrinal faith. How tormented John Henry Newman was about genuine 'development apostolical' as something neither creeds nor Canon had resolved.

What of these adventures of faith itself in the caring of entrusted souls, the vigilance of loyal minds such as ordinands are sworn to be? They will not be preaching the sermons of a Lancelot Andrewes, not merely because they lack his wit and Latin but in that there is no 'obedience of time' that way. Nor would the sylvan tones of Newman fill a University Church to its whole pew capacity today as once they did. Oxford is no longer a precinct of a precious inter-Anglican introspection that matters deeply to its quadrangles. The architecture of churches and colleges blessedly persists to charm and dream but its denizens reside otherwise. *Dominus illuminatio mea* only sentimentally endures. What founders meant by it was always more than the psalmist had in mind.

How does a novice deacon deal with theses volatile texts, these shifting sands of culture and the times? And what, in that care, of the flux of his/her own tides of mood, despair and hope? Just as Christian marriage as a life-long will to mutuality exists to enable what it demands by its own quality whereby intent and attainment are one, so the engagement of faith with ministry and of ministry with faith must do likewise. Both have a present continuous tense. Such is the theology of the Ordinal in the very 'laying on of hands'. But how is the inner sufficiency of office to be achieved in the long exercise of its commission? 'This naughty world' where 'Christ's sheep' are worldwide 'scattered' means, in the language of archaism, a world that brings so many things 'to nought'. Ministry is closer to that experience in often sharing it, the more so with those conspiracies of enmity and malice we studied in Chapter 6. The more engaged to care in society and

---

[3] De Quincey, *loc. cit.*, p. 160, quoting Samuel Taylor Coleridge.

there to commend a faith, the more liable to the burdens of the one and the more prone to the stresses of the other.

There is a special Anglican (or 'Free Church') quality to this situation, given its long tradition of a 'learned clergy' ready to let the interrogation of the pew enter the thinking of the pulpit and to integrate the ministry of the sacrament with the ministry of the Word. The Roman—and other—'Catholic' tradition has entrusted all such final, faith office, and indeed its scholarship to the *magisterium*, the kind of mind-sanctuary which Newman sought and believed himself to find in Roman authority, infallible whenever it said it was. By so doing, he sought relief from his great fear, the hard onus of 'private judgement' and, with it, the risky 'liberalism' which was his arch-foe. But how did the solution of 'submission' resolve the matter? For there was, inevitably, an act of 'private judgement' in opting for the authority which was to give him relief from it. Its worth, its credentials, its right to rule him—these, as he long struggled to identify them—had evoked his own decision. Must it not always be so with the things of faith, whether this proceeding relates to a guarantor of doctrine or to doctrine as its own 'persuader'?[4] Ever since the worthy Richard Hooker, or indeed since Archbishop Anselm, Anglicans have wanted personally to understand in order corporately to believe. William Tyndale had striven at great cost in suffering, and with eminent skills of language, to give the Scripture to the ploughboy in the confidence that ideally he could understand, even if the text had to be 'chained' in churches for the literate to read it to him.

It is true that, by long structural design, that lectern and the pulpit are kept distinct on either side a crossing or an arch. That 'space' is also honoured in the rubric which routinely distinguishes what is being 'read' from what may be added in comment as homily. 'Here begins ... here ends ...' may be tedious to hear but they are appropriate where what is read is to be 'ministered' through the mind and heart of a deacon/priest/bishop. These must belong with it but it will register through them. Such is the partnership of 'the Word', lest reliance on the sacrament of 'bread and wine' alone should lack its message to the mind in its symbols to the soul or the deep emotion that dwells in their unison.

---

[4] Echoing Paul's familiar *pepeismai* of Romans 8. 39: 'For I am persuaded ...'

II

Leadership of worship in this way is, by the same token, a steady exercise in faith-possession. We have seen many aspects in all the foregoing pages of such faith-possession in converse with Jew and Muslim and the 'banishers' of articulate conviction concerning God and Christ. The 'cares' of sustaining studies we have also pondered, as 'office' commands both mind and will. There is comfort in the fact that the puzzlements of time and place which bewilder and oppress are no less there for those faith's 'office' serves. Blessedly, the task is not to impose or guarantee its meanings-in-trust, but only to 'commend'. Paul's intriguing word is *sunistesin* which has the sense of 'establishing together', as both God's strategy and the ministry's (Romans 5. 8 and 2 Corinthians 4. 2). Faith, rather like a wooer, goes out to solicit what hopefully has the ability to reciprocate and to find its yearnings confirmed. Does 'faith comes by hearing' (Romans 10. 17), have this implication—'by heeding', to be sure, but in that heeding is found to be akin? The Christian faith brings its own *argumentum*,[5] as we have seen in the first two chapters but that 'theme in presentation', being 'the wisdom of God' concerning 'the gentleness of Christ' is 'standing at the door to knock.' Whatever loss of nerve may come about discharge of ministry there need be none about the nerve of its meaning. The world as it is ensures its perennial relevance.

It follows that all likely issues of personal integrity, as we noted them in the 'Therefore' Chapter, are best resolved in the fidelity of the faith itself, invested—as that fidelity is—in the trust it places in the heart and will of its 'faithful people'. Thanks to this mutuality, it is right to read 'the obedience of faith' as not only the one our 'obedience' brings in tribute to it, but also a resilience it possesses to respond to all that changing times and scenes require of it. We studied in Chapters 4, 5 and 6, how readily its resources met the claims adversity or contradiction laid upon it. Making itself good in every vicissitude of thought or action worked to refine its language or reformulate its metaphors. The Fathers' formula *Per necessitatem Christiani* is thus no rigorous dictum but the logic of a truth responsive to what finds the 'necessity' unproven or illusory. Since ministry serves no 'coward thing',

---

[5] In the original Latin sense, not of a 'conflict' but 'a setting down and setting forth of a case'.

we draw courage in the fears and the failures of office from the very quality of the truth we serve.

It is not that truth somehow changes or adapts but only that it proves always and everywhere perennial, having—as the 'suffering servant' in Isaiah yearned—its own 'word in season' in the weariness of the world, the 'word' of its own 'learning', as never to be unlearned, either in the mind of God or in the being of the Church.

If, then, in the vagary of mood or hesitations of mind, our *Introibo ad altare Dei* of 'Word and Sacrament' we reach the end of *our* tether, it will never be as with Jeremiah, crying: 'O Lord, Thou hast deceived me and I was deceived.'[6] By beginning with deacons, ministry leaves room for the novice and the apprentice. It sponsors a growing and ripening intelligence and ever renews its 'learning' invitation as to those Jesus first recruited, addressing them as 'weary and heavy-laden'. The call was never oblivious of the future it concealed in its present. What grew with it would survive by virtue of it. 'Waxing wiser and stronger' was how the Ordinal itself prayed concerning the ministry it conveyed. Re-assuringly it bids us

> 'From thy first simplicity
> Surer vision finding,
> Let thy soul's perplexity
> Be My Spirit's minding.'

When in his *Doctrine of Christian Liberty*, that ever self-interrogating soul, John Milton, wrestled with the honesty of liberty, he seemed to doubt whether resolving to 'love the Lord God with all one's soul and mind' might be enacting the very self-love it thought to have renounced. Yet, utterly sure of his own poetic vocation, his 'argument'—as he called it—invoked 'the Heavenly Muse' of Horeb with 'Sion Hill' and 'the brook that flowed fast by the oracle of God' to be the 'aid' of his 'adventurous song'.[7]

---

[6] Jeremiah 20.7, 'deceived' with the sense of 'enticed', 'lured' into what had not been understood at the outset. The situation in exilic Judah was entirely different in his case from what may emerge of forlornness in Christian ministry. Unbeknown to Jeremiah, the despair to which he gave such eloquent expression in his 'Confessions' was the very crux of his abiding significance.

[7] John Milton, opening of *Paradise Lost*, Book 1, lines 6-13.

Are the prosaic, patient, sustained and splendid adventures of deacon, priest and bishop to draw a less enabling reliance from 'the wounded hands of Christ'? Or, after Alan Paton, dwell in the precincts of their 'yoke' and ever so 'learn'.

> 'This kneeling, this singing
> This 'burden that is intolerable,'
> This 'humble access', this putting out of hands,
> This taking of the bread and wine
> This dedication and my apostasy
> Take them and accept them all, O Lord.
>
> They are a net of holes to capture essence,
> A shell to house the thunder of the ocean,
> A discipline of simple acts to catch Creation,
> A rune of words to hold one living Word.'[8]

These are 'the means of grace' that tell and translate what is mutual in love between God and ourselves, 'the love that God has towards us and we toward Him' and all in and with these 'four human virtues of delight'.

It is noteworthy that Alan Paton's lines came from the tense situation he so long laboured to redeem in South Africa. Some have detected a close parallel between that world of conflict and the long tragic years and decades of Palestine/Israel, Israel/Palestine. There are crucial features in common. There was/is the same will of a people to 'dwell apart' in a calculated apartheid which did not want to co-inhabit. There was a self-insertion into territories where an indigenous population had long been at home and by ethnic tenure, custom and determination. That self-insertion claimed it had warrant by its own lights and was effectively pursued by tactics of settlement which did not scruple from violence when resisted. Inevitably the situation sharpened into armed confrontation.

At long last—and by help of international pressure—a leadership emerged ready to 'negotiate' a co-existence in hope of ordering some common good. Blessedly there was on 'the other

---

[8] Alan Paton, 'Meditation for a Young Boy Confirmed', published in *The Christian Century*, 15 October 1954 and in *Knocking on the Door*, London, 1959. See further Peter F Alexander, *Alan Paton: A Biography*, Oxford, 1994, pp. 256-57.

side', out of long bitter years of solitary incarceration a leader ready and capable for response. The tragedy in Palestinianism is that it has produced no Nelson Mandela. As for Israeli Zionism, it vetoed by assassination the leadership which, via Oslo, brought it to the most hopeful it reached on the road to an agreed co-existence. The death of Prime Minister Rabin had the consent of a sizeable element in Israel's population, as evident in the vituperation to which he and his policy were subjected antecedently.[9]

Now the search—if such it be—for how and when and whether the positives of South Africa (for all their inevitable frailties) might attain to be in the other locale—is darkly beset by ever multiplied and multiplying enmities and hatreds.

There is no conclusion for a ministry of 'the wounded hands' in this maelstrom, neither in fact nor in logic. There is only a mind for the meaning and the mission of those hands by their measure of how God is God in so man-marred a world.

---

[9] Witness also how, in November 2005, settlers gathered in the hills of the West Bank to celebrate the tenth anniversary of the murder of a 'traitor'. An Israel-wide poll at the same time registered nigh twenty percent of Israelis agreeing that Yigal Amir, the Jewish assassin, should be pardoned.

BIBLICAL REFERENCES

Old Testament

Exodus	3.1-15	19, 23, 56, 60, 97
Leviticus	7.17	77
Deuteronomy	21.18-23	21, 22
Psalm	2.6	16
	3.4	14
	15 all	71
	18.36	60
	23 a11	131
	24.1f.	16, 17
	26.8	12, 14
	33.2	13
	39.3.	1, 3
	40.12	14
	42 all	15
	43 all	15
	45.8-16	16
	50.1f.	16, 144
	50.8-16	16
	51.14	15
	51 all	71
	61.6	17
	68.23	14
	69 all	71
	72 all	74
	73.26	14
	84.3	14
	87.1	14
	90.17	158
	92.3	14
	96.6	14
	99.4	17
	103.13	141
	103.20	68
	119.176	127
	135.10f.	17
	136.17f.	17
	150.4	14
Isaiah	8.18	66
	18.7	19
	43.24	97
	60.13	19
	63.9	58
	63.15	141
	66.1	19
Jeremiah	8.15-21	22
	11.19	22
	15.18	22
	20.7-9	22, 164
	28.3	19
	29.14	19
Amos	9.7	56
Hosea	1.9	56
Malachi	2.10.	141
Ecclesiasticus	51.23-27	76

New Testament

Matthew	5.48	57
	9.36	112
	11.28f.	4, 67, 75, 145, 155
	16.13-28	71
	19-14	7
	27.36	14
Mark	1.28	37

Luke	6.35	76	13 all	72
	9.62	40	2 Corinthians 4.6	30, 163
	13 34	93	Galatians 3.26	71
	15.20-23	21	4.25	10
	22.28	33, 39	Ephesians 2.19	71
John	1.1-18	16, 71	4.26	47
	1.29	22	4.30	52
	3.17	1, 54	Philippians 2.5-11	60
	4.34	33	3.10	67
	12.47	33, 150	2 Thessalonians 3.13	155
Acts of the			Hebrews 2.3	66
Apostles	2.36	38	5.8	76
	4.12	104, 105, 142	9.12	13
	6.6	39	10.25	77
	13.3 and 15	38	12.3	76
	21.16	26	12.24	77
Romans	2.4	76	13.12	77
	5.8	163	13.13	37
	6.11	135	13.15	77
	7.22-24	71	1 Timothy 4.12-16	39, 138
	8.39	162	5.22	39
	10.17	163	6.12-21	138
	12.21	50	2 Timothy 1.6	2
	14 all	72	1.12	41
	14.10-23	153	2.15	138
	16.1	140	Titus 1.5	39
1 Corinthians 6.20		38	2.10	155
	10.19-31	153	1 Peter 2.3	76
	11.24	133	3 John 6	28
			Revelation 1.18	133

QURANIC REFERENCES

Surah	2.87	93, 142	Surah	19.1-36	10
	2.272	143		19.39	108
Surah	3.33-66	101	Sizrah	22.74	82
	3.19	94	Surah	29.52	86
Surah	4.82	141	Surah	36.67	103f.
	4.156	118	Surah	39.67	82
	4.165	44	Surah	47.4	86
Surah	5.52	47		47.111	99
Suran	6.91	82	Surah	68.4	86
Surah	7.172	1.91, 98	Surah	69.50	103
Surah	17.111	45, 46	Surah	76.24	86
			Surah	92.18-31	143

169

INDEX OF NAMES, TERMS AND PHRASES

Aaron 38, 45, 78
'Abba, Father' 78
'Abd al-Sabur 5
Abel 77
Aberglaube 66
Abigail, and David 72
Abraham 13, 55, 75, 77
Acts, Book of 28, 20
adhan 45, 46
Adorno, Theodor 110
Al-Ahad 81
akedah 144
akedia (accidie) 129
Al-Akhirah see 'the Last Day'
Alexandria 75
'Ali 90
Allah 1, 35, 44, 45, 48, 81, 82, 103, 104
—Names of 97
Allahu akbar 45, 46, 81, 89, 99, 139
Allah and His apostle 113 *(Shahadah)*
altar 17, 109, 140
Amalek 67
American University of Beirut 4, 6
Amos 54, 56, 58, 84
Amsterdam 135
Andrewes, Lancelot 161
Angelus, the 150
Anglican Communion, the 39
Anti-semitism 22, 54, 73, 74
Anselm 162
Arabic 5
Arabism 6, 9
Aristotle 124
Armada, Spanish 90

Armenians 9
Arnhem 72
Arnold, Matthew 111
—*Dover Beach* 111
Asbab al-nuzul 100; see also Names of Allah
Ascension, the 28
awzar, spoils of war 86
Al-Awwal wa-l-Akhir 106
Ayah, ayat 122; see also signs
Al-Azhar 139

Badr 87, 90
Baghdad 5
Bait Hanun 4
balagh 46, 84, 95
Bafour Declaration, the 8
Bar Kockhbar 62
Barnabas 29, 39, 71
Beatitudes, the 72, 153
—and Paul 72
Beckett, Samuel 128, 129
Beethoven 110, 142
—*Missa Solemnis* 110
Beirut 1, 3, 6, 10
Bellow, Saul 131
Bethlehem 35
Bismillah 102
Blake, William 101, 102, 106, 149
Bloch, Ernst 126, 159
Book of Common Prayer 2, 133
—Collects in 2
'bond of peace' 41, 154
'bond of the law' 73

170

Index of Names, Terms and Phrases

'bread and wine' 17, 35, 36, 49, 77, 122, 158
British Mandate, the 8
Browning, Robert 105, 147, 158
—*Bishop Blougham* 158
—*The Ring and the Book* 147
Buber, Martin 18, .63, 150
Bunyan, John 90
Byron 129

Caesar 36
Caesarea 26
Caliphate, the 45, 87, 90
Calvary 76
Camus, Albert 5, 128, 135
Canaan 58, 75
Canon, the role of 127, 161
Canterbury 5, 139, 153
Catholics (Roman) 90, 110f., 148, 161
Chaldea 27
Chadwick, Owen 119
Chester 15
Chesterton, G K 147
Christ, mind of 3, 5, 12, 25; see also Christhood, Christology
Christendom 48, 89, 93, 96, 107
'Christ our Passover' 69
Church, the 3, 13, 38
Church of England 39, 90, 149, 158
Cicero 134
Cohen, A A 64
Coleridge, S T 129
consensus fidelium 30, 154
Constantine 48, 89, 96
Corinth 26
Council of Christians and Jews 70
Cranmer, Thomas 134
Crete 39
Cross, the 3, 18, 23, 75, 44, 48, 49, 57, 66, 70, 72, 77, 99, 104, 118, 135, 149
—as 'place of the Name' 13
—*titulus* over 13
'cup his Father gave' 32; see also Gethsamane

Cyprus 29
Cyrene 29
Cyrus 56

Damascus 40, 41, 71
Dar al-Islam 46, 96
Darwin, Charles 119, 123, 124
Darwish, Mahmud 5
David 12, 20, 61, 74, 142
—and Davidism 15, 93, 96
—Son of 62, 65
Da Vinci code 132
Dead Sea Scrolls 127
'death of God' 119, 124
Decalogue, the 47, 48, 75
Defoe, Daniel 45
De Quincey, Thomas 160, 161
Deuteronomy, Book of 21, 22
Dhimmi system, the 106, 107
dominion, the human 44, 87, 91; see also *khilafah*
Dominus Illuminatio mea 161
Donne, John 59, 130, 156f.
Druses, the 9
Dryden, John 80, 82
Dublin 110

East/West, inter-reality 10
Easter 39, 133f., 159
—Anthems of 134
Eban, Abba 8
Egypt 5, 55, 60
—and Exodus 18, 60
ekpetasis 57
'elders in every church' 28, 39
England 1
Eliot, T S 5
English literature 5
emathen, epathen 76, 78
Ephesus 26
epieites 67
epiousios 32, 33; see also Lord's Prayer
Eucharist 18, 20, 68, 74, 77
—and Easter 104, 133f.
Europe 9

171

Eve 131
exegesis 138
Exile 15, 36, 62, 164
Exodus 12, 18, 56, 60, 97
—Book of 38
Ezekiel 13
Ezra 62

'face of Christ' 30
Fascism 50
'Father, Son and Holy Spirit' 80
Father, the 40
fitnah 86
Five Pillars, the 46
Fox, George 139
Freud, S 55

Galatians 40
Galilee 26, 27, 32 , 40, 62, 65, 112
Gaza 4
—Hospital 4
'Gentiles' 34, 35, 56, 70f., 114, 118
—admission of 28, 29, 43, 72, 73
Gethsemane 3, 13, 21, 23, 32, 34, 35, 39, 49, 56, 58, 66, 67, 76, 97, 108, 126, 136, 154
Gettysburg 25, 105
Gibbon, Edward 119
Gide, André 5
Gilead 56
'God in Christ' 19, 23, 29, 30, 31, 42, 43, 45, 49, 57, 69, 70, 82, 98, 101, 104, 126, 138, 147, 155
God, of Exodus 18, 19
'God's funeral' 119, 121
God, 'knowledge and love of' 5
God, measures of 99; see also 'esteeming aright'
Good Friday 19, 78
Gospels, the 4, 19, 27f., 32
—synoptic 19
Greece 6
Greek 17, 19, .32, 37, 53, .67, 71

Hadrian 27, 62

Al-Hallaj, Mansur 5
Hamas 10
Hamlet 4, 5
Hanina Ben Dosa 125
'handmaid of the Lord' 30
Haqqa Qadrihi 99, 104; see also esteeming Allah aright
Haram al-Sharif, al- 108
Harries, Bishop Richard 70
Harvard 7
Hasmoneans 62
Hastings, James 61
Hebrews, the Letter to 15, 18, 20, 24, 49, 67, 74f., 77
Hemingway, Ernest 109
Herbert, George 145
Hermon, Mount 15, 32
Herodotus 76
Hertzberg, Arthur 4, 7
Herzl, Theodor 8
Heschel, Rabbi Abraham 17, 59, 60, 61, 62, 65, 74, 94, 97
—*The Prophets* 59, 97
hiereus 49
Hijrah, the 35, 46, 85, 91, 113
—pre-and post situations 95
Hitler, Adolf 72
Hizballah 10
Hobbes, Thomas 119
Hocking, W E 7
Hodgson, Marshall 83, 84
—*Venture of Islam* 83, 84
holocaust, in Leviticus 18, 77
Holocaust, the 72
Holy Communion, the 17, 18, 149, 159
Holy Cross Day 2
Holy Spirit, the 2, 30, 42, 52, 143, 152
—grieving of 52
—'and us' 30
Hooker, Richard 162
Hopkins, G M 130, 159
Hosea 17, 35, 56, 60
Hoskyns, Sir Edwyn 37
huda 92; see also guidance

Index of Names, Terms and Phrases

Husain, Imam 89, 90
—and martyrdom 90
Husain, Taha 5
Huxley, Thomas 119

Idris, Yusuf 5
Introibo ad altare Dei 17, 20, 35, 75, 109, 139, 158, 164
Iraq 90
Ireland 19, 112
Isaac 144
Isaiah 17, 35, 58, 145
Islam 6, 16, 44, 51, 80f., 93, 94, 103
—Sunni/Shi'ah 7
Israel 7, 8, 9, 25, 57, 60, 63, 78, 166
—apartness 8
Italy 75

Jahiliyyah 44, 81, 96
Jenkins, Simon 149
Jeremiah 17, 22, 35, 58, 61, 84, 143, 164
Jericho 48
Jerusalem 1, 3, 4, 6, 9, 12, 30, 92
—Christian relation 10f., 108
—Council in 29, 30, 73, 78
—all of 55, 73, 75, 93
—Islam in 107, 108
—and Jesus 52, 72
—Judaisation of 107f.
Jesus 32, 34, 37, 76; see also Messiah
—as the Christ 12, 31; see also Christology
—death of 118; see also the Cross
—lament over Jerusalem 94
—and *lex talionis* 35
—ministry of 19
—and 'remembrance' 133f.
—trial of 33, 94
—wounds of 3; see also wounded hands
Jewish Revolt, the 125
Jewry 8, 12, 22, 29, 53f., 70, 118
—and the early Church 73
—and supersession 70
Job, Book of 71
Johannine accents 20, 22, 32

John the apostle 29, 133, 151
John the Baptist 22, 31
John, Letter of 97
John of Patmos 144
Jordan, River 8, 15, 55
Joseph 55, 58, 142
Joshua 12, 62
Joyce, James 109, 112
—*Ulysses* 109
Judaism 8, 29, 44, 48, 51, 53f., 69, 93, 118
—and Messiah 62f.
Judas 35
—kiss of 76
Judea 72, 164
judgement day 103
'judgement of God' 35, .48, 116

Kafka, Franz 128, 129
kairos 26
Karbala' 90
kenosis, divine 60, 70
Khan Yunis 4
khilafah 44, 81, 91, 98, 102
Kierkegaard, Soren 134
Kipling, Rudyard 98
kufr 103, 104

la'alla 124
'Lamb of' God', the 22, 57, 144
Larkin, Philip 130, 150
Last Day, the 46
Latin 17, 91, 121, 154, 161, 163
Latin Mass, the 110
Lawrence, D H 102
Law of retaliation, the 3, 7, 21, 34, 35, 47f., 78
'laying on of hands' 3, 38, 137f., 161; see also Ordinal
Lebanon 4, 6, 7, 9, 10
—civil war in 7
—French Mandate 6
—in 2006 1f.
Leibowitz, Yeshayahu 65, 68, 70
'Let God be God' 113

173

Leviticus, Book of 13, 20, 21, 22, 23, 54, 74, 75
Lewis, C S 65, 147
Lincoln, Abraham 17, 25, 50, 105
Litany 38
logikes latria 156; see also worship
Lord's Prayer, the 32, 50, 65, 72, 92
—as Messianic 32f., 65
—and *epiousios* 32, 33
—and *peirasmos* 65, 66
Lord's Supper, the 133
Luke the evangelist 29, 71, 93, 104
Luther, Martin 137

magisterium 48, 140, 162
Mahfuz, Najib 5, 145
Malchus 3
Malik, Charles 4, 6, 7, 9, 10
—Declaration of Human Rights 6
Malvolio 155
Mandela, Nelson 166
Mann, Thomas 148, 149
Maronite Church, the 6
Marx, Karl 135
Marshall, D E 114
Mary 30
Masefield, John 40
Mecca 75, 46, 84, 85, 87, 90, 95, 108, 113, 114
Medina 46, 47 87, 88, 90, 93, 113, 114
—these two as *Haramain* 90
Mediterranean, the 5, 6, 8, 9, 27, 72
Melchisadek 75, 77
Messiah 17, 22, 31, 35, 62, 105, 126, 133; see also Index of Themes
—bread of 32, 33
—as suffering 36, 43
Methodism 3
min duni-Llahi 84
Milton, John 131, 156, 164
'mind of Christ, the' 154
Mnason 26
Mosow 25
Moses 18, 55, 58, 75, 78, 97, 142, 143
Moule, C F D 125

Mount, the holy 13
Mount of Olives 84
Muhammad 35, 84, , 85, 86, 88, 90, 91, 92, 100, 108, 142, 143
—supreme exemplar of *islam* 101
munafiqun 85
Murdoch, Iris 123, 135, 136
mushrikun 45, 81

Napoleon 25
'this naughty world' 112
Nazareth 26, 27, 31, 35, 134
Nazism 50, 71, 139
Nehemiah 62
Neher, André 68
Neusner, Jacob 64, 69
Newman, J H 161
New Testament 2, 82, 23, 48, 67, 69, 72, 98, 104, 118, 125, 133, 141, 152, 155
—dual meaning of the words 26, 126
—Gospels in 26, 126
—Letters in 26, 27, 57, 71, 126, 133, 156
—Old Testament relation 61
—scholarship and 125f.
—'therefore' in 37f.
'Next Year in Jerusalem' 62
Niebuhr, Reinhold 70
Noah 142
Normandy beaches 72
Al-Nuwaihi, Muhammad 103, 104

old covenant, in James Parkes 70f.
Old Testament, and Biblical unity 61
Ordinal, the 2, 3, 24, 28, 38, 40, 42, 68, 112, 137f., 156, 160f.
Oslo 9, 166
Oxford 161

Palestine 8, 11, 23, 107
Parkes, James 70f.
—two covenant theory 70f.
Parousia 67
Passover 69, 127

Index of Names, Terms and Phrases

Passion, the 26, 51, 67, 76, 80, 95, 99, 101, 104, 135, 144, 148, 165, 166
—narratives 23
Pastoral Epistles 2, 39, 138
Pater, Walter 132
Paton, Alan 165
Paul 2, 10, 13, 19, 26, 29, 35, 37, 39, 40, 41, 48, 50, 61, 67, 71, 75, 148, 153
Pawlikowski, John 69, 70
peirasmos 65, 92
Pentateuch, the 15, 22
Pentecost 70, 39, 40
Per necessitatem Christianus 42, 163
Peter 26, 32, 39, 71, 105, 133, 142
Pharisees, the 127, 135, 154, 155
Philemon 28
Pilate 33, 99, 108
'place of the Name', the 18, 19, 33
Plato 6
Ploughman, Piers 40
praotes 67
presbuteros 49, 50
Prior, Michael 54
Psalms of David 15, 16
Pseudepigrapha 127
Pushkin 105

Quarles, Francis 80, 81, 82
quarrel, God's 93, 94
Quick, O C 23, 31
Quraish 84, 113
Qur'an 44, 45, 46, 48, 78, 81, 82, 100, 101, 113, 141, 142
—authority of 6
—as Arabic 92, 98
—and Biblical tradition 97
—Jesus in 78, 100
—Mecca/Medina distinction in 47
—status of, as Book 100

Rabb al-'Alamin 81
Rabin, Yitzhak 7, 166
Al-Rahman al-Rahim 46, 97, 102, 106
Ramsay, Michael 139

Al-Razzaq 141
regnare, servare 42, 121
Rhine, River 72
Rome 26, 27, 28, 33, 34, 35, 39, 62, 75, 108, 125, 155
Romans, Letter to 28, 153
Roosevelt, Eleanor 10
Rushdie, Salman 116

Sabbath 35, 99
Samaria 72
Samaritans 72
Samuel 18
Sartre, J P 5, 135
Satan 32
Sayers, Dorothy 12
—Mind of the Maker 12
Sayigh, Tawfiq 5
Scholem, Gershom 63
'second mile, the' 35
Sermon on the Mount 20, 48, 61, 134, 143
Shabbatai Zvi 62
Shahadah 81, 113
Shakespeare 4, 5, 82, 93, 102, 130, 147, 155
—*King Lear* 102
—Sonnets 147
Shari'ah 87
Shi'ah Islam 9, 89f.
Shelley P B 129
shirk 45, 89f.
Sidon 7
Sinai 16, 71, 75
'sin of the world' 57, 76, 77
Sirah 86, 87, 100
Skinner, John 22, 61
Solomon 12, 18, 20, 74
Sophocles 128, 131
sophomores 4
Sorbonne, the 5
South Africa 165, 166
Stalingrad 72
Stephen 40
Sufism 90, 91

175

Sunistesin 51, 140

'a table before me' 121
Takbir 99
Talmud, the 47, 60
Tanakh, the Hebrew 54, 56, 98, 141
Tanzil 92, 100
Tawhid 45
tefillah 66
teleios 37
'Temple of his body' 19
Temple, the Jerusalem 1, 12, 14, 38, 20, 22, 55, 135
—as 'place of the Name' 18
—ritual of 13, 21, 74, 75, 107
Temple Mount 107, 108
Temple, William 1
Temple Area and 1967 107, 108
Tennyson, Alfred Lord 110, 116
Timothy 2
Titus 27, 62
Tolkien, J R R 148f.
Torah 68, 69
—ethics of 73; see also Law of retaliation
Traherne, Thomas 146, 160
Tranmere 1
Trinity Sunday 2
Tripoli, Lebanon 7
Tyndale, William 162
Tyre 7

Uhud, battle of 87, 90
Umayyads, the 90
Unio sympathetica 59, 60, 78
United Nations, the 6
—Declaration of Human Rights 6, 10
—Partition Vote 1947 8
Upper Room, the 133

Vaughan, Henry 146

Versailles, Treaty of 67
Veni Creator Spiritus 2, 137
Verms, Geza 123
Vital, David 56
vineyard parable, the 84f., 93, 94
'virtues of delight' 101, 102, 106; see also Blake, William
Vulgate, the 3

wahy 92, 100
'The Wall' 9
Al-Wahhab 141
Wesley, Charles 2, 3, 132
Wesley, John 3
West, the 10, 112
Whitehead, A N 7, 119
Wisdom literature 76
'Word made flesh, the' 20, 30, 60, 84, 100 101, 139
Wordsworth, William 124, 146, 152
'wounded hands of Christ' 20, 39, 49, 50, 52, 78, 96, 137, 146, 160, 166

Yahweh 12, 15, 16, 21, 68, 75, 93, 98
—'bearing the people' 58, 59
—holiness of 54
—and kingship 16
—and Moses 18, 19, 97
—and Torah 68
Yathrib 87, 113

Zachariah, Song of 56, 57
'zeal of God's house' 20
Zealots, the 31, 35, 62, 76, 112, 145
Zion 8, 70, 78, 94, 108
—'holy hill of' 16, 17
—and Israel 78
—and psalmody 14, 15, 16
Zionism 6, 7, 8, 53, 70, 93, 96, 166
—and Judaism? 8

INDEX OF THEMES

abrogation, of *lex talionis* 154
absence from self 127f.
absolute, the 16, 111, 114, 118, 141, 149
—claims of 127
adoption 101
adulthood 122
adventures of faith 161f., 165
agency, human/divine 30, 43, 58, 92, 100
agnosticism 109f., 115
alienation in the mind 128
allegiance, religious 147, 148
alternatives, to Eucharist 134, 135
amenability, of nature to man 119, 121; see also sciences
analogy 14, 76, 77, 111, 112, 144, 158
ancestry 54, 97
anointing 43; see also 'Messiah'
anxiety 128
apartheid 139, 165
—Israeli 55, 56, 89, 114
apostolate 26, 28
Arabism 6
argumenta, of faiths 25, 37f.
arts, the 122, 156
atheisms 78, 110
atonement 23, 75f.; see also redemption
atrophy, of feeling 128, 138
authority 3, 26, 28, 29, 38, 40, 42, 49, 51, 91, 117, 141, 142, 157, 162
—of Qur'an 6
—sequence in 38, 39
awe 82, 122

banality, in media 150
'banquet, God's' 121
'bearing the evil', God's 34, 36, 67
—His people 58
belief, as act of will 123
bigotry 113
birth 117, 160, 161
—royal 16
—of New Testament 125; see also Christology, 'Messiah'
blasphemy 110
blood, cleansing—analogy in 144
—'his own' 77
Body, the 19, 38, 101
—as sacrament 152, 153, 157
Book, in 'descent' 100, 103; see also Qur'an
boredom 128

celebration 122
certitude 111
change, desire for 150, 151
chastity 158
'chosenness' 55f., 90, 97
—and creation 98
'chosen peoples' 98
Christhood 27, 49, 155; see also 'Messiah'
Christ drama, the 13, 23, 25, 49; see also Gethsemane
Christianity 6, 25, 36, 56, 148
—role in Lebanon 6
'Christ-learning' 6, 23, 67, 76, 100, 145, 154

177

—and Messiahship 67f.
Christology 69, 70; see also New Testament, *kenosis*
Church, the Christian 2, 112, 126
—faith with, faith in 3, 112, 124
—imagination of 11, 39, 43, 126
circumcision 29
coercion 85, 94, 95, 96, 105
co-existence 117
commendation, faith 51, 52, 105, 114, 138, 162, 163
—problem in 148
'common sense' 116
compassion 34, 43, 45, 49, 50, 88, 94, 97, 101, 104
—in *Bismillah* 102
compensation culture 157
community, Christian 31
—Messianic 69
conscience 46, 48, 76,
—in law and society 95
—monitors of 90
consecration 121, 122
consensus 124, 140
consolation, in Shi'ah Islam 90
continuity, in ministry 2, 3, 40, 41, 161
controversy 57, 93, 119, 152f.
—in Qur'an reception 100
conversion, as moral 72, 73
counter-culture 150, 155
courage 4, 107, 122, 164
courtesy 150
covenant 12, 59, 66, 70, 73, 79, 93
—in inter-faith 139
cowardice 115, 142, 163
creation 16, 35, 42, 43, 44, 46, 60, 62, 74, 87, 96, 122, 165
—and death 131
—and evolution 123, 124
—human tenure in 41, 46, 91, 92, 93, 94, 122
creaturehood, human 46, 91, 92, 96
—inclusive 98, 99
credentials, of faith 57, 78, 114, 139
credulity 113

criticism, New Testament 123, 124, 125, 126
cynicism 109, 122, 150

death 112, 130f.
—delay in 131
—'last curiosity,' the 132
—loneliness of 132
—to sin 136; see also self-love
deconstruction 126
democracy 10, 149, 150
—and the State 149
demographic factor in Palestinianism 9
desert, Jesus 'trial' in 32
destiny, sense of 6, 13, 40, 54, 59; see also covenant
devotion, loss of 119; see also *accidie*
diaconate 1, 13, 28, 138, 139, 142
dialogue 27, 51, 52, 54, 114, 138, 139, 142
—changed attitudes to 139
—and co-existence 94, 114, 117f.
—and honesty 152f.
—power issue in 87, 81f.
diapason in theology 95, 97, 99, 113
diaspora, Islam in 95, 97, 99, 113
disciples: of Jesus, the 30f., 39, 126
—education of 39, 43
—role in faith 50f., 135
—their sense of Jesus 32, 35
—in emulation 66
discipline 38, 41, 43, 52, 116, 117, 145, 150, 157
discounting of faith 109f., 147, 148
disenchantment about Messiahship 62f.
diversity, religious 113, 142
—issues in 117f.
documenting of faith 25f., 125; see also New Testament
doctrine, disillusion over 112f.
dogma 114, 144, 162
—distrust of 147
doubt 111, 115, 125
—via scholarship and criticism 125f.
drug culture, the 157

Index of Themes

earth, the good 92; see also 'dominion'/ *khilafah*
East and West 10
—in 'clash'? 10
educational patience 4f.
education against prejudice 109, 110, 145, 153
election 12, 55, 59, 66
empiricism 119, 120
end's and means 120f.
enigma, of death 131
enmity 34, 51, 57, 67, 88, 110, 115, 119
ennui 127
eschatology, and human regret 103, 104
—the tragic in, Quranic view 103; see also pity
Establishment 149
esteeming of Allah, a right 82, 86, 99
ethics, Christian 47, 48, 147, 148
—guardians of 121
evil, problem of 1, 20, 36, 88
—how overcome 30f, 66f.
evolution 124
exclusivisms 141, 142
expectation 66, 67; see also hope

fact and faith 25f., 30, 31, 37, 57, 68
—in ministry 161
—and unfaith 112
faith and fidelity 3, 35, 68, 117, 118, 139
—and fact 25f., 30, 31, 37, 57, 68, 126
—logic of, from Christ 35, 126
—loss of 111
—option in 123, 124
fallacy in *lex talionis* 89
fallacy in memorials 134
Father/Son relation 35, 75, 100, 141, 142
—at the Cross 49
feminism, Islamic 6
finality 47, 114, 118
—Islamic 142
finitude 123, 124
forbearance, divine 95f., 104; see also transcendence

forgiveness 14, 20, 22, 49, 50, 72, 73, 88, 97, 144
freedom, of self 129, 130
'fundamentalisms' 114
futility 127
futurism, perpetual 63; see also Scholem, Gershom

'gay', the word highjacked 152
genesis, of the Gospels 27
God, as 'Messiahed' in Christ 42, 43, 69, 126
—'death' of 119, 124
—'knowledge and love of' 43
—love economy of 130
—recession of the sense of 119f.
God being God 51, 69, 126
governance 106; see also power
grace 30, 38, 60, 67, 70, 98, 104
—case for in eschatology 103, 104
gratitude 121, 122, 151; *shukr*
greatness, divine 45, 46, 99
—measures of 46, 98, 99
—and suffering 95f.
greed 116
greeting, unrestricted 72
grief, human 128, 151, 152
guidance 43, 44, 92, 95, 96, 114; see also *huda*
guilt 21, 73, 88
—Christian 73
—and sacrifice 19f.

hand, significance of 38, 39, 43; see also 'laying on of hands'
—on the plough 40, 157
hegemony, of religion in politics 91, 94, 95; see also power
'hereness', our 123; see also Iris Murdoch
history, role of 17, 25, 49, 53, 67, 69, 84, 88, 104, 126, 143
—Jewish 54, 55, 64, 93
—and 'Messiah' 60, 126
holiness, divine 21, 39, 54, 122

179

The Order of the Wounded Hands

Holy Orders 1, 36, 42, 69, 148, 149
—as life-long 41, 160
homosexuality 152f.; see also sexuality
—condition 152f.
—practice 152f.
honesty 122, 126, 128, 164
—intellectual 5, 149
hope 11, 35, 88, 161, 165
—and despair 161
—in dialogue 51, 140f.
—Jewish 53, 62f.
hopelessness 127, 128, 129
hospitality, God's 121, 140
humanism 9, 72
human role, in science 120
hybridisation 115
hypocrites, post-Hijrah 86

identity 6, 15, 19, 27, 43, 52, 56, 72, 73, 117
—Jewish 8, 43; see also election
—subversion of 117
idolatry 29, 84, 101
—veto on 81f.
idol meats, precedent in re homosexuality 152f.; see also Romans 14
illiteracy 3, 116
illusory faith 110
imagery 2, 19, 25, 143, 157; see also metaphor
—Tolkien's use of 148
—of washing 144
inalienable things, in Jerusalem 108
Incarnation 16, 19, 30, 49, 80, 99, 104, 139, 145, 154, 155
—and annunciation 30
—and the Muslim mind 99, 100
—and suffering 76, 99, 159, 144
inclusion, 'Gentile' 72, 73
incompatibles, acknowledgement of 118, 119
integrity
—and criticism 124f., 127
—in dialogue 119

—in Islam 87
—of sceptics 114
intellectual, the, in ministry 138f.
intention, the divine, in creation 123, 124
internalising conviction 114
interrogation, self 118
intolerance 47
—Islamic 82, 118
irony 53, 107, 110, 149
—in science concerning 'data' 120
Islam
—and Christian relation 44f., 118
—ethics post Hijrah 84, 85, 86, 87
—great positives of 44f.
—image of 147
—new politicised? 90, 91
—original Islam powerless 89, 149; see also Hijrah
islam (small 'i') point of 94
Islam and the West syndrome 46

Judaica 52f.
—debt to 53f.
—fulfilment from 53f.
judgement, criteria in 115, 117
justice 36, 50, 88, 106
—modicum of possible 50, 93
—power as means to 92, 93

kingship, concept of 15

Lamb/Throne paradox 57, 64, 144
land 9, 54, 71
—and promise 70; see also covenant
language and faith 62; see also metaphor
'last curiosity', death as 132
law 36, 62, 76, 117; see also law of retaliation
—limits of 88, 89
—and order 62, 105, 106
learned clergy, tradition of 162
learning the Christ 23, 43, 67, 76, 145, 164

Index of Themes

liberalism 162
liberty, and inclusion 152, 153
life-sacrament 157; see also ministry
limits of power 36
literature, comparative 5, 128, 144, 147, 148
liturgy 117, 137
long-suffering 139, 142
lostness, moral 5
love 88, 105; see also things Messianic
—as self-expending 46; see also vicarious

malaise, contemporary 150f.
man, a theological. theme 80, 81; see also diapason
—divine stake in 91, 102
—'pity' in, with William Blake 101, 102
marriage 158, 160, 161
martyrdom 8, 90
—pseudo 35
meaninglessness 122, 123, 128
—as impracticable 123
mediation of faith 6, 139; see also commendation
memory, role of 15, 19, 20, 25, 27, 55
—and festival 19
—and historians 25
mercy and its measure 47, 97, 105
Messianic issue, the 17, 22, 31, 33f., 36, 39, 43f., 54, 57, 62f., 76, 78, 126, 142, 145, 154
—alleged silence over 31, 58
—alternative measures of 31, 32
—Messiah's 'bread, 33, 149
—Messianic futurism 63, 65
—in the Lord's Prayer 32, 33
—pathos and 17
—and priesthood 157, 158
—Messianic seclusion 63
—'realised' 64, 65, 67, 68; see also Christhood
—whether quantitative or qualitative 66f.
—and 'woes' prior to 65

metaphor 2, 41, 100, 111, 131, 138, 144, 157
mind, the divine 31
mind, a growing, open 41, 114
ministry, Christian 1, 38, 43, 49, 50, 51, 52, 112f., 129f., 131, 138f., 144f.
—cares and studies of 137f.
—commitment in 160; see also Ordinal
—continuity in 2, 40, 41, 164r.
—for Jerusalem 10, 11
—of Jesus 27, 32, 33, 47f., 76
—origins of 25f.
minority/majority relations 106, 107
mission 27, 110, 141
—in Christ quality 27, 36
morality via neutral nature 120
mortality, ministry and 130f.
mysticism, nature 117

Name, the divine 18, 92, 97, 101, 120
—known in event 19, 97, 101; see also 'place of the Name'
narrative, and faith 25, 26, 35, 59, 99
nature 88, 120
—and humankind 92; see also dominion/*khilafah*
—neutrality and consistency in 120
necessity, an inter-, between God and man 81f., 91, 94, 104
negation, Islam's supreme 81f.; see also *Shahadah*
neutrality, in dialogue 139f.
non-religion 36;

obduracy, human 82, 83, 84
obedience 69, 76, 149
—community of 69
—issue of Islam post-Hijrah 86
—of time 160f.
—Torah
oblivion, issues in 133, 134
obscurantism 113
omnipotence, whole meaning of 96, 119; see also sovereignty
order, sense of 119, 120

Ordination 1, 39, 40, 41, 49, 50
—past and future in 41f., 160f.
original sin 143
orthodoxy, and conspiracy 127

paradox 19, 47, 80, 81, 82, 117, 130, 133f., 148
parables 55, 72, 92, 93, 142, 145, 146
pardon 20, 104; see also forgiveness
parody 109, 110
particularity 9, 117; see also identity
pathos, divine 59f., 93, 97, 98, 102
patience 3, 34, 58, 75, 82, 86, 92, 119, 127, 138, 148, 153, 154
—of Jesus 34
peace 11, 36, 104
—making 50
—'king's peace' idea in 151, 152
peoplehood, divine 58, 59, 118; see also chosenness
perhaps, the grand 111, 124
perplexity 3, 118, 163, 164
persecution 28
personhood 19, 21, 74
—engaged as envoys, see prophethood
—and office 157, 158
—and sexuality 152f.
—truth through 40; see also Incarnation
piety 123, 124,
—pseudo 149
pilgrimage 15f.
pioneers, egoism in 153; see homosexuality
pity, and theology 102, 103, 105; see also eschatology
plurality of beliefs 117
poetry 111
political religion 89f., 95, 96
positivism 116
poverty 3, 116, 147
power and faith 32, 36, 61, 85, 86, 87, 89, 90, 96, 105
—and the Hijrah 46, 84
—issue at Karbala' 90

—orbit of 35, 50f., 61, 88
—and schism 96
power-suasion 84, 85, 86, 93, 142
preaching 23, 35, 148, 161, 162
—apostolic 35
—of Islam 84
—of Jesus 37f.
—vagaries of 23
priesthood 1, 13, 75f., 156
—Aaronic 38, 75
—Levitical 13
—the public/private in 41, 62
prisons 151
prophethood 17, 35, 43, 58, 60, 83, 87, 92
—hazards of 84, 85, 93, 144
—precedents of Messiah in 35, 58
pro-Semitism 72

realism, theological 45, 55, 63, 66, 122, 147
redemption 23, 33, 36, 43, 49, 51, 55, 57, 66, 68, 74, 80, 97, 106, 116, 132, 142
—cost of 13, 43, 49, 74f.
religion(s)
—guilt of 112f.
— reproach of 148
reluctance, against life 131, 148
remembrance in Eucharist 138f.
rendezvous, divine/human 14
repentance 58, 144
restlessness, contemporary 128
Resurrection 36, 78, 133f.
retribution 88
revelation 60, 83, 92, 143
—views of 83, 84
revenge 21, 22, 48, 89, 142
—'one for one' no formula/remedy 89
ritual, as theatre 149
romanticism 148, 150
rule of law 50

sacrament 23, 28, 29, 37, 50, 122f., 131, 152, 153, 158

Index of Themes

—of redemption 23, 35, 66, 67, 77
sacrifice 75f., 149
—animal 13, 44
—Temple 20
salvation 6, 104, 142, 143
—will to 127, 129
sanctuary, psalmist and other 12f., 24, 109, 127, 144, 156
—landscape as 14
—Yathrib as, for Muhammad 85
sanity 10, 113, 150, 151, 156
—in Islam 10
scapegoat, idea of 22, 38
science, esteem of 119f.
—and 'data' 120, 122
scepticism 110, 114
scholarship, and doubt 125f., 150
scruple, and liberty 153f.
secular, the 109f., 112, 119, 122, 130
secularity 41, 91, 109f., 112, 115, 119, 122, 123
self-identity 127, 128, 157 155, 156
—loss of 127f.
—offering in death 132
—in the Ordinal 138
self-consistency, divine 43
self-esteem, traps in 135
servant-king 37, 43
—prosperity of 61, 144
sexuality, human 6, 151
significance, and 'sign' 124; see also *ayat*
silence, of God 68
sin, seriousness of 20, 23, 54, 55, 76, 78; see also wrong
sincerity 52, 112, 114, 120
society, power in 88, 89
'Son of Man' 57, 58
souls, care of 144f., 161
sovereignty, divine 14, 16, 36, 55, 62, 66, 144
—'of the good' 121; see also Iris Murdoch
—and Islam 45, 51
—and Shari'ah 87
species, in Darwin 120, 124

statehood 9, 84, 112
status in office 114
stoicism 142
submission, in Islam 82, 94, 114; see also *islam*
suffering 13, 22, 36, 45, 45, 60, 76, 98, 100, 142
—and 'Lamb of God' 22, 57
—in truth-serving 35, 144; see also prophethood
supersession 69, 70
surrender, self 129f., 135, 136
—and-self-possession 129, 135, 136

technology, impact of 115
—mind-set of 119
territory, for identity 13, 54
terrorism 10
theism, Semitic 46, 91, 113, 148
—case against 122, 123
—Christian 105; see also the Christ drama
theodicy 96f.
—and history 64f., 69
theology, Christian 11, 19, 43f., 112, 120, 121
—and sense of order 119, 120, 121; see also sacrament
—and suffering 97
'therefore' logic in 39f., 46
time, obedience of 160f.
tolerance 117
—and rule of power 10, 107
tourism 108, 128
tradition 39, 41, 151
tragedy, in human history 63, 64, 101, 128, 151, 166
—at Karbala' 90
transcendence 60, 61, 62, 113, 147, 148, 149
translation, Tyndale 162
triad, of people, places and past 55f., 62
truth, in history 25f., 67, 83, 84, 105, 113, 114, 126, 144
—capacity for 112, 11?

—role of will in 126f.
'truth for': 'truth of' distinction 118, 119
'two covenant' theory 70f.
tyranny, of mind 113, 152f.

ultimacy 114
unbelief, incentives to 110f.
unforgettable, Jesus the 133, 134; see also Eucharist
unilateralism, Israeli 108
unity, divine 45, 80, 81
—Islamic sense of 45; see also *Shahadah*
—negative imperative in 81f.
—and worship 45
universe, the—and us 122, 123, 124, 131
unredeemedness, of the world 63, 64, 69; see also Jewish futurism
unselfishness, the one great 124, 130

veracity 126
verbalism, divine 86, 91, 92
verdicts, of affirmation 122, 123
—of negation 111; see also grand perhaps, the
vicarious, the 13, 21, 48, 49, 138, 142, 155
—in dialogue 142, 143, 144, 154
vindictiveness 50, 106
—rejection of, at Karbala' 90
—repudiation of 50
violence 67
virgin birth 101
vocabulary 17, 138, 144; see also 'words and the Word'
vocation 137, 138
—and homosexuality 151f.
—prophetic, cost of 144
vulnerable, the 48, 50, 138, 144, 154
—divine 49, 82, 83, 96, 97, 155
—of the prophets 84, 86, 142

war, spoils of 86; see *awzar*
waywardness, human 44
—stressed in Islam 44, 45
well-doing 155
West, the 10
—contempt for 151
wisdom, in ministry 129, 130
—political 150
wonder, sense of 82, 112, 121, 124, 151
words and the Word 49, 155, 162, 163, 164
—at large 83, 88, 92, 99, 100, 101, 118, 138
—in season 145, 147
worldwideness, Christian 27, 28, 29, 40, 52, 56, 63
worship 28, 45, 74, 112, 117, 122, 149, 153, 163
—imperative for 80f.
—indifference to 109f., 129, 148
—pitfalls in 148, 149
wrong, human 21, 23, 54, 88, 97, 126
—necessity of the Cross in 49, 81f., 126
—and state power 88, 126

yoke, analogy of 145, 165